P9-EMG-984

DISCARD

GUANTANAMO'S CHILD

GUANTANAMO'S CHILD

THE UNTOLD STORY OF OMAR KHADR

MICHELLE SHEPHARD

John Wiley & Sons Canada, Ltd.

Copyright © 2008 by Michelle Shephard

All rights reserved. No part of this work covered by the copyright herein may be reproduced or used in any form or by any means—graphic, electronic or mechanical without the prior written permission of the publisher. Any request for photocopying, recording, taping or information storage and retrieval systems of any part of this book shall be directed in writing to The Canadian Copyright Licensing Agency (Access Copyright). For an Access Copyright license, visit www.accesscopyright.ca or call toll free 1-800-893-5777.

Care has been taken to trace ownership of copyright material contained in this book. The publisher will gladly receive any information that will enable them to rectify any reference or credit line in subsequent editions.

Library and Archives Canada Cataloguing in Publication Data

Shephard, Michelle
    Guantanamo's child : the untold story of Omar Khadr / Michelle Shephard.

Includes bibliographical references and index.
ISBN 978-0-470-84117-4

    1. Khadr, Omar, 1986–2. Political prisoners—Cuba—Guantánamo Bay Naval Base—Biography. 3. Political prisoners—Legal status, laws, etc.—United States. 4. Canadians—Legal status, laws, etc.—United States. 5. Detention of persons—United States. 6. War on Terrorism, 2001– —Prisoners and prisons, American. 7. Afghan War, 2001– —Prisoners and prisons, American. I. Title.
HV9468.S54 2008   341.6'50973   C2008-900603-8

Production Credits
Cover design: Ian Koo
Interior text design: Tegan Wallace
Typesetting: Thomson Digital
Cover photo of the White House: Digital Vision/Getty Images
Design of Omar/letter cover image: Devin Slater/Toronto Star
Printer: Friesens

John Wiley & Sons Canada, Ltd.
6045 Freemont Blvd.
Mississauga, Ontario
L5R 4J3

This book is printed with biodegradable vegetable-based inks on 55lb. recycled cream paper, 100% post-consumer waste.

Printed in Canada

1 2 3 4 5 FP 12 11 10 09 08

Contents

Acknowledgments

Journalism can be a cutthroat, competitive and ugly business. That has not been my experience in writing this book, which would not have been possible without the help of other reporters. My thanks first to *Miami Herald* journalist Carol Rosenberg. She has been to Guantanamo hundreds of times and remains a thorn in the U.S. administration's side. Carol deserves a Pulitzer for her relentless work. The *New York Times'* Tim Golden has also helped both personally and through his excellent investigative work from which I've quoted often. Then there are those who have shared the surreal reporting experience that is Guantanamo. Thanks especially to my Canadian pals, Paul Koring, Beth Gorham, Sheldon Alberts and Bill Gillespie. Also to Andrew Selsky, Carol Williams and Bill "Number One" Glaberson.

I feel especially grateful to Tabitha Speer. Thank you for introducing me to your husband Chris and for your trust, Tabitha. To the Utah soldiers who welcomed me into their homes and brought me as close as I could come to being at that firefight July 27, 2002. Layne and Leisl Morris are wonderful people and I will always be touched by their hospitality.

Although they were not happy with my writing this book, Maha Elsamnah and Zaynab Khadr eventually took me into their confidence and spent hours explaining Omar's upbringing. I appreciate the time they spent trying to explain a world I'm not sure I'll ever completely understand. Thanks to Abdurahman Khadr for our many cups of coffee and for attempting to set the record straight.

The *Toronto Star* has been my home for a decade and was incredibly supportive while I was writing this book. Thanks to Editor-in-Chief Fred Kuntz and Foreign Editor Martin Regg Cohn. To Tom Walkom for leading me to this beat. To Tim Harper for his generous help and Washington hospitality. To Susan Delacourt, Tonda MacCharles and Bruce Campion-Smith for helping me navigate Ottawa.

Thanks to friends Linda Diebel, Marina Nemat, Scott Simmie and Julia Nunes for encouraging me to write a book. To Isabel Teotonio for so capably taking over in my absence.

To my good friends and London "fixers," Jennifer Quinn and Simon Hunt.

Thanks to Tanya Talaga, Rita Daly, Patty Winsa and Jenny Guerard for their encouragement and friendship. To Betsy Powell. I'm glad we're going through this together.

When history judges Guantanamo, the leading characters will be the lawyers who have endured such frustration and personal sacrifice. Thanks especially to Dennis Edney, Nathan Whitling, Muneer Ahmad and Colby Vokey for our many long talks. To Rick Wilson, Bill Kuebler and Rebecca Snyder for their patience and help. To Clive Stafford Smith and Michael Ratner for their advice.

To Moazzam Begg, Ruhal Ahmed and Abdullah Almalki for trusting me with their stories when trusting must be hard after all they've been through.

Thanks also to Jack Hooper for explaining his world to me and for his hospitality in the West. To Cmdr. J.D. Gordon, Lt. Catheryne Pully, Col. Dwight Sullivan and Col. Moe Davis for helping me fill in the blanks.

To Peter Bergen, Larry Wright and Nazim Baksh, whose work I have so greatly admired, for their advice.

This book would not be possible without the guidance of two very special editors. I had heard publishing was an even tougher business than journalism, but that didn't seem so at Wiley. Don Loney, for your skill, kindness and patience, thank you. To my friend Lynn McAuley. Your blue marker is wicked. This book was not possible without your brilliance, Lynn.

Thank you to my family. To my sisters Meg, Suzanne and Mary, for their love. To my parents, Dawn and Ron. I grew up thinking that being the daughter of an English professor and English teacher was a curse. What a blessing. No one has read this book more often than they have. Thank you, mum and dad, for your love and help.

Lastly, to Jim Rankin, a wonderful reporter, writer, photographer and friend. Thank you Jimmie, for everything.

Introduction

The Khadr family lives in east end Toronto in the suburb of Scarborough, crammed into a second-floor apartment where posters of Saudi Arabian mosques cover the walls and the youngest son controls an army of video-game commandos from his wheelchair. Every so often, a slight, grey-and-white cat named Princess will wander into the living room, trying to avoid her brother, Slim Shady. Most days the cats seem to be the only ones who will venture close to the family that has been vilified in Canada. Most days the Khadrs don't seem to care what other people think.

The apartment is a reflection of the life the Khadr family has lived, shuttled between East and West, the children brought up memorizing the Quran and *Green Eggs and Ham*. It is a dizzying clash of culture and it is often hard to fathom that this family, who named a pet after an Eminem rap, once counted Osama bin Laden a friend.

On leaving their apartment you don't know whether to laugh or cry. The Khadr family is endlessly fascinating, infuriating, belligerent, simple, and yet complicated, sometimes naïve, sometimes savvy. While some Canadians believe the Khadrs have been victimized, persecuted for their opinions and for crimes that have never been proven in court, the majority thinks they are dangerous and wants them kicked out of the country.

The Khadrs defy traditional description. Which is okay, because this isn't a book about them.

This is the story of only one Khadr, Omar. He is the soft-spoken, dutiful, second youngest son of the Khadr clan who has spent a quarter of his life in the U.S. prison in Guantanamo Bay. Omar was fifteen when he sat with heavily armed and bearded men in a mud house in a small village in Afghanistan on July 27, 2002. Someone in that compound had shot dead two Afghan soldiers who had demanded they put down their weapons and surrender. That sparked a long battle with U.S. Special Forces soldiers who eventually called in air support and reduced the compound to rubble.

Somehow Omar survived. The Pentagon alleges that the soldiers approached the rubble, believing everyone dead, and that Omar emerged and threw a grenade that killed Sgt. 1st Class Christopher Speer. Speer, a twenty-eight-year-old Delta Force soldier, had two young children in North Carolina waiting for him to come home. He wanted to become a doctor and was trained as a military medic. This was his first time at war.

Omar was shot at least twice before he collapsed and was captured. He had two massive holes in his chest and a wound that caused near-blindness in his left eye. The Toronto-born teenager was interrogated and held in the U.S. prison at Bagram air base in Afghanistan before being transferred to Guantanamo Bay in October 2002.

The U.S. administration is determined to try him for war crimes before a military commission, despite numerous court setbacks and a restive worldwide public that has grown weary of President George W. Bush's assurances that justice can be carried out at Guantanamo. If the case proceeds, it will be the first U.S. war crimes trial since the prosecution of Nazi commanders in Nuremberg. The world is immeasurably different from what it was in 1945, but it is hard to believe that history will equate a fifteen-year-old Canadian alleged to have killed a soldier with concentration camp commandants who exterminated thousands of innocent civilians.

I was introduced to terrorism, and eventually to the Khadr story, the same day most of the Western world first heard of Osama bin Laden. About twelve hours after the World Trade Center collapsed, a dusty rain of the building's pulverized parts still fell at Ground Zero and coated my arms. The image of an exhausted firefighter slumped on the curb, framed by that gruesome mountain of paper, twisted metal and wires, is seared into my memory.

New York City turned into a wounded small town in the weeks after 9/11. In a scene that now seems plucked from a melodramatic B movie, I remember watching a blur of faces and ribbons of light stream past my taxi window. Hundreds of people had lit candles and stood silently in front of shops, apartment buildings, parks and stores, remembering the victims of 9/11. Billy Joel's "New York State of Mind" came on the taxi radio and I began to cry. There was no way to imagine during those first weeks that five years later, sympathy for the United States would turn to blame, tens of thousands of civilians would be dead in a country with no connection to the 9/11 attacks, and one afternoon I would be sitting on a military jet over southeastern Cuba about to land in Guantanamo Bay.

The first of the half a dozen trips I have taken to Guantanamo to report on Omar's case was in January 2006. Like the journalists who came before me, I was initially struck by the beauty of the terrain. There's always something incongruous about bad things happening amid natural splendor, which is why murders just aren't supposed to take place on quiet, tree-lined streets.

But I would quickly learn that the notorious jail's pristine Caribbean real estate was one of many jarring contradictions at Guantanamo. There were undefined, evolving rules as to what constituted the torture of detainees, yet the regulation regarding the care of the island's other inhabitants—the iguanas—was crystal clear. If a soldier hit one of the lounge lizards that sunned in the middle of the road, he faced a $10,000 fine and a possible jail sentence.

There were inconsistencies in how the Geneva Conventions—the international treaties that govern the treatment of prisoners of war—were applied. The Bush administration declared that since detainees were "enemy combatants" and not PoWs, the conventions weren't binding. But the officials cited the conventions when convenient, such as the rule that no detainees could have their faces photographed or be interviewed by journalists. The Pentagon argued to do so would violate the convention that PoWs were not to be exploited. They would not relent even after some detainees signed waivers saying they wanted to tell their stories.

As with the experience in the Khadr family apartment, Guantanamo could be both tragic and comical. On my second trip to Guantanamo in 2006, our group of about twenty reporters was under the supervision of a public affairs military unit from Hawaii. Daniel Byer, a captain with a shy smile and round brown eyes, and wound tighter than a drill sergeant, was our chief guide. To be fair, journalists and soldiers are usually a bad combination. The military trains its soldiers to follow the rules and not question authority. Life trains journalists to do the opposite. Byer grew more tense and terse as the week progressed. *He'll figure it out*, I thought. *Growing pains.*

A year later, I was back and Byer was near the end of his tour. I was with a clever and soft-spoken *Daily Telegraph* journalist who bore an uncanny resemblance to Harry Potter. On our first morning, the British journalist had the misfortune of asking one of the workers in a mess hall where he could find milk for his coffee. Byer went ballistic. "Did I not tell you to not talk to anybody but me? I'll tell you where the milk is." I was stunned. In a manner that perhaps was too cheeky, I asked Byer if it was okay that I get a yogurt. It was half in jest, but I also worried he might yell again if I just wandered off. Byer's face grew red. He scolded me as if I were a petulant teenager. As I walked away, I heard him say that if I kept up that attitude I would be sent to my room and not let out. I referred to the incident thereafter as the "dairy meltdown."

Byer did apologize, but his aggressive manner continued for the rest of the week. Inside the prison, we watched a detainee, who was wearing goggles and earphones, taken into a portable. I asked where he was going and Byer took great offence, barking finally, "Why don't you ask him yourself?" One of his underlings explained quietly it was a "need-to-know situation." Apparently, I didn't need to know.

Byer's frayed nerves were emblematic of just how Guantanamo could challenge one's sanity. Most Military Police hate being posted there, and taking command of Gitmo, as it is known, is a thankless job. But soldiers usually don't spend more than a year on the island, unlike the prisoners, some of whom have been there for six years without a trial. No one really knows what effect such indefinite detention has on the prisoners. Four have committed suicide and others have tried. Some continue lengthy hunger strikes but are force-fed. Those are the adults. What about Omar, who has been alone for his teenage years, locked up beneath the glare of fluorescent lights often for twenty-four hours a day?

Before Omar's first appearance at the military commission on January 11, 2006, his only public image was a photograph his family had given the media. It shows him at age twelve or thirteen, staring impassively at the camera. His hair is short and there is the fine fuzz of a pubescent mustache.

The tall, thin nineteen-year-old who walked into the Guantanamo courtroom in 2006 looked very different, stuck between youth and manhood. His attempt at a beard consisted of scraggly wisps of hair on his chin and bare patches around the corner of his mouth. My eyes were drawn to his feet which were covered in massive, glaringly white running shoes his lawyers had brought for him. They seemed too big, and he looked like an awkward puppy whose body hadn't caught up with its paws.

Guantanamo's chief prosecutor, the always-quotable Col. Moe Davis, had chided the media for portraying Omar as a fresh-faced teenager, calling the coverage "nauseating." "You'll see evidence when we get into the courtroom of the smiling face of Omar Khadr as he builds bombs to kill Americans," he told us. "When these guys went to camp, they weren't making s'mores and learning how to tie knots."

But Omar did seem like a teenager. As the proceedings unfolded around him, Omar remained transfixed by the television before him that carried the hearing live. When I later watched his younger brother Kareem glued to his computer playing video games in the Khadr apartment, he reminded me of Omar.

In June 2006, the U.S. Supreme Court dismissed the military commission process as unconstitutional, throwing Omar back into legal limbo. Early the next year, he was again facing trial, this time as one of only three detainees charged under the new Congress-endorsed military commissions that Bush had signed into law.

In June 2007, a very different Omar Khadr returned to the courtroom. He was wearing pyjama-like khaki prison garb and flip-flops. He had filled out, grown up, and his beard and hair were shaggy. Some reporters described him as defiant. I thought he looked despondent. Just before the hearing—that would end with his charges again dismissed and the case thrown back for appeals—Omar's Canadian lawyer, Dennis Edney, came up to me. He had just met Omar for the first time but had spent four years fighting for him in Canada. "I think he's lost. I'm not sure I can pull him back," he said. Edney, an Edmonton lawyer with a Scottish brogue, is a scrapper and likes nothing more than a good legal battle. But on that day, Edney looked more tired than angry.

The public has rarely been sympathetic to Omar or taken much interest in his case, largely because of the outrageous comments made by his family and revelations about their connections to al Qaeda. Thus, although this is a book about Omar, the story of how he grew up and the actions of his family are important.

Over the years, almost every development in Omar's case that should have sparked debate has been diminished by news stories about the other Khadr family members. A year after Omar was transferred to Guantanamo, his brother Abdurahman returned to Canada and was profiled in a documentary by Canada's public broadcaster, the Canadian Broadcasting Corporation (CBC), where he talked about his "al Qaeda family." The Khadrs thereafter became known as "Canada's First Family of Terrorism." Omar's mother appeared in the documentary saying she would rather raise her kids in

Pakistan than Canada where they could become drug addicts or homosexuals. A few months later, she returned to Toronto so her fourteen-year-old son Kareem could get free medical care. (He had been paralyzed after a battle with Pakistani forces in 2003 during which his father was killed.)

There's no doubt many Canadians view the Khadrs as Canadians of convenience, accepting subsidized housing and health care with outstretched hands, while wagging fingers at Canada's morally corrupt society. "The Khadr family is like a rugby team at an all-you-can-eat buffet," Canada's former top spy, Jack Hooper, told me in describing the Khadr's use of social services.

Canadians have grown weary of the Khadr family. Even at my newspaper with its century-old tradition as defender of the underdog, editors sometimes receive my story suggestions with rolled eyes as if to say, *Why can't the Khadr stories just go away?*

I understand the fatigue, and how the public gets tugged in one direction, only to be yanked in another. That happened to me when I met Tabitha Speer in her North Carolina hometown and her story broke my heart. Her soldier husband was an Elvis fan, a romantic who left her love notes around the house and a dad who wanted nothing more than to watch his little daughter and son grow up happy.

In Utah, I was graciously welcomed into the home of Layne and Leisl Morris. Layne had been blinded in one eye by shrapnel from the July 2002 battle, forcing his retirement from the army. He has a beautiful family and four children whose lives would be so different today if he hadn't come home. Scotty Hansen, a Vietnam vet not prone to long emotional discussions, talked to me in detail about the battle while sitting on his living-room couch, his granddaughter snuggled on one side and a grey teacup poodle on the other. The Bronze Star that he was awarded for his bravery in recovering the bodies of the two dead Afghan soldiers was displayed on the mantle.

The soldiers all want justice, which they too have been denied. Locking up a fifteen-year-old and holding him for more than five years without trial isn't justice. It's retribution. Omar has become a victim, too.

And that's why understanding Omar's case is so important. It speaks to Canada's relationship with the United States. The fact that the Canadian federal government and the public have never been able to separate Omar from his family has left Canada standing virtually alone in its support of Guantanamo Bay, while other Western governments have condemned the prison and managed to bring their citizens home. The silence also means a Canadian teenager has been interrogated, abused and jailed in conditions worse than those afforded convicted rapists and murderers. Canada has lost the moral high ground we once enjoyed.

The case also reveals the fundamental problem with the Bush administration's post-9/11 policies. By flouting traditional law cherished by democratic governments, the United States has managed to turn its enemies into symbols of oppression. Iraq's Abu Ghraib prison and Guantanamo are gifts for al Qaeda propagandists. Intelligence experts now believe terrorism is a greater problem for the West today than it was on September 10, 2001.

For me, Omar's age has always been the greatest factor. He was indoctrinated into his father's war, like a child soldier forced to fight for a corrupt government or guerilla organization. But Omar has always been treated as an adult. Canada is a signatory to the Convention on the Rights of the Child, an international treaty that protects children under the age of eighteen, yet Canadian politicians deliberately steered the public away from that issue in Omar's case. An e-mail sent by a high-ranking Canadian Foreign Affairs official soon after Omar's capture warned her political bosses to "claw back" on public comments that reinforced that Omar was a minor.

At the Guantanamo press conference, I asked Col. Davis about the fact that Omar was only fifteen when he was captured. He answered, "He's nineteen now." I thought the reply was outrageous, but Ottawa gave the standard government response that amounted to little more than "no comment."

Now he's twenty-one, and it's hard to know who Omar has become. His childish letters say little more than "pray for me." Edney promised Omar that once he is released, he would take him to his lakeside retreat in Western Canada. Edney told him that to give him hope. Privately, he said it was part of a plan to re-humanize him after years of being detainee No. 766.

Former detainee and British citizen Moazzam Begg was held in a cell in Bagram with Omar in 2002. He remains haunted by the last conversation they had as Omar was taken from his cell to board a plane to Guantanamo. Omar told Begg he was lucky. "You know you're fortunate because there are people who actually are concerned about you," he said. "I don't have anyone."

Toronto,
January 2008

Author's Note

The world of national security and terrorism is murky. Skilled terrorists can be skilled propagandists. Intelligence is sometimes deceiving or simply wrong. Politicians have lied and lawyers can distort.

All this makes writing a narrative about a controversial prisoner in a controversial prison difficult. In trying to get at the truth I have attempted to rely only on government and intelligence reports that could be independently verified. Where there are allegations or statements that could not be substantiated, I have included them only if the details seemed plausible based on supporting documents.

Using unnamed sources can create doubt in the mind of the reader so I have tried to quote everyone by name, although I have relied on the expertise of a handful of people not mentioned in the book.

In writing dialogue, I have relied on court transcripts or my own taped interviews. In other cases where there is no record, I approached the interview subjects more than once to ensure their recollection was the same each time.

Even with these precautions, however, there are the unavoidable pitfalls when writing a non-fiction narrative. Memories can sometimes fade or be revised and therefore will be disputed. Many of the government's records remain censored under claims that releasing the information would jeopardize national security.

And finally, this story cannot fully be told until the Pentagon allows access to Omar Khadr and until his fate is determined.

1

"Shoot Me"

THE GRENADES CAME down in a shower burst in the early morning heat, falling one after another with sickening thuds. The U.S. Special Operations Forces under attack couldn't believe how many were being thrown, seemingly tossed by a company of soldiers, not the five or six men housed in the compound built of mud, straw and stones.

Sgt. Layne Morris took cover behind a house with his unit's executive officer, Capt. Mike Silver. The men had known each other in Utah, their friendship strengthened during the past few weeks by the bond that forms between soldiers in places such as Afghanistan.

Amid the thunder of explosions, Silver crouched over Morris's left shoulder and explained where he wanted him to shoot. It wasn't an easy target, but a shot over the wall and into the front of the house would trap the suspects inside and maybe stop the onslaught. The soldiers needed time to regroup, settle down and plan their assault.

In the fields around them, the rest of the team was taking cover behind buildings, in ditches, careful not to get caught in the crossfire. For Morris and Silver, though, their focus was narrow. *Hit the front porch. Keep the suspects trapped inside.*

They didn't see the grenade when it landed at their feet.

The force of the blast sent Morris flying backwards, landing in Silver's lap. A black curtain closed over Morris's right eye and it took him a few minutes to realize his eyelid was still open; he just couldn't see anything. Both men were momentarily dazed and stared at Morris's M4 rifle lying in the dirt, thinking it had somehow misfired. Morris was more confused than in pain. "What's wrong with my eye? Why can't I see?"

But Silver wasn't worried about the eye; instead he was pressing a bandage hard against the gash on Morris's nose. He yelled into his radio,

"We've been hit, we're hit." They crouched lower to the ground. The firing continued.

Sgt. Scotty Hansen hadn't heard the call and came running around the corner, almost tripping over Morris and Silver as he took cover. A Vietnam vet, Hansen had killed and seen others kill, but that seemed a lifetime ago. Now, as he slumped down and leaned against the wall clutching his gun, everything was different. He was a grandfather of five, nearing retirement, and beside him was Morris, a friend of two decades wounded with a bloody rag held to his face.

Morris needed to be moved out of there. Hansen offered to take him to the "combat casualty point," a sheltered area about 200 yards from the fighting that was designated for medical triage. With Morris secured at his side, Hansen lurched forward and kept low, as Silver and the other soldiers laid down cover fire.

There was no question the soldiers outnumbered those inside the compound. In addition to Morris, Silver, Hansen and another dozen soldiers from Utah's 19th Special Forces, there were at least ten soldiers with the 82nd Airborne Division and a half-dozen local Afghan fighters with experience in guerrilla warfare and a lifetime of fighting behind them. There was also a handful of fighters from the elite Delta Force, the best counterterrorist troops the U.S. Army has to offer. Just days earlier, a Delta Force medic had saved the lives of two Afghan children. Sgt. 1st Class Christopher Speer had run into a minefield to grab the children who had been injured by one of the explosives. He treated them until he flagged down a passing ambulance and then stayed with the children after one hospital refused to admit them. By the time he left them at a hospital run by Spanish doctors, he was optimistic they would live.

Speer wanted to be a doctor some day but on this morning as he crouched with the others surrounding the compound, he was a soldier, and Delta Force were trained to kill with stunning precision. Although he had been with the army for eight years, this was the first time the twenty-eight-year-old Speer had seen battle.

DESPITE THEIR NUMBER and skill, the soldiers weren't gaining much ground. They had to move quickly. News of the battle would spread, and if those inside were connected to al Qaeda or the Taliban, there was a good chance reinforcements were on the way. The soldiers had called for ground support but their base was more than an hour's drive away. Who would arrive first?

Too many men were dropping. Morris was hit the worst, but others were being dragged to medical care. Silver and another commander with the Utah soldiers made a call. They couldn't wait for ground support. They wanted the area leveled. Air support was summoned.

Minutes later, the sky began to thump with the drumbeat of heavily armed Apache attack helicopters. The hulking flying tanks hit the target, then retreated. But the walls of the house, about three feet thick near the base, were remarkably resilient, and Silver, lying nearby, could hear shouting. "They're still firing," Silver yelled into his radio.

As the smoke cleared, the next wave of air support was called. Two A-10 Warthog fighter jets whistled low, pockmarking the dusty ground. Morris, unable to move, watched warily as the Warthogs approached, firing as they came. They looked like massive hunched-back birds precariously rocking back and forth. "One gust of wind," he thought, "and I'm dead." With remarkable accuracy, though, the fighter jets fired on the walled-in compound.

Still, the grenades came and Silver could hear shouts. In the end, it took two F-18s and their 500-pound bombs to finally destroy the compound, save for a couple of stubborn walls. Who could have survived that onslaught?

Everything went quiet. The only sound was the whop-whop-whopping of the Medevac helicopters. Through swirling clouds of dust, the wounded at the casualty staging area were loaded on to stretchers destined for the Bagram base. Morris's last view was of the smoldering compound. *Good, we got them.*

The soldiers slowly emerged to survey the remains. Mike Silver joined Chris Speer and a small group of Delta Force and 82nd Airborne soldiers, and they moved cautiously toward the compound. One by one, with weapons drawn, they gingerly stepped through a hole that had been blown in a wall. Silver went right, following the path of the first Delta Force soldier. Speer went straight, covering the two in front of him. Debris from the collapsed house provided a low wall of cover. Then someone from a nearby alley began to shoot at the soldiers, sending dust flying into the air.

Pop. Silver heard a faint noise. The two soldiers in front ducked, either realizing that the sound was the crackle of a grenade when first lit or because they saw something move.

Speer didn't see the grenade coming, or if he did, he didn't have time to react. It landed, the explosion sending searing chunks of shrapnel into his torso and skull. One of the commandos heard moaning from the back of the compound. When the dust cleared, he saw a man lying on his right side, with an AK-47 beside him, and began shooting with his own M4 rifle.

The soldiers had killed three men now buried among the debris. They looked to be in their thirties or maybe even their forties, but it was difficult to judge since they were covered in blood and dust. One man had a scraggly mustache and beard, his open mouth revealing a prominent overbite and big gaps between his teeth. Another looked older, his mustache and beard trim, caked dirt sealing his eyes shut, giving him a peaceful look in death. Blood covered half of another's narrow, prominent nose and pooled in his matted mop of long hair and unruly beard.

There was another body behind a wall, breathing and conscious, despite two golf-ball sized holes in his chest. Lying on his side covered in a thick layer of dust, his eyes closed, was a fifteen-year-old Canadian named Omar Khadr.

FOUR WEEKS AFTER THE SEPTEMBER 11, 2001, terror attacks on New York and Washington, the U.S. military launched Operation Enduring Freedom in Afghanistan. B-52 bombers began the assault, followed by fighter jets and Tomahawk cruise missiles dispatched from U.S. and British ships and submarines. The first ground troops were Special Operation Forces, soldiers trained in unconventional warfare and skilled at aligning themselves with local opposition forces. Although their mission was supposed to be covert, pictures soon emerged of American soldiers on horseback fighting alongside the anti-Taliban forces of the Northern Alliance.

In New York, Ground Zero still smoldered and throughout the city pictures of hundreds of the dead remained taped to walls and lamp posts. Each day in Washington, the men and women making military decisions had to walk past the charred entrance of the Pentagon. U.S. president George W. Bush made it clear that al Qaeda's leaders and their hosts, the Taliban, would pay.

On October 7, news of the first bombs scrolled across the ticker tape of New York's Times Square. The ABC News feed read simply: "The United

States has launched massive military strikes in Afghanistan." New Yorker Lucille Ferbel stopped and stared at the words as she pulled her scarf tight against her shoulders and began to cry. "I hate the idea that we're going into a war, but what could we do? Look what they did to my city. It's my city. I'm heartbroken." So too was much of the world.

Taliban leaders at first offered to negotiate the handover of al Qaeda leader Osama bin Laden if the United States would stop bombing, but the offers were met with angry rebukes. "There is nothing to negotiate. They are harboring a terrorist. They need to hand him over," Bush told reporters.

Within one month and two days of Operation Enduring Freedom's launch, Mazar-e-sharif became the first Afghan city liberated from the Taliban's rule. Others soon followed, and by November 14 both Kabul and Jalalabad were under the control of the Northern Alliance, with the substantial help of U.S. and NATO forces.

On December 22, Hamid Karzai was sworn in as the prime minister of the interim government, becoming the face of a post-Taliban Afghanistan. Karzai was a man who had been born into privilege and politics, and his elegance in manner and eloquence in speech were greatly admired in the West. Gucci fashion designer Tom Ford called Karzai "the most chic man in the world."

By the spring of 2002, the U.S. forces were deep in Afghanistan's mountains, targeting al Qaeda's labyrinthine cave hideouts in an offensive known as Operation Anaconda. "In the end, it took U.S. army infantrymen—inching up rocky mountainsides, crunching through snow patches, and blasting the enemy out of caves and rock piles—to pull off Operation Anaconda, which began March 1. It took army helicopter aircrews, flying through ground fire and sleet with rocket-propelled grenades exploding around them and sometimes bouncing off the fuselages. It wasn't technology that finally pried hundreds of Taliban and al Qaeda fighters from their stronghold—it was the tenacity and bravery of individual American soldiers," *Army Magazine* reported in April 2002.

The soldiers lived up to the operation's code name. They squeezed out the enemy by sheer force. The military announced hundreds of al Qaeda and Taliban supporters had been killed and their hideouts all but destroyed. Yet al Qaeda's leaders, rumored to be hiding in the mountains along Afghanistan's border with Pakistan, remained elusive. This lawless tribal region had a history of resisting outsiders and harbored a generation of youth who had grown up with war. Across the mountains lay Pakistan's

Federally Administered Tribal Area, where Pashtun tribes had autonomy from Pakistan's government; the barren badlands are known as Ilaqa Ghair, the land without laws.

In early 2002, the military established a base camp about ninety miles south of Kabul in the Paktia Province near Pakistan's border. These soldiers were responsible for hunting down the remaining al Qaeda leaders hiding in this dangerous and highly unpredictable terrain. It was here that a group of Delta Force soldiers landed in July 2002. It was here that Sgt. 1st Class Christopher Speer first went to war.

THE U.S. ARMY WON'T DISCUSS, or even acknowledge, the existence of Delta Force, the elite counterterrorism unit that operates out of Fort Bragg in North Carolina. But since its creation in 1977, the mystique of Delta Force has whetted the appetite of countless journalists, Hollywood producers and even video-game manufacturers, making the name of the covert unit one of the army's most recognized. Secrecy seemed especially ludicrous after army Col. Charlie Beckwith, Delta Force founder, wrote a memoir that described in detail how the counterterrorism unit defined itself. Beckwith, who died in 1994, wrote that his unit had a simple goal: "Put two head shots in each terrorist."

"They do not serve warrants and they do not make arrests," one former Delta Force soldier told the *New York Times*. "Their job is to kill people we want killed."

The Special Operations Forces has more than 30,000 soldiers on active duty and includes the Army Rangers, Green Berets and other units trained in guerrilla warfare. Only the Delta Force and the Naval Special Warfare Development Group, better known by their former name of Seal Team Six, are trained specifically to combat terrorism. Estimates vary on Delta Force members but most believe there are no more than 2,000.

Delta Force's failed missions are better known than the unit's successes. In 1980, the mission to free fifty-three American hostages held by Iranian Islamic revolutionaries at the U.S. Embassy in Tehran ended in disaster. Malfunctioning helicopters and a collision with a plane while refueling in the Iranian desert claimed the lives of eight soldiers and only bolstered the hostage taker's confidence.

In 1993, Delta Force embarked on the ill-fated mission to apprehend Somali warlord Mohamed Farah Aidid. The joint operation with the

U.S. Army Rangers ended with two downed Black Hawk helicopters and the deaths of eighteen U.S. servicemen and hundreds of Somalis. Mark Bowden's bestseller *Black Hawk Down* brought to life this devastating mission in painful detail.

But the successes have not received equal attention. Operation Just Cause involved Delta Force soldiers helping to capture Panamanian dictator Manuel Noriega in 1989 and three years later, during the Persian Gulf War, Delta Force was credited with demolishing scud missile launchers. There could be many more missions but even the families of the soldiers involved don't know about them. The words "Delta Force" are never uttered by the unit's soldiers and wives are forbidden to acknowledge its existence.

While Delta Force were developing into a highly skilled international force, Chris Speer, the youngest of three boys born to Betty and Richard Speer of Denver, Colorado, was finding his way into the military. Unlike his rambunctious older brothers, Speer was a shy, observant child whose mother held him back from kindergarten for a year because she didn't think he was ready. While Speer was in grade school, his family moved to Albuquerque, New Mexico, where his father opened an antique furniture refurbishing shop. When tiny hands were needed to fit in an especially tight corner, Speer was his dad's eager assistant.

Speer grew into a well-rounded teenager, both athletic and artistic, which helped him fit easily into high school cliques. However one passion overshadowed all others—his love of Elvis. Even as a little boy, he would run gobs of Vaseline through his hair to imitate his favorite singer. (After he was married, his wife Tabitha was mortified to see a matted and framed poster of Elvis being carried into their first home. "Tabitha, you have to let him have this," a wise aunt told her and the poster was hung without debate.)

By the time he finished high school at eighteen, Speer knew he wanted to join the military. His eldest brother Todd had enlisted but it wasn't sibling hero worship that took Speer to the recruiting offices. Speer wanted to be a doctor and by enlisting he would get basic medical training and have his education paid for. After training in San Antonio, New Mexico, he moved to a base in Pennsylvania and then to Fort Bragg, where he signed up for the Special Operations Forces. He underwent eighteen months of training, which for him included advanced first aid, scuba diving and French, since all Special Forces are required to speak more than one language.

In many ways, Speer was a paradox. He was the quiet Elvis impersonator, the six-foot-one athlete who liked to sketch, the soldier who joined the most lethal army unit to learn how to heal. With all his quirks, he is, however, a man well remembered and admired. His roommate at the Carlisle Barracks in Pennsylvania's Army War College named his first son Christopher after Speer, whom he describes as "tall, strong and honest," always "full of love and hope."

At Fort Bragg, Speer and the other soldiers often spent their free time by unwinding in nearby towns that looked like backdrops in a Norman Rockwell painting. Speer especially liked Southern Pines, with its clapboard train station in the center of downtown, fudge stores and barber shops marked by the red-and-white poles. In 1996, Brooks Bar was the place to go on Saturday night.

One December evening, Speer found himself bellied up to the bar when Tabitha Hansen walked in. Speer was twenty-three and scheduled for tours in Africa the following year. He wasn't looking to settle down or even to meet anyone, but when the twenty-seven-year-old curvy cosmetician with jet black hair and nearly translucent blue-green eyes introduced herself, Speer couldn't see anything beyond her. By the end of the night, Speer had his arm around Tabitha and her phone number in his pocket. By the end of the week, they were dating, by the end of the year, in love. Nine months later, they were engaged. He would later tell people that he knew that first night he had found the woman he would marry.

Tabitha became Speer's priority and partner but the military remained his mistress. Throughout their engagement, he was often abroad, helping train local forces in Uganda and Kenya. Tabitha didn't like his job but she respected it because he was so passionate. When he found out he would be sent abroad in May 1998, the month they were supposed to get married, they decided not to wait. They set a date and, within four weeks, Tabitha's mother had planned everything back home in Michigan, contacting a Baptist minister friend to perform the ceremony, reserving a spot at a new resort that could take a booking on short notice, selecting the cake and making sure there was champagne for toasts. There wasn't time to buy a wedding dress, so she bought Tabitha a black evening gown. Even Tabitha's great-grandmother, who was horrified by the non-traditional garb, said the romance of the ceremony overshadowed the details.

Speer continued his missions abroad. When he returned from Portugal soon after they were married, Tabitha met him at the airport with a gift bag. Inside were two baby bibs. One said, "My daddy loves me." The other: "If you think I'm cute, you should see my daddy." Eight months later, their daughter, Taryn, was born and Speer was smitten.

Speer climbed quickly through the military's ranks. By the time he was twenty-eight, he had become one of the youngest members of Fort Bragg's Delta Force unit. When the attacks happened on September 11, 2001, every Delta Force soldier knew he would be called to duty soon and Speer was looking forward to finally putting his skills to the test. But Tabitha was just a month away from giving birth to their second child, son Tanner, and they were devastated when they learned Speer would be among the first to depart for Afghanistan. Knowing his predicament, his friend J.K., Robert J. Kennedy Jr., offered to take his place. Tabitha was relieved, not realizing that it would be J.K. who would again bring her a small measure of comfort during a devastating time.

The next July when Tanner was nine months old, Speer got his chance to fight. As he did before all his lengthy deployments, Speer left love notes all over the house for his wife and children, some of which remained hidden for more than five years. When he told his three-year-old daughter Taryn he was going to the desert, she exclaimed excitedly: "You'll be riding camels!"

On July 12, he took his children to the hair salon where Tabitha worked so Tanner could get his first haircut. Speer videotaped the milestone. A picture from that day shows Speer in front of his house hugging Tanner with Taryn leaning close to the camera beaming, her face slightly out of focus. Speer, tanned, with a trim goatee, wearing a white tank top that shows off his tight biceps, looked the picture of health. But his expression is somber, unlike many of the pictures in the family photo album where he is grinning broadly with his arms draped around his wife and kids. "There's something in his eyes. It's like he knows," Tabitha's father later said.

The evening before his flight to Afghanistan, he gave his children a bath and as they sat in their pyjamas, he spoke to them quietly. "I love you more than anything, please remember that," he said. "But I have to go away to work and I might not return."

FOR MANY AMERICAN SOLDIERS, their first experiences outside of American borders come in times of war, when they are sent to fight for their country.

But Layne Morris had been traveling since he was born. His father was an agricultural engineer with the U.S. State Department, which meant

Morris spent his childhood living in a new country every couple of years. By the time he joined the army at twenty-one, he had experienced more of life abroad and had picked up more life skills than most of his commanders. While living in Thailand, he became fluent in Thai and while in Jamaica learned what it was like to live with guard dogs. In Nepal, he once asked for directions from Tenzing Norgay, realizing only later that he had spoken with the world's most famous Sherpa, the first to reach the summit of Mount Everest with Sir Edmund Hillary.

Morris had even visited the U.S. navy base in Guantanamo Bay, Cuba, as a kid. While the family was living in Jamaica in the 1970s, Morris's father, ever the Boy Scout, had formed a troop of his four sons and some of the local kids. Since he worked at the U.S. Embassy, he had the military contacts to make a quick call to the navy base known as Gitmo, for its acronym GTMO. The boys arrived on a U.S. military-chartered C-130 from Jamaica for an island camping adventure. The base's sailors saw the visit as a pleasant distraction, and the sailors' children who lived on the base were delighted.

"You could tell everybody was just bored out of their gourd. We'd go to the bowling alley and the kids of the soldiers that were there, you'd almost have to pry them off you, they just wanted to be friends," Morris said. "You really had the feeling that everybody there really wanted to get off that rock."

In 1985, Morris met Leisl Budge at Brigham Young University, the Mormon college in Utah. Leisl, a blonde, lithe runner, worked at a nearby store but lived in the same student housing complex and often took long jogs around the campus. Leisl asked Morris for a date. He suggested the shooting range.

Not long after they graduated and married, Morris enlisted and eventually became a Green Beret. The Green Berets, also known as Special Forces, believe the military was as much a calling as a career. Though highly trained for combat, they prided themselves on their intellect. "Your Most Powerful Weapon Is Your Mind" is the Special Forces recruiting pitch. "Afghanistan was the Holy Grail. This was the situation that was tailor-made for Special Forces," Morris later recalled. "That's our mission to go into a country like that and hook up with disaffected groups, train them, turn them into a military force and then overthrow the government."

Morris was attached to the National Guard 19th Unit Special Forces out of Camp Williams, a sprawling base on the west slope of the snow-capped Traverse Mountains, about a forty-minute drive south of Salt Lake City. The unit's deployments since Vietnam had been mainly two-week or month-long stints in safe locales throughout Europe and Asia. The assignments were much like their routine lives in suburban Utah: safe and predictable. Many of them, like Morris, were Mormon and had married and started their families young. Monday nights were reserved for family time, which usually meant playing a board game together.

The unit had been passed over during countless conflicts, including Panama and the Gulf War. When New York's World Trade Center collapsed, the men cynically shook their heads and told each other there would soon be another war they would watch from afar. "The Boy Scouts are going to be called up before us," Morris's friend Mike Silver said.

There may have been surprise, but there was no hesitation, when the call came in the fall of 2001, just after the first bombs fell on Afghanistan. Morris's wife and four children remember him jumping with excitement when he told them he would be deployed. He "wha-hooed," Leisl recalled.

Many of the soldiers knew it was probably their last big war since the unit was aging. Morris would celebrate his fortieth birthday in Afghanistan, his wife Leisl cheekily sending black balloons to mark the milestone. But Morris was by no means one of the older guys.

There was Sgt. Scotty Hansen, the plain-talking favorite, with thick forearms and crinkly eyes. When he grew his white beard and hair for the Afghan mission, he joked that he looked like Moses. He celebrated his sixtieth in August 2002 during that tour. Then there was The Prospector, Master Sgt. Delbut Jay, formerly known as Deljay until he acquired the new nickname in Afghanistan. Like the others, he grew his beard to better blend with the Afghan locals and to distinguish themselves from the clean-shaven soldiers, but somehow Deljay, in his Tilley hat and wild mane, looked like he was mining for gold rather than terrorists.

From Utah, the unit first went to Kentucky where they trained for a few weeks and then to Uzbekistan. In May 2002, they crossed into Afghanistan and took charge of a former Soviet runway. The base had been christened Chapman Airfield, as a tribute to the first U.S. soldier slain by hostile fire in Afghanistan since 9/11. Nathan Chapman, a thirty-one-year-old father of two, had been a Special Forces soldier and communications specialist who was killed on January 4, 2002. He had been riding in a pickup truck with a CIA agent near a mosque when a fourteen-year-old boy reportedly fired at him. "I can assure the parents and loved ones of Nathan Chapman that he lost his life for a cause that is just and important, and that cause is the security of the American people and that cause is the cause of freedom and a civilized world," President George W. Bush eulogized after Chapman died.

There were unconfirmed reports about the fourteen-year-old, including one that the teenager was avenging the deaths of relatives who had died during the American air strikes. It's believed the teenager fled to Pakistan and news reports said a local warlord arrested three of his cousins and turned them over to U.S. forces for questioning.

Chapman's death served as a constant reminder that in Afghanistan insurgents blended easily with civilians and a calm situation could suddenly turn.

THE MORNING OF JULY 27, 2002, began with a tip from a local Afghan, a "walk-in" as the soldiers called it, about a local bombmaker who used a wheelchair after a clumsily handled bomb had ripped away most of his lower legs. The information led directly to a white-haired man wearing medieval-looking metal contraptions to hold the remnants of his legs together. Mike Silver and his team searched the house and recovered a few rifles but not the stockpile they had hoped for. Outside, soldiers were receiving word that a satellite phone, which was being tracked in Washington, had been used nearby. The National Security Agency, America's secretive electronic eavesdropping security service, routinely tracks phones suspected of belonging to terrorists and can send satellite images to soldiers in the field pinpointing locations.

Morris went with five other soldiers to secure that site, and once Silver and the others completed the search, they set out to join them. "We've been to hundreds of these places and I'm not exaggerating. I personally had probably been into about a hundred of these compounds," Silver said. "So, we pulled right up to it and Layne said, 'Hey, a couple of guys had guns.'" That also wasn't uncommon since it would have been difficult to find a house in the area without at least one AK-47 or some relic of the Soviet war in the 1980s.

Calls for those inside the compound to come out went unanswered. Once the soldiers learned that "unfriendlies" might be inside, there was debate about what to do next. "We didn't want to be storm troopers unless we had to. We like to get permission, go in and check the compounds out," said Hansen. Two Afghan soldiers volunteered to enter through the front gate to act as interpreters. But they didn't get very far. Just a couple yards from where the others waited, the Afghans fell, killed in a hail of gunfire.

Amid bullets and grenades, a handful of women, screaming as their colorful *abbayas* flapped around them, ran from the compound, miraculously escaping the gunfight.

Hansen didn't know if the Afghan soldiers were dead, but he was driven by the soldier's creed to never leave a comrade behind. Hansen ran to retrieve the bodies of the Afghans with another sergeant. Morris couldn't believe his eyes. *There goes Scotty. We will be telling his wife the sad story.* But somehow they returned, dragging the dead Afghans. "He was the hero of the day. He should not have made it out," Morris said later.

The fight was on. The soldiers spread out and set up a casualty collection point, coordinated by the team's medic who everyone called Doc. Morris and Silver ended up on the backside of one building and began planning their shot.

LEISL WAS AT HER mother-in-law's home in Vancouver, Washington, attending a Morris family reunion when her cell phone rang. A soldier told her he was a friend of Layne's. Leisl thought, *Okay, not a very good friend since he doesn't know he's not here.* Then the soldier said, "Layne wanted me to call to say everything's okay," and it dawned on Leisl that this wasn't a call from Utah but a friend who was with Morris in Afghanistan.

That soldier could have been in trouble. News of casualties was supposed to travel through official channels. But Morris had begged his friend to contact Leisl. He and Leisl had a system which required him to call home whenever there had been a big battle somewhere in Afghanistan. He wouldn't give details and would only say he was checking in. She would know he wasn't one of the wounded or dead. Morris knew this fight was big enough to make CNN and he knew his wife would be worried.

The call frustrated Leisl at first because the soldier wouldn't say much. She pressed him for details, unsure if her husband really was okay. "Layne wanted me to tell you something," the soldier finally said. "He wanted me to reassure you that the family jewels are okay." And Leisl knew instantly that was something Morris would say, and if he said something like that he was going to be fine.

Morris was flown from Bagram to Germany where he would undergo eye surgery and that was where Leisl would meet him. Morris's eldest son Tyler was twelve, and it took him and his younger siblings a while for reality to set in. "I was still at the stage where dad's Superman, dad's invincible, he can't get hurt. We've grown up watching Rambo and that's what your dad can do. So you just think dad's not going to get hurt; he's just doing the stuff dad does."

Doctors in Germany determined that shrapnel had entered through a cut on Morris's nose and bounced behind his eye severing an optic nerve. His sight would be lost and his career with the military was over, but Morris would go home.

TABITHA SPEER also received news about her husband's injury while surrounded by family. She had gone with her kids to Michigan to spend time with her brothers and parents and was on her father's boat on Torch Lake when her cell phone rang. Taryn kept swimming and playing but watched her mother closely. "Why is mommy crying?" she asked her grandparents. Tabitha was told her husband had been hit in the head but no one would describe the extent of the injuries.

Speer's friend J.K. arrived that evening to escort Tabitha to Germany. Tabitha had been warned her husband was heavily sedated and likely not aware of his surroundings but when she walked into his hospital room and touched his face she was sure he felt her presence. Although his injuries were severe, Speer didn't look like some of the other wounded soldiers who were covered in bandages and tubes. The wound where shrapnel had punctured his skull was dressed in gauze but the rest of his face was largely unscathed and the cuts to his body looked superficial.

For a week, Tabitha walked in a haze, the voices of friends droning together in incomprehensible murmurs. Doctors started to make plans to transfer Speer from Homburg University Hospital, the civilian hospital in Germany where he had been admitted, to the military's Walter Reed Memorial Hospital in Bethesda, Maryland. But Tabitha couldn't think about that. She had already come to a terrible realization: too much of her husband's brain had been damaged and while other relatives clung to hope, Tabitha knew the man she loved would never be the same. *How do I explain to a three-year-old that Daddy doesn't know you?* Her husband wouldn't have wanted that.

On August 6, the doctors told Tabitha to go for breakfast with J.K. and not return that morning since they had to conduct tests. When Tabitha came back, she no longer recognized Speer. Fluid had pooled around his brain and the pressure had made his head balloon grotesquely. She knew he didn't have long and asked a nurse about organ donations. The nurse sighed and thanked her, since she had been fretting over how to raise the subject.

Ten days after Speer's first wartime battle, five people received his heart, liver, lungs and kidneys. Tabitha Speer returned to North Carolina a widow.

ONCE THE FIGHTING STOPPED, Doc had gone immediately to Speer's side, but he knew that Speer would not recover. His head wounds were just too extensive. "He wouldn't want to live," Doc later said to Mike Silver.

The bodies of the three men killed in the compound by U.S. Forces were wrapped in garbage bags. They were photographed, their dusty, bloodstained faces recorded with signs held over them as KIA (killed in action) 1, 2 and 3. In Bagram, soldiers would try to identify them.

Doc did what he could for Speer and then moved to work on fifteen-year-old Omar Khadr. Omar had been pulled from the compound to a dusty patch of level land where he lay with his knobby knees pressed together. He appeared to be critically injured but Doc noted the location of the entry and exit wounds and believed the boy would live.

Silver had searched Omar's body for potential booby traps since many fighters were eager to become martyrs. Silver's job was to guard Omar but he was certain that Omar was incapable of escaping. *These are killing wounds*, he thought to himself.

When the other soldiers saw Doc working on Omar, they began to shout. They were furious Omar was receiving care from the chief medic, when Speer, one of their own, was down and receiving only cursory treatment.

Tired and with adrenaline from the fight having not yet subsided, the soldiers looked menacing. Gripping their weapons, more than one soldier took a few steps toward Doc and Omar. It took Silver and a few others to prevent an attack on Doc. "It's worse for him to live," Silver told the others. Silver wasn't just trying to talk down a bad situation; he really believed Omar wanted to die so he could become a martyr. He didn't see an innocent teenager on the ground. He saw a hardened warrior, trained to fight, to kill Americans and die trying. The other soldiers didn't know that minutes earlier Silver had been the first to hear Omar talk. He was surprised the teenager spoke English.

Omar Khadr had looked at him and said, "Shoot me."

2

Al Kanadi

MAHA ELSAMNAH WAS A SHY teenager whose round face and rosy cheeks were framed by her tightly secured hijab when she first arrived at T.L. Kennedy Secondary School in Mississauga, a leafy suburb west of Toronto. Born in Egypt to parents of Palestinian descent, Elsamnah moved to Saudi Arabia when she was young and immigrated to Canada with her family two days after she turned seventeen, arriving on August 1, 1974. Her parents wanted Elsamnah and her siblings to finish their education in the West and had heard Canada was a good place to raise a family. Elsamnah told them her dream was to become a doctor.

She was the high school's only Muslim student, but it didn't take long for her to make friends who were as curious about her as she was about them. After a few months, she found her hijab embarrassing and began to wear a small scarf that she would tie under her chin instead. The next year, she began tying the scarf at the nape of her neck to mimic the style worn by the other girls, but with her hair covered, she could still honor her religious belief of female modesty.

Elsamnah graduated in the summer of 1977 when she was twenty, and decided to volunteer as a counselor at a Muslim camp southwest of Toronto on Lake Erie; a perfect place, she thought, to contemplate her future and reconnect with the roots of her faith. The camp was run by Qasem Mahmud, a Palestinian engineer who had come to Canada from Egypt a decade earlier. He had a full-time engineering job with the Canadian government but the forty-four-year-old father of six had also started the camp for new immigrant children. Most Muslim families who came from the Middle East moved to the cities of Toronto or Ottawa so the camp was the first time the children could sit around a campfire and experience the wilderness. The camp offered canoeing, kayaking and swimming, and while religious lessons were not part of the program, some children and their counselors would read the Quran. It seemed a perfect blend of their parents' traditional upbringing and their own exploration of the country they now called home.

One of the volunteer counselors, a confident man with intense dark eyes, was a friend of Mahmud's. Ahmed Said Khadr had come to Canada at twenty-seven to continue his engineering studies and obtain his Canadian citizenship. He arrived in the summer of 1975 in Montreal, where he lived for a few months before moving to Toronto. Although Khadr liked Toronto, he had been accepted into the master's engineering program at the University of Ottawa, so had settled in Canada's capital.

Khadr was the son of Mohamed Zaki Khadr, an Egyptian civil servant from the rural province of Menoufiya who had three sons and a daughter before his first marriage ended in divorce in 1937. A few years later, Mohamed Khadr met his second wife, a polite and beautiful young woman named Munira Osman. She would become Ahmed Said's mother. Mohamed loved to tell the story of the couple's chance encounter, and his children, no matter how many times they heard it, loved to hear the tale.

The story began in the early 1940s, when Mohamed Khadr was asked by a man in his village to vet a prospective husband for his daughter Munira. Mohamed Khadr did as asked and reported back that the man was unworthy. As a gesture of thanks, Mohamed Khadr was invited to dinner and met Munira for the first time. They were immediately attracted to each other and married soon after.

Ahmed Said Khadr was the second-born son, and like all the children from this second marriage, he was showered with affection. "You see, in nature I think when someone remarries he just loves his new wife, his new children more than the old ones," Khadr's half-brother Ahmed Fouad recalled. "Or maybe we were old enough to take care of ourselves."

None of the Khadr children was athletic or extroverted, but Ahmed Said Khadr was particularly shy and quiet, partly due to a speech impediment that made pronouncing some words difficult. He was raised in the sprawling Cairo neighborhood of Shubra and since Khadr's father was protective of his children, he rarely went outdoors. As Ahmed Fouad was seventeen years older than Khadr, he was more a father figure than a half-brother. He married when Khadr was just three and used to take him to stay at his house with his new wife. Together, they would visit the local Japanese garden and Khadr would delight in being outdoors. They were a close-knit family; all eight children from the two marriages and their father wanted to keep it that way. But Ahmed Fouad left Egypt for the United States in the 1970s. He had two sons and wanted his children to be raised with the freedoms and education the West could offer.

Ahmed Said Khadr wanted to leave, too, but his father would not hear of it. "I immigrated to the United States, my father was okay, no problem. But when [Ahmed] tried to immigrate to Canada, my father was not happy," Ahmed Fouad recalled. Khadr was forced to plan his move behind his father's back, only telling him he was leaving Egypt just as he departed for Canada. His father did not bless the move and was furious at his son's deception.

In Ottawa, Khadr found comfort in the city's tight-knit Muslim community, which at the time numbered no more than a few thousand. He met Mahmud, the camp director, soon after arriving. In the summer of 1977, Khadr had a specific reason for assisting at the camp: he was almost thirty and desperately wanted a wife.

Mahmud was watching when Elsamnah and Khadr met for the first time and he knew it was love at first sight. "I could sense that he was attracted to her," he recalled. "I can't remember the details but I knew he was going to get engaged." Despite his early speech impediment, Khadr had become a forceful speaker. But it was how well he listened that impressed Elsamnah. "He was very much calm. We talked and talked; he was a very patient person," she said. "I loved his company. He had a way of making things so challenging. He made me feel like I could prove to myself how much I could do, not for him, but for myself."

By the end of the week, the couple had settled on each other and knew they would marry. In November, following Islamic tradition, a marriage contract was signed binding them and they later wed in a ceremony at Toronto's Jami Mosque. A photo from the day shows a beaming Elsamnah; a salmon-colored hijab loosely covers her head and cascades down her shoulders, blending into a matching gown. A bearded Khadr is more serious and wore a black suit. None of his relatives attended the wedding.

IN MAY 1978, Elsamnah moved to Ottawa where Khadr would finish his studies, and seventeen months later their first child, daughter Zaynab, was born. Elsamnah delighted in her role as mother and threw herself into domestic life, while her husband became increasingly unsure that he wanted a career in engineering. Khadr had joined the University of Ottawa's Muslim Student Association, or MSA, a student group founded by members of Egypt's Muslim Brotherhood. The student group started in the United States in 1963 but by the 1970s had established chapters in schools throughout North America. The Muslim Brotherhood was an Islamist group that believed Egypt should be governed by the religious principles of Sharia law. Many of its members fled persecution in Egypt by immigrating to Canada and the United States. Khadr had arrived in Canada as an observant Muslim, but largely secular in his beliefs. The MSA opened his eyes to the politics of Islam and by the time he graduated he was a proponent of Sharia law.

Khadr landed a job with Bell Northern Research, a leading telecommunications company then jointly owned by Bell Canada and Northern Telecom, which would later become Nortel. It was a challenging job, made more so because his mind was elsewhere—in Iran and Afghanistan, where dramatic insurgencies were taking place that would alter the fate of Muslims worldwide.

The Iranian revolution of the late 1970s saw the collapse of Shah Mohammad Reza Pahlavi's rule and the establishment of the first modern Muslim theocracy. In December 1979, when Zaynab was two months old, Ayatollah Ruhollah Khomeini became the Supreme Leader of the country.

A very different fight was underway in Afghanistan. On Christmas Day 1979, the Soviet Union's Airborne Forces of the Red Army landed in Kabul, setting off a nine-year conflict that eventually saw their defeat but divided Afghanistan and left it crippled by landmines and weapons discarded by the warring factions. The Soviets had come to the aid of the Marxist People's Democratic Party of Afghanistan, the PDPA, who were in power during the late 1970s. The PDPA was battling Islamic insurgents who were trying to topple the government. The Soviets wanted control of Afghanistan, since it gave them access to an Indian Ocean state and would greatly increase their influence in Southeast Asia, a strategic Cold War advantage.

The Soviet invasion became a rallying call for the world's Muslims who felt it was their religious duty to fight for the oppressed Afghans. They considered it a call to *jihad*, a word that has many meanings within the Islamic faith. In one sense, jihad defines the inner struggle of each Muslim to become a better human being by helping others. Jihad can also mean waging war against an unjust ruler and is often defined as a holy war.

These Muslim warriors, the *mujahideen* or *jihadis*, arrived by the thousands in Pakistan, where they would receive substantial help from Pakistan's intelligence service and a way into Afghanistan. Most were from Arab states, in particular Saudi Arabia whose government helped finance their travels, but they also came from Europe, the United States and Canada. The CIA covertly provided millions in funding, weapons and training to help support the Afghan mujahideen.

In 1982, Bahrain had opened its first institute of higher learning, the Gulf Polytechnic, and its administrators traveled to Europe, the United States and Canada in search of teachers. In Ottawa, they found Khadr. Impressed by his degree, language skills and Canadian citizenship, they offered him a position. Khadr liked the idea of living in the Middle East and becoming an educator and Elsamnah liked the idea of being closer to her Saudi relatives. In what would become a life of travel, the couple moved with their two children, Zaynab and their first son, Abdullah, who had been born in Ottawa. In Bahrain, they would have another son, whom they called Abdurahman.

Although Bahrain had a predominantly Muslim population, Khadr was dismayed to find Western influences. While living in Canada, he had become less tolerant of views other than those that were in accordance with Islam's teachings and took personal offence to the sale of alcohol and pork products in Bahrain.

The war in Afghanistan was covered extensively by the media in Bahrain. The nightly news told stories of jihadis' valor and Friday prayers in the mosque were devoted to victims of the war. Khadr soon became obsessed with the battle for Afghanistan, and deeply affected by the stories of the oppressed Afghans. He would cry as he listened to stories about the victims, cursing his own inaction.

Like hundreds of thousands of other Muslims, Khadr started to believe this wasn't just a dispute over the territory of a faraway land, but a war against Islam. As a devout Muslim, Khadr abided by the five pillars of Islam: faith, fasting, charity, daily prayers, and making the Hajj pilgrimage to Mecca in Saudi Arabia. The Islamic concept of charity, the third pillar of Islam known as *zakat*, is the duty of every Muslim. Khadr would ask his wife, was it not his religious obligation to help the Afghan orphans, widows and injured? He started to feel guilty about living comfortably while so many Muslims suffered and decided he had to go to see how he could help.

Azzam Tamimi, a British citizen of Palestinian descent and now the director of London's Institute of Islamic Thought, was living in Bahrain at the time. When he first met Khadr, he was struck by how passionately the Canadian spoke of Afghanistan. "I remember this very well. He said he was going to go to Afghanistan to join the jihad because this was our duty as Muslims because our brothers were fighting for their freedom and independence. I had a very long argument with him. 'You have a very successful career, you are a Canadian, there are so many people there in Afghanistan; they don't need you, why do you want to go?'" Tamimi recalled. "He didn't say he was going to fight. He said he was going to help; now what exactly he did there I wasn't sure. He was very sincere; his intention was just to help. We used to get all these images of the Afghanis suffering, so he went."

Khadr sent his family to stay with Elsamnah's parents in the Toronto suburb of Scarborough during the summer of 1983 so he could make his first trip to Pakistan alone. He called Elsamnah at the end of August to say he would meet the family in Bahrain for the start of the school year. But in the summer of 1984, he returned to Pakistan, while his wife and three children summered again in Canada. During that second trip, Khadr made up his mind. A Kuwaiti relief organization was looking for volunteers in Pakistan, so Khadr signed up. Engineering and teaching were merely professions; he had a calling. He wanted to devote his life to easing the suffering of fellow Muslims and no one was going to change his mind, he told his wife. Once he declared that the family would move to Peshawar, the family visited Elsamnah's parents in Canada to tell them the news.

As the snow and cold of a Canadian winter tightened its grip in late 1984, Khadr and his wife took their three children for one last trip to Bahrain, then to Kuwait to meet the charity organizers. In January 1985, the Khadrs left for Pakistan.

LIKE OTHERS DRAWN to the capital of Pakistan's North-West Frontier Province, Elsamnah had been romanced by Peshawar's rich history and the idea of helping Muslims fight an oppressive superpower. Peshawar teemed with Afghan refugees, aid workers and idealistic Muslims from across the world who were prepared to offer their lives in the fight against the Soviets.

Throw in the spies and foreign journalists on their way to or from the war and Peshawar during the 1980s was a city running on adrenaline.

The city is populated mainly by Pashtuns, a proud and fierce tribe that has remained independent despite years of attempted occupations. Peshawar sits on the edge of the Khyber Pass, the mountain road that links Pakistan to Kabul in Afghanistan, one of history's most fabled trading routes and a path for invading forces since the days of Alexander the Great. The chaotic markets, shrieking merchants and streets clogged with vividly painted rickshaws weaving around the odd camel create a city seemingly untouched by the years of modernization that have transformed Pakistan's other main cities such as Islamabad and Lahore.

Elsamnah also embraced the idea of living in a community of devout Muslims but when she first arrived, with three young children and pregnant with another, she was unhappy. The family lived in a second-floor apartment in a concrete building that housed the Kuwaiti Red Crescent Society. They enjoyed certain amenities such as running water, but at the center of the apartment was a courtyard where a cloud of flies, mosquitoes and dust hung. The family had to walk through this room to reach the bathrooms which Elsamnah often had to visit in the middle of the night. "I was prepared to live without electricity and in difficult circumstances but it was very, very hard," Elsamnah recalled. "At the time, I also had morning sickness. I had it with all my pregnancies. It was awful."

In Pakistan, Khadr become known by his *kunya*, an honorific more commonly used in the Arab world than a given first name. Typically, a *kunya* begins with father (*Abu*) or mother (*Umm*), followed by the first son's name. So Khadr should have been known as Abu Abdullah, but for some reason others mistook Abdurahman as Khadr's first-born, so instead Khadr became Abu Abdurahman and Elsamnah became Umm Abdurahman. By the time they tried to correct the mistake, the name had stuck. Since Abdurahman was such a common name, Khadr was also given an additional title—the Canadian, *al Kanadi*.

Khadr became Abu Abdurahman al Kanadi.

Khadr was jubilant, having finally found the excitement and purpose he craved, which only made Elsamnah feel guilty about her unhappiness. He tried to pull her out of depression and engage her in his passion for the people of Afghanistan. "He wanted me to feel the cause," Elsamnah recalled. He persuaded her to volunteer at the Red Crescent Society hospital, even offering to care for the children while Elsamnah worked a few hours every day. "When I first went there, I felt so helpless. I had never seen anything like that in Canada or Saudi before—people with TB, amputees. When they would change the dressing wounds without anesthesia people would scream and the kids, they were so skinny. I was crying all the time. They had to tell me you're here to make these people feel better, not worse."

Canadian journalist Eric Margolis was in Peshawar in the 1980s writing columns for the right-of-center tabloid, the *Toronto Sun*. Margolis was dismayed by the dearth of media coverage of the war and in awe of the Afghans' courage. "I've covered fourteen wars in my time so I'm not a newcomer to this, but it was emotionally draining. This was the hardest one," Margolis said two decades later. He knew Khadr and said he had a reputation as "a man of respect" among other Muslims. "He just seemed like your ordinary pious Muslim, not a rabid firebrand or Islamist, [but] conservative in his views. I don't know if he got radicalized in Afghanistan or subsequent to the time I met him but then he was quite middle-of-the-road and his interests as he expressed them to me were entirely humanitarian and not ideological at all."

OTHERS IN PESHAWAR were also starting to make a name for themselves. Osama bin Laden, the seventeenth of fifty-seven children born to an incredibly wealthy Saudi construction magnate, had set up a base in Peshawar to support the jihad. Backed by his family's fortunes and his own fundraising efforts, bin Laden brought money, construction equipment and recruits with him. But the twenty-three-year-old was not recognized as a military or spiritual leader. "Bin Laden was conspicuous among the volunteers, not because he showed evidence of religious learning, but because he had access to some of his family's huge fortune" the *9/11 Commission* that investigated the September 11, 2001, attacks concluded in its report.

The most influential spiritual leader was a charismatic Palestinian cleric named Abdullah Azzam. He had issued a *fatwa*, or religious ruling, at the start of the fighting declaring that every able-bodied Muslim had an obligation to protect Afghanistan from the Soviet invaders. In his late thirties, Azzam was the founder of the Hamas guerilla group that operated in the occupied West Bank and Gaza. Bin Laden had been greatly influenced by Azzam's sermons that he had listened to on tape while at university, and Azzam was responsible for convincing the wealthy, and somewhat impressionable, bin Laden that he should focus his attention and resources in Afghanistan.

Working with Azzam, bin Laden offered residence and living expenses for every Arab who joined the jihad in Afghanistan. Together they set up an organization called the Mektab al Khidmat, the "Office of Services," or "Services Bureau," to coordinate fundraising and channel recruits into Afghanistan.

Khadr worked for a Kuwaiti organization called Lajnat al Dawa, one of the largest of dozens of charities operating in the area. Lajnat al Dawa employed more than 1,000 workers in Pakistan and was responsible for some of the major reconstruction and refugee projects. (Almost two decades later in 2003, the U.S. Treasury Department and the United Nations included the Lajnat al Dawa on their lists of charities alleged to fund terrorism. Several of the early Peshawar members had allegedly joined al Qaeda once it was created, including Khalid Sheikh Mohammed, the suspected planner of the 9/11 attacks. His brother Zahid al-Sheikh was the charity's director during the late 1980s.)

A Canadian charity called Human Concern International (HCI) was another well-known humanitarian organization. Formed in 1980 by two Muslim doctors from Calgary, Alberta, HCI received grants from the Canadian government for specific projects in Afghanistan or Pakistan but relied mainly on private donations. While working at Lajnat, Khadr started to enquire about opportunities with HCI. He was impressed by HCI's work and, since he could easily travel back and forth to Canada, he approached them with an offer to help the charity fundraise. HCI was delighted to have him and he joined permanently in 1988.

Although Khadr had lived in Canada for only about seven years, he stood out from the other Arabs in Peshawar. Bin Laden, Azzam and other foreign leaders wore the loose-fitting clothing common in Pakistan, but during his first few years in Peshawar Khadr continued to wear Western pants and dress shirts.

Abdullah Anas, now a British citizen and an imam in London, met Khadr in Peshawar in 1985. Anas was an Algerian whose leadership in northern Afghanistan had earned him the reputation as a brave and skilled warrior. He recalled that the first time he met Khadr he was struck by his Western air but impressed by his charity work. "He was just presenting himself everywhere as not a man of training, not a man of fighting, not a man of jihad, just a man of charity work, aid," Anas said. "Twenty-four hours a day, he's talking just about this in Peshawar. It was usual there. There were many, many charities."

Anas was one of Azzam's most devoted followers and even married the Palestinian religious leader's daughter so he could become part of his family. Khadr also adhered to Azzam's teachings and wanted to get close to him.

CANADA WAS NEVER far away for the Khadr family. Almost every summer, and sometimes two or three times a year, the family would return to a small red-brick home on Khartoum Avenue where Elsamnah's parents lived after moving from Mississauga. The house in Scarborough, a suburb about a thirty-minute drive east from Toronto's downtown, was on a quiet cul-de-sac with mature trees and wide streets perfect for ball hockey or kicking around a soccer ball. A Canadian flag flew from the porch.

During the 1980s, as new citizens and immigrants from Asia, the Middle East and Caribbean settled there, Elsamnah's parents had no trouble fitting in. Mohamed and Fatmah Elsamnah ran a bakery in a strip mall on Eglinton Avenue East, a six-lane thoroughfare lined with stores and businesses that reflected the neighborhood's diversity. Beside the bakery, there was a Jamaican restaurant, and on the corner, the old-fashioned barbershop where the Khadr children had their hair cut. At Shuler and Gomes Optical, the Khadr boys would spend long summer days in the cool storeroom questioning owner Don and his brother Mike. The gregarious Gomes brothers from Guyana never turned away visitors and would patiently explain to the boys how all the machines in their store worked. Sometimes the conversations shifted to Guyana or the boys would talk of their life in Pakistan.

The bakery was known not just for its sticky coconut buns but also as a meeting spot where Arabs would linger and loudly debate throughout the day. Mohamed Elsamnah was unfailingly generous and regular customers would go home with more than they paid for.

The Elsamnahs never liked the idea of their daughter living in Pakistan because they had brought their children to Canada for a better life. So no matter how crowded and chaotic their home would become, the couple always looked forward to visits from their grandchildren. And so, in the summer of 1985, after only six months of first moving to Pakistan,

Elsamnah arrived with Khadr and their three young children: Zaynab, five; Abdullah, four, and two-year-old Abdurahman. She was near the end of another pregnancy and wanted her child born in Canada.

On July 6, 1985, she gave birth at Scarborough's Centenary Hospital to Ibrahim, her fourth child and third son. While the pregnancy had been largely uneventful, the birth was traumatic. The newborn was diagnosed with a congenital heart defect and the doctors weren't optimistic he would survive. Had the family been in Pakistan for his birth, he most likely wouldn't have. But Ibrahim was admitted to the world-renowned Hospital for Sick Children in Toronto where he successfully underwent open-heart surgery.

Khadr always spent his time in Canada fundraising for his Afghan projects. As Elsamnah cared for the children, her husband delivered speeches at mosques and community events, trying to collect money. By the time Ibrahim underwent the risky heart surgery, he had already returned to Peshawar with the funds he raised. Elsamnah's parents tried to convince her to stay a little longer, but three months after Ibrahim's birth she brought her family back to Peshawar.

IN PESHAWAR, now with the three toddlers, a fragile newborn and quickly pregnant again, Elsamnah was miserable. She continued to visit refugee camps with her husband but most of her energy was devoted to Ibrahim and she worried how she would handle another baby. She couldn't wait to return to Canada, and when that time came in the summer of 1986, Elsamnah was exhausted. Ibrahim was fourteen months old and scheduled for another open-heart operation at Toronto's Sick Kids and she was again ready to give birth. On the morning of September 19, as Elsamnah was preparing to take Ibrahim to the hospital, her contractions started. She reluctantly went instead to Centenary Hospital, while her mother took Ibrahim for his surgery.

Elsamnah's thoughts remained with her baby in a hospital across town even during her labor. She felt helpless and feared that her next baby would also emerge from her womb sick. But the birth was quick and painless and Elsamnah was shocked when the nurses told her it was all over and she had another son. From that very moment, her new baby, Omar, became the favorite child. Elsamnah called him *Yasser*, Arabic for "comfort" or "easy," which her life was anything but. Omar was a content, gurgling baby and for a few brief moments nothing else seemed to matter to Elsamnah except the newborn bundled in her arms.

Despite the family drama, Khadr again used the trip to Canada to fundraise. Five days after Omar's birth, Khadr was featured in the pages of Canada's largest circulation newspaper lamenting the lack of attention Afghanistan was receiving. He described landmines left by the Soviets that were disguised as toys in an effort to target children. "Some of them are quite pretty, particularly ones that look like a butterfly," he told the *Toronto Star*, identifying himself as A.S. Khadr. "They don't kill the children but they blow off their arms when they pick them up or their feet if they tread on them."

Ibrahim made it through his second surgery and, although fragile, recovered sufficiently to leave the hospital. Before fall ended, the family returned to Peshawar.

THE YEAR OMAR WAS BORN, Khadr met the man who would help shape the family's future. Ayman al Zawahiri was an Egyptian surgeon and senior member of the Islamic Jihad, one of two militant groups trying to overthrow Egypt's secular government. The Islamic Jihad had roots in the Muslim Brotherhood movement and was led by the Blind Sheikh, Omar Abdel Rahman. The spiritual leader's fiery rhetoric was said to have inspired the assassination of Egyptian president Anwar Sadat in 1981. Both Rahman and Zawahiri were among the hundreds of Islamic militants rounded up after the assassination and tried.

The raucous trial was covered by the international media and broadcast around the world. Since Zawahiri could speak English he emerged as the spokesperson and addressed the television cameras directly from the crowded caged pen inside the courtroom. On the opening day, he began: "Now we want to speak to the whole world. Who are we? Who are we? Why did they bring us here, and what we want to say about the first question: We are Muslims! We are Muslims who believe in that religion in its broad meaning, as more than ideology and practice. We believe in our religion, both as an ideology and practice, and hence we tried our best to establish this Islamic state and Islamic society."

Between his pronouncements, the other prisoners chanted in Arabic, *la illah ill Allah,* "There is no God but God!" At one point they cried out, "We will not sacrifice the blood of the Muslims for the Americans and the Jews."

Most of the accused received sentences of two or three years. Rahman, the Blind Sheikh, moved to the United States after serving his time in prison and he preached from a New Jersey mosque. (A decade later, he was arrested and convicted for his role in the 1993 World Trade Center bombing that killed six and injured more than a thousand people. He is currently serving a life sentence in a Colorado prison.)

In 1986, Zawahiri was in Peshawar treating the wounded mujahideen streaming out of Afghanistan and into the Red Crescent Society hospital. The Egyptians in Peshawar, many of them educated professionals, were a particularly close group. Khadr was impressed by Zawahiri, and sympathetic to his fight against Egypt's government. The two men became fast friends and would spend long evenings talking about the plight of the Afghans and their dreams of an Islamic government.

OSAMA BIN LADEN sometimes lectured at the Red Crescent where Zawahiri worked, but the two were not yet close. Bin Laden had a stronger alliance with his mentor, Azzam. Zawahiri competed with Azzam for bin Laden's considerable wealth and tried to get him to finance his own cause in Egypt.

Zawahiri and Azzam had different ideas on how the jihad should continue once the war with the Soviets was over. Azzam was focused on Palestine, while Zawahiri had a pan-Islamic view, vowing to bring Islamic governments to power worldwide, beginning with Egypt.

During most of the Soviet occupation, foreign leaders such as bin Laden and Zawahiri were mainly responsible for setting up guesthouses or channeling funds and fighters into Afghanistan. The mujahideen were predominantly Afghans or Pakistanis. It was not until the Battle of Jaji in April 1987 that the Arabs fought as a group against the Soviets. The fight may not have been an important military battle, but it gave the Arabs credibility that only increased as the stories of their victory became exaggerated in the telling. Jaji was where bin Laden had set up a base which he called *maasada*, meaning den. Since Osama means "lion," the base became known as the Lion's Den.

There are different accounts of the battle, which lasted more than a month, including wild exaggerations about the number of Soviet troops who tried to seize the base. But there is no doubt the Arabs were outgunned. Initially, they suffered a series of crippling defeats, but slowly the group, numbering no more than one hundred, managed to repel the Soviets and bin Laden gained a reputation not just as a financier but as a fighter.

When Khadr visited Canada, he would praise the bravery of the fighters in Jaji. His son Abdurahman always believed his father fought alongside bin Laden, but Zaynab said she repeatedly asked her father if he took part since he had been in Afghanistan at that time and would not tell them where. But Khadr never answered her questions directly and would only smile and walk away.

As the 1980s drew to a close and with the Soviet forces all but conquered, Elsamnah was no longer able to cope. Ibrahim was weak and required constant care, a duty that seemed to consume all her time.

Khadr decided Pakistan wasn't a place for a sick child, so he bought a plane ticket to Canada and flew back alone with his son to leave him in the care of Elsamnah's parents. "My mom agreed to take care of him. It was very hard. My mom didn't want to take the responsibility of a sick child. With a sick child, you're so occupied it's all you can do," Elsamnah recalled. "I feel sometimes it's not fair. It's true when I'm keeping Ibrahim I'm looking after one. But when Ibrahim was with my mother I was helping one hundred other Afghan children. That's my husband's mentality."

Every day, Ibrahim's grandparents would take him with them to the bakery so he could play and entertain their clientele as they worked. The staff at a Scarborough hospital also became familiar with Ibrahim, since every cold or flu seemed to land him in the emergency room.

Elsamnah threw herself into volunteering and tending to the sick, wounded and orphaned. She became a midwife and helped with the deliveries of the children of the mujahideen. Omar was always at her side. "I was all over the place, into camps and houses and all this. I would take Omar everywhere with me because he was breastfeeding. The others were in school. I guess I put all my love for the children in him because Ibrahim was taken away from me, sent away."

In January 1988, Elsamnah's parents called to say they were going to the Middle East to visit relatives. They couldn't take Ibrahim with them so Elsamnah returned to Canada with Omar. In a blurry photograph taken during that visit, the two curly-haired brothers sit on the carpeted floor of their grandparents' home wearing fuzzy jumpers and staring at the camera with blank expressions. Omar was sixteen months old, more than a year younger than Ibrahim, but in the photo he is larger and older looking. Although she missed the rest of her children, Elsamnah was happy to be with her sick son and away from the chaos of the war. Life in Canada was certainly simpler.

But one winter evening, Ibrahim suddenly became very sick and Elsamnah rushed him to Centenary Hospital. The next morning, he was transferred to Sick Kid's, the hospital that had saved her son twice before. Doctors said Ibrahim's heart was weak but he was stable and they encouraged her to go home to rest. Later that afternoon, she returned with Omar, but became frustrated when both her babies began to cry. "I shouted at Ibrahim, may God have mercy on me," Elsamnah recalled. Exhausted, depressed and lonely, she left the hospital late that evening only to be called back at 3 a.m. Ibrahim was in the intensive care unit and fighting for his life. Soon after she arrived, one of the doctors gently told Elsamnah her son's brain was no longer functioning and he was only being kept alive by machines. "Take him off of them," Elsamnah said. She held Ibrahim close to her chest as he died.

The next day, she bathed Ibrahim's body, dressed him in white and left him in the care of her brother at the Jami mosque, where she had been married a decade earlier. Her brother buried her son as she called the airline to book a flight. The next morning, with Omar in her arms, she returned to Peshawar.

OMAR WAS NOT ONLY his mother's favorite but his siblings' too. They called him the "good son" and it seemed he could do no wrong. Even before he could talk, he had a habit of clenching his teeth and letting off a high-pitched wail to get attention. But his behavior was seen as a source of entertainment rather than an irritant. The family taped Omar's outbursts and sent them back to Elsamnah's mother and father; the recordings were talked about for years.

For the first five years of his life, Omar and his siblings were shuttled between Peshawar and Scarborough on their father's fundraising excursions. Omar, like all the Khadr children, was comfortable in both worlds. Omar's favorite pastime was to have *The Adventures of Tintin* read to him. His father had been a fan of the stories about the fictional Belgian reporter and was delighted when he found the Tintin books at a market in Islamabad. After hearing the story countless times, Omar began doing impressions of Tintin's best friend, the seafaring whiskey-drinking Captain Haddock. Hearing the wide-eyed boy cuss with a lisp "billions of bilious blue blistering barnacles," or "ten thousand thundering typhoons" would dissolve his siblings and parents into fits of laughter.

It didn't matter that Omar lost his status as the baby of the family when Abdul Kareem was born in Peshawar in March 1989 and Maryam in Scarborough in August 1991; he still remained the most loved. Maryam would try for years to win her grandmother's affection but could not dethrone the dutiful Omar.

As OMAR AND HIS SIBLINGS grew up in Pakistan, a terrorist organization was coming together around them. On August 11, 1988, Abdullah Azzam met with bin Laden and five other prominent leaders to discuss how they could build on what had been created in Afghanistan. If their army of Muslim fighters could defeat the Soviets, what else could be accomplished?

Not much was agreed upon during the meeting as the men bickered about their goals. The only common thread was that the training that had begun in Jaji the year before should continue. "I am only one person," bin Laden told the group. "We have started neither an organization nor an Islamic group. It was a space of a year-and-a-half—a period of education, of building trust, of testing the brothers who came, and a period of proving ourselves to the Islamic world." They wanted to continue to train the most promising of the Afghan-Arabs, as the foreigners in Afghanistan came to be known. Their camp would be called al Qaeda, meaning "the base." "The name 'al Qaeda' was established a long time ago by mere chance," bin Laden told an al Jazeera television reporter in October 2001. "We used to call the training camp al Qaeda. And the name stayed."

A series of discussions that followed the August meeting brought more structure to their vision. All members would swear an oath, known as the *bayat*, to bin Laden, who had assumed the position as leader.

Bin Laden's vision of the jihad, which was shared by the Egyptians, was taking on a dramatically different form from what Azzam or Abdullah Anas envisioned. When Anas returned from fighting in northern Afghanistan, he met with Azzam in Peshawar and they talked about rebuilding instead of future fighting. Anas had discovered during his travels that Western organizations were delivering aid in northern Afghanistan not local Muslim charities. "I said beside the fighting we need to focus on the society to have our own schools, our own projects for the society because the Westerners are working and doing well there. Only fighting is not going to work. One day, jihad is going to finish, but after that we should have something there," Anas recalled. Anas didn't want Afghans to rely on handouts of non-government organizations from the West. It was a question of Muslim pride that Azzam understood.

Azzam sought advice from Khadr, who had also been talking about starting a new grassroots organization. Together they decided on a Peshawar-based charity that they would call al Tahaddi, which in Arabic means "the challenge."

According to Anas, Khadr offered to fundraise for the new charity during his next trip to Canada and the Middle East. But first he wanted Azzam to endorse his trip. "He said: 'Look, Sheikh Abdullah Azzam, I'm going now to the Islamic world, I'm going to Canada, my credibility is not the same as yours, I need a letter from you saying I'm sending Abu Abdurahman. Please all Muslim brothers help him.'" Azzam was one of the most well-known Muslim leaders worldwide and his support of Khadr would carry much weight. He agreed to write the letter.

But when Khadr returned to Peshawar with the funds, he told Azzam that he wanted to make the final decision on how the money was to be used. Azzam felt betrayed and some of his followers, furious at the deception, became wary of Khadr. They questioned out loud how someone who came to Peshawar as a Westerner could have so many connections, but so little loyalty. Perhaps he was a spy for the Americans, an accusation that enraged Khadr. He told Azzam directly that the issue had to be settled once and for all. "I'm not a spy," he said. "If you can prove it, kill me, and if you can't, then the person who is spreading this has to be punished."

The city buzzed with the controversy. In the mosques and guest homes, flyers were posted demanding that Azzam be brought to trial for spreading allegations against Khadr. Anas started to fear that the confrontation was part of a plan hatched by Zawahiri and the other Egyptians who were vying for bin Laden's attention and wanted to discredit Azzam. Even bin Laden worried for his mentor's safety. Bin Laden said he had no choice but to hold a trial as Sharia law dictated but warned Azzam not to attend. If convicted, Azzam could be sentenced to death and bin Laden did not believe he had the power to stop an execution.

What followed was justice, Peshawar-style. The trial was held at bin Laden's home and Khadr alone was given a chance to present his case. A jury of elders quickly found Azzam guilty of spreading false claims but agreed to spare his life. The al Tahaddi soon collapsed and Khadr eventually became the director of HCI's Peshawar office.

In November 1989, Azzam and his two sons were killed in a mysterious car bombing in Peshawar. Zawahiri was one of the suspects since the bombing finally eliminated his rival and cleared the way to bin Laden. No one was ever charged for the killings. Despite his past conflict with Azzam, Khadr was visibly distraught when he learned about his death. He was among the hundreds who attended Azzam's funeral, sobbing loudly throughout the day. "He cried without limits," Anas recalled.

WHEN THE LAST OF THE SOVIETS withdrew from Afghanistan on February 15, 1989, the mujahideen waged a bloody internecine battle and the humanitarian crisis continued unabated. A short article published in October 1989 in the *Toronto Star*, again profiling Khadr's involvement with HCI, began:

> Ahmed Khadr is a fighter in a forgotten war, whose living casualties make up almost half the world's refugee population. The Afghan children he battles to protect have the highest mortality rate in the world, he says. Almost one in three dies . . . The never-ebbing human tide had long since engulfed the meager resources Khadr has at hand. "Still we continue," he said. "What else can we do?" He was to fly home this past Saturday after almost two weeks in Canada and the United States lecturing on the Afghan civil war and pleading for help. "I've had people come up to me afterward and say, 'What war? The war is finished,'" he said. "It's not finished at all. It's getting worse. It was in the headlines for so long, 1.5 million people killed. Now it's going unnoticed."

Khadr now spent much of his time fundraising in Canada and often came alone. He no longer wore Western clothing, but instead dressed in a long, white *kurta* and an ivory *pakol*, the woolen cap favored by the mujahideen. Khadr was revered in Canada for his charity work, but his long, passionate fundraising speeches did not focus solely on the widows and the children he vowed to protect. In a September 1991 appearance at the Markham Islamic Centre, north of Toronto, Khadr spoke for forty-five minutes in a speech he titled "Afghanistan, The Untold Story," where he told the crowd, "Muslim people have given their life very cheap."

Although he spoke of the overpopulation of the refugee camps in Pakistan and of Afghan women struggling to raise their children alone, most of his talk focused on the mujahideen's valor. He blamed the media for covering Afghanistan only when there was American interest during the fight against the Soviets. He blamed the United States for withdrawing its support of the mujahideen, for stopping the delivery of ammunition and arms before the mujahideen had achieved their goal of creating a true Islamic government within Afghanistan. If Muslims around the world stopped donating, the mujahideen would be "forced to give up the battle and go back to Peshawar because of starvation," he said.

"You must think about the cause," Khadr said as he leaned into the microphone. "Afghanistan's cause is not an Afghan cause, it's your cause; it's my cause, too. It's every Muslim's cause." After his speech, he collected donations.

ONE EARLY DEFINING MOMENT in Omar Khadr's life, the first traumatic experience from which some say he never recovered, happened in 1992 when he was five and his father came close to dying.

Afghanistan remained in the grip of the civil war as various warlords tried to wrest control of the country. What exactly happened to Khadr in April 1992 is the source of some debate. HCI officials maintain Khadr was surveying one of the charity's refugee camps when he stepped on a landmine. His son Abdurahman says his father was part of a military battle and was hit by a bomb. Whatever the circumstances, Khadr was severely injured. Shrapnel tore through his right arm and leg and punctured a kidney and his bladder. His arm was probably the worst injured and most believed it would have to be amputated. Doctors in Peshawar were unsure how to treat him so he was taken to Karachi. But Khadr's condition didn't improve and Elsamnah was eager to get him to Canada. A month later when he was stable enough to travel, Elsamnah brought him to Toronto's top trauma hospital, Sunnybrook Health Sciences Centre.

Orthopedic surgeon Dr. Terry Axelrod saved Khadr's arm, during an operation that later became the subject of one of Axelrod's medical lectures. Khadr's half-brother, Ahmed Fouad, recalled that when he drove from the United States to visit Khadr, he was surprised to walk into his hospital room and find Elsamnah and all the children crowded together on his hospital bed. Khadr didn't talk much about his time in Pakistan with his brother but did say he was furious with the civil war.

Omar sat close to his father and listened, although at such a young age it's hard to know what he absorbed. It was certainly the first time he had seen his father fragile and it frightened him. For the brief times they weren't visiting him, all the children begged their mother to go back to the hospital. "Let's go see papa," Omar would cry until his mother relented.

Khadr didn't want to stay in Canada and was frustrated by the length of his recovery. "There was some time when they thought he was not able to walk again. When he started to get better, everyone convinced him now you're disabled, you know, you have done enough for Afghanistan, now you need to spare some time for the family," Elsamnah recalled. "But it was in his blood."

On his weekends away from the hospital, Khadr would visit community centers and tell anyone who would listen about the victims of Afghanistan. "It's your duty, you have to help them," he would say. Khadr stayed in Canada only as long as it took him to learn to walk again before returning with his family to Peshawar in the fall of 1993.

Some say he returned a different man.

3

The Khadr Effect

THE KHADR CHILDREN had grown accustomed to the comforts of Canada and were happy in 1993 that they didn't return to the apartment above the Red Crescent Society. Khadr had rented a house in Hayatabad, a suburb northwest of Peshawar that was divided into seven zones or "phases." Phase II, where they settled, was popular with Egyptian, Arab and wealthy Afghan families. The houses were spacious, each with its own backyard, and Elsamnah was delighted she could grow vegetables while Khadr was happy he could indulge his weakness for rabbits. Rabbits were mainly raised in Pakistan to be eaten but Khadr couldn't bear to kill them so instead he brought two home as pets. The pair quickly multiplied into a herd and the Khadr children loved having so many furry companions, even if their mother fumed about the loss of fresh vegetables from her garden.

Soon the rabbits with distinctive markings had names such as Pistachio and Bandit. There was also one named Khattab, after the Jordanian who gave it as a present to five-year-old Kareem. Ibn al Khattab was a scrawny teenager who had come from Saudi Arabia to join the jihad in the 1980s and became a battle-hardened warrior. He was just one among hundreds of young jihadis who lingered in Peshawar in the 1990s, spending most of their time in guesthouses for foreign fighters. Khadr often visited these homes as well and one day he brought Kareem along. When Khattab noticed Kareem looking at his rabbits, he offered one as a gift.

Within a decade, Khattab would have an international reputation. He left Peshawar to fight in Tajikistan in 1994, then on to Chechnya, a disputed territory where Muslim separatists were battling the Russian government. Khattab emerged a robust and heavily bearded Chechen warlord and one of the most familiar faces in Russia. Fluent in Russian, Arabic and with a good knowledge of Farsi and English, Khattab became a charismatic leader who understood the power of publicity. He often held one of his hands behind his back to hide the fact that two of his fingers had been blown off, concealing any sign of his fallibility.

The Russian government claimed that Khattab had links to Osama bin Laden's al Qaeda and denounced him as a terrorist. The Chechens regarded Khattab as a hero in their "war of liberation." In early 2002, Russia's Federal Security Service reportedly killed Khattab by slipping him a poisoned letter.

Khattab, the rabbit, also met a dismal fate. Kareem's little sister, Maryam, was just a toddler and used to play roughly with the rabbits. She was especially fond of grabbing Khattab by his hind legs and suspending him, until one day, the stress on the rabbit's legs crippled him. Khadr was devastated. He loved the rabbits and would often return from work with a bushel of corn and go directly to the backyard to feed them, without saying hello to his children or wife. After Khattab's injury, Khadr would sit in the backyard, with tears rolling down his cheeks, staring at the rabbit struggling to pull itself around by his front paws. The connection between their recently disabled father and the injured rabbit was not lost on the Khadr children. They would watch him from the window and not know whether to laugh or cry.

THE STAFF AND VOLUNTEERS at the Peshawar office of Human Concern International (HCI) were delighted to have Khadr back. Khadr carried clout both within the community of Western humanitarian workers and among Afghanistan's leaders vying for power. HCI had suffered during Khadr's absence, losing its status within a powerful organization called the Agency Coordinating Body for Afghan Relief, or ACBAR. This coalition worked to coordinate the dozens of projects undertaken by non-government organizations, and it wasn't uncommon for top United Nations officials or representatives from the Afghan and Pakistani governments to attend meetings. Khadr had chaired the ACBAR meetings in the province of Logar before his injury but while he was convalescing in Canada the position had been turned over to a U.S.-based charity.

Abdullah Almalki was in his early twenties and among a handful of Canadians working with HCI when Khadr returned to Pakistan. He had first heard of HCI while studying electrical engineering at Carleton University in Ottawa after he sponsored an Afghan refugee through the charity. Carleton offered a program that allowed students sixteen months of work experience as a break from their studies. Almalki decided to put his engineering skills to the test with HCI, and because a friend's mother worked with the charity, getting a placement wasn't a problem.

Almalki had grown up in an upper middle-class neighborhood in Damascus before arriving in Ottawa with his family in the summer of 1987 when he was sixteen. He obtained his Canadian citizenship a few years later. His upbringing left him unprepared for what he saw when he first arrived in Peshawar in the fall of 1992. He had never seen such poverty and desperation.

The following winter, Almalki returned, this time helping to build an irrigation system in Afghanistan as part of a United Nations Development Program reconstruction project whose contract had been awarded to HCI. He only took a break in his work to return to Canada to marry Khuzaimah Kalifah, a Malaysian-born student with almond-shaped eyes and a quiet disposition whom he had met at Carleton.

By the time Almalki and his wife returned to Pakistan, so too had Khadr. Almalki was the director of HCI's engineering division of Afghan development projects and Khadr, as director of the HCI's Peshawar office, was his boss. From the moment they met, Almalki and Khadr did not get along. Khadr was a micro-manager, a workaholic and a stickler for detail, but now he was also impatient and demanding. "You can't operate a project and engineers with wanting to know every detail and being in control of everything. It just doesn't work that way. He wanted things done and he wanted them done now. He was very pushy, not easy to deal with," recalled Almalki. People who had worked with Khadr for years didn't know how to handle him once he returned. Two senior managers soon quit and the local employees who were accustomed to working regular hours were forced under Khadr's new management to stay late most days without compensation.

It seemed much of Khadr's frustration stemmed from his disability. The area was awash with crippled victims of the war; no other country has been more heavily planted with landmines than Afghanistan. Khadr had come to help these victims not become one. Some days it seemed his pride had been the most injured. He had to wear specially designed shoes and he walked with a profound limp. His injured arm and hand made it difficult to process the charity's paperwork. Much to his embarrassment, he also had to travel with his own chair. It was a tell-tale sign that Khadr was going to Afghanistan if a plastic fold-up chair was packed along with other supplies. "He needed a chair to go to an outhouse, if there was an outhouse. In many cases, it was just bare land. He needed something to sit on," Almalki explained.

Almalki had intended to stay with HCI for most of 1994, but Khadr's overbearing management sent him back to Canada earlier. Almalki didn't realize that wouldn't be the last he would hear of Khadr's name.

ALTHOUGH HE FRUSTRATED HIS STAFF, Khadr still maintained good relations with Afghanistan's political players. The period in the early 1990s between the Soviet Union's withdrawal and the Taliban's rise to power was one of bloody confusion. Many Western-based humanitarian and human rights agencies were forced to leave even as the refugee crisis worsened. When the last of the Red Army limped out in February 1989, the international community turned its back on Afghanistan. Other conflicts, such as ethnic cleansing in the former Yugoslavia, dominated the headlines. Afghanistan became one of the "world's orphaned conflicts; the ones that the West, selective and promiscuous in its attention, happens to ignore in favor of Yugoslavia," UN Secretary General Boutros Boutros-Ghali said in 1995.

Most expected Afghanistan's Communist government under President Mohammad Najibullah to collapse once the Soviets withdrew. Najibullah had been the leader of KHAD, Afghanistan's notoriously brutal secret police, and his government was seen as a Soviet puppet regime. But Najibullah's army dug in with surprising force during the mujahideen's first attempt to seize power, sparking a period of brutality and continually shifting alliances during which various mujahideen factions fought amongst themselves.

For a brief period, Osama bin Laden and Ayman al Zawahiri remained in Afghanistan. Bin Laden focused his attention on a training camp called al Farouk, near Khost, where he began to cultivate an army to fight the next, still unidentified jihad that had first been discussed at the meeting in August 1988. The genesis of al Qaeda may be traced to that meeting but it would be years before it developed into a terrorist organization with a defined goal. Recruits at al Farouk, however, had to sign an oath of loyalty to bin Laden and, in return, they received a salary, a round-trip ticket home each year and even a month's vacation. The camp's constitution was simple: "To establish the truth, get rid of evil, and establish an Islamic nation." For the young Muslims who had come to Afghanistan, enticed by the stories of the mujahideen's bravery, the camp was a welcome opportunity.

But bin Laden didn't stay in Afghanistan long, returning to Saudi Arabia in the fall of 1989 to what he thought would be a hero's welcome. Instead, the pious thirty-one-year-old found himself at odds with the Saudi royal family, who were fearful of a fundamentalist uprising and concerned about bin Laden's influence. Bin Laden made no secret of his disgust for the king's lavish, alcohol-fueled lifestyle. When Saddam Hussein invaded Kuwait and Iraqi forces occupied its oil fields a year later, bin Laden offered his army of Islamic militants as protection for the Holy Kingdom. But the royal family rebuffed his offer which could not compare to the thousands of U.S. troops who had been invited into Saudi Arabia. Bin Laden was incensed at the end of the Gulf War when a large contingent of U.S. troops remained in Saudi Arabia, home to Islam's two holiest sites. In 1991, he fled to Sudan. Bin Laden would not return to Afghanistan until the Taliban were in control five years later.

AFGHANISTAN'S FATE was in the hands of seven mujahideen leaders who could not agree how to share the power. Two of the most powerful leaders were Gulbuddin Hekmatyar, a native Pashtun, and Tajik Ahmed Shah Masood. Hekmatyar commanded the Hizb-i-Islami party, which was supported by much of Afghanistan's Arab community and had the backing of Pakistan's powerful intelligence agency, the ISI. Hekmatyar was an Islamist whose disdain for the United States didn't stop him from accepting substantial CIA funding. Masood, a French-speaking leader who inspired a faithful following, was based in the Panjshir Valley north of Kabul where he enjoyed a modest lifestyle. Masood's closest ally was Abdul Rasul Sayyaf, an Afghan who had spent most of his life in Saudi Arabia. During the 1980s, the Saudi government supported Sayyaf's move to Afghanistan where he established the Ittehad-e-Islami or "Islamic Unity," which introduced the strict Saudi Wahabbi interpretation of Islam to Afghanistan, where the mystical Sufi interpretation had been the most common form of Islam practiced. Sayyaf's reputation seemed even larger than his substantial girth. Despite his wealth, he shunned air conditioning and other comforts and lived modestly like Masood. Each night, he slept on a small slat of wood instead of a mattress. His only indulgence seemed to be a nightly match of tennis.

Najibullah's government managed to fend off the mujahideen leaders for almost three years until the warlords realized they had to put their differences aside and join forces. Masood aligned himself with Tajik leader, Burhanuddin Rabbani, and an Uzbek named Rashid Dostum. They came together under the umbrella of a newly created party called the Northern Alliance and managed to take control of the capital of Kabul. Najibullah fled to the safety of Kabul's UN compound where he remained for four years. (When the Taliban took control of Kabul in 1996, they slaughtered Najibullah and his brother and hanged their bodies from a pole in the center of town. Cigarets were stuffed in their mouths and money in their pockets to serve as an example of the excesses the Taliban would not tolerate.)

Rabbani was appointed president of the Islamic State of Afghanistan in June 1992 and the other warlords were given positions of power in the uneasy alliance. Hekmatyar was appointed prime minister but the Pashtun leader was angered that Rabbani, a Tajik, was in power instead of a Pashtun. Hekmatyar refused to come to Kabul and attempted his own coup by launching a merciless bombing campaign on the capital. Then Dostum defected from the Northern Alliance and joined forces with Hekmatyar. Together their attacks left thousands of innocent Afghans dead. In 1994 alone, it's estimated 25,000 died in Kabul.

ALL THE LEADERS had a history of violence, but Dostum's brutality was legendary. A muscular mountain of a man, taller than six feet, Dostum had a booming laugh that Uzbeks swear had frightened men to death. When Pakistani journalist Ahmed Rashid visited Dostum's compound he noted bloodstains and pieces of flesh on the muddy ground of the courtyard. "I innocently asked the guards if a goat had been slaughtered," Rashid wrote in his book *Taliban*. "They told me that an hour earlier Dostum had punished a soldier for stealing."

Dostum survived by pledging loyalty to only one man—himself. At the beginning of the Soviet invasion, Dostum was a hard-drinking committed Communist. A decade later, he emerged as a devout Muslim. Switching sides again, he joined Hekmatyar before retreating to the north where he created his own mini-state. Only the Taliban were capable of driving him out of the country, to Turkey where he sought shelter until he returned to join the Northern Alliance.

Sayyaf's history typifies how quickly sides could change in Afghan politics. Sayyaf's forces, with their substantial Saudi backing, had been vital in the war against the Soviets. During Rabbani's tenure, Sayyaf aligned himself with Northern Alliance leader Masood. But once the Taliban took over, it was reportedly Sayyaf who encouraged bin Laden to return to Afghanistan from Sudan.

Despite this history, Sayyaf became part of Afghan president Hamid Karzai's U.S.-backed government in 2004. In March 2007, he helped pass an amnesty bill shielding former warlords from being tried for war crimes, enraging human rights groups that held him accountable for the slaughter of thousands of Afghan civilians.

During the confusion in the early 1990s, Khadr managed to deal with all the mujahideen leaders. He was especially close to Sayyaf, whom he had known since the early days in Peshawar, but it wasn't uncommon for officials with President Rabbani's government to also visit HCI's headquarters to talk with Khadr. Khadr's diverse connections enabled HCI to work in areas of Afghanistan where many Western agencies wouldn't attempt to visit.

When Khadr arrived in Canada he was largely secular in his beliefs, but by now he was devoutly religious and determined to live in a country ruled by Sharia law. He believed the only true form of government was an Islamic one. He would joke with his children that Canada was perfect as an Islamic nation since the CN Tower, Toronto's lofty landmark, resembled a mosque's minaret.

He talked with his children about the beauty of living and dying for Islam. If you died fighting for Islam, you would die a martyr and the rewards in heaven would be wonderful, he told them. For the men, seventy-two perfumed virgins would be waiting in heaven. But the afterlife could also be whatever you wanted. Khadr said he envisioned a paradise with a beautiful waterfall and rare white elephant. Abdullah would chime in that his heaven was a place filled with fancy cars. Omar said his paradise would be a swimming pool of Jell-O, his favorite food.

Khadr believed that with the Soviets out of Afghanistan the path was clear for the Islamists and a pure society ruled by Sharia law. He was furious when the fighting broke out among the Muslim factions. "When I was there [Khadr] was totally against the civil war that was happening," said Almalki. "He felt they were destroying everything that they'd worked for."

THE KHADR FAMILY was well known in Peshawar as The Canadians. Even the children, who attended private Arab schools, were seen as Westerners, not Arabs. The youngest daughter, Maryam, was listed on school report cards as Maryam al Kanadi.

Like most families, birth order greatly affected the Khadr children's upbringing; their personalities developed in part because of the responsibilities imposed upon them. Abdullah was the eldest son and, as such, shouldered the majority of responsibility. Quiet and obedient, when his father needed a driver, Abdullah was behind the wheel. Zaynab became like a second mother to the children and cared often for her younger siblings when her mother traveled on missions with Khadr. She was also determined and confident, most like her father. Maryam and Kareem were the babies in the family and allowed such indulgences as the youngest often receive. Then, there were the middle sons—Omar and Abdurahman—and they couldn't be more different.

Omar was closest to his mother and, as such, was doted upon by the women in the family. By contrast, Abdurahman was closest to his father, but not because there was a natural parental bond. Khadr kept Abdurahman close out of necessity. Rambunctious, hyper and prone to running away, Abdurahman was the family's problem child from the beginning. "My dad always did like a challenge and I was a challenge in his case because everybody else listened, but I had all the questions to ask," Abdurahman later said. "I respect my dad as blindly, I think, as they do. But in the end, I was the only one who said, you know, 'Let's not do that.'"

In 1994, when Abdurahman was only eleven or twelve and Abdullah thirteen, Khadr decided to send them to Afghanistan to learn how to fight. While it wasn't uncommon for young Afghan boys to learn how to shoot AK-47s, Khadr sent his sons to Khalden, a prestigious training camp. When the Khadr boys were at Khalden, the camp was run by a Libyan named Ibn al Sheikh al Libi. He introduced them to others at the camp personally. Everyone at the camp used aliases, or *kunyas*, their true identities known only to the leaders. "This is Hamza," the camp leader said, pointing to Abdullah, then to Abdurahman: "This is Osama."

ONE OF THE MEN at the camp was a Moroccan who went by the name Abu Imam. Unbeknownst to Ibn al Sheikh al Libi and the others, Abu Imam was a spy who had infiltrated the camp and was reporting to the British and French intelligence services. He was shocked at the arrival of the Khadr brothers, who were much younger than any of the recruits he had previously encountered. He was also shocked by how immature they were. The Khadr boys fought incessantly and bitterly. One day, their shouting drew the attention of the whole camp. "As usual, they were less interested in the training than in fighting with each other," Abu Imam wrote in his book, *Inside the Jihad*, published under the pseudonym Omar Nasiri.

> After a few minutes, they stopped firing at the targets and turned towards one another. Even though we were far away, we could hear them yelling. Suddenly, Osama lifted his PK and pointed it at his brother. Hamza immediately pointed his Kalashnikov back at him. We were all shocked. We never turned our guns on each other this way. The boys were screaming more and more loudly. Their fingers were on the triggers of their guns.
>
> I think every brother on that hill believed that the boys were actually going to kill each other. And they probably would have if the trainer hadn't jumped in between and pushed them apart. When it was over, we all turned to each other in dismay. We had never seen anything like this at the camp. They had broken all the rules we had learned since our first day of training. Soon, we were laughing about it, even though it wasn't funny at all. It made us nervous.

Abu Imam watched from afar one day when Khadr arrived with a few men, driving up in a four-wheel-drive truck. He wasn't there to visit his sons but instead quickly disappeared with the camp leader into the area that housed the camp's explosives laboratory. "Nobody ever talked about the explosives laboratory. It was behind the mosque, near the entrance to the munitions caves. We were strictly forbidden to go inside. In fact, we weren't even supposed to look at it," Abu Imam reported. Although Abdurahman does not remember Abu Imam, he did recall the day he described in his book. His father came to talk to the camp leaders, not his sons. But Abdurahman assumed his dad went in a meeting room adjacent to the explosives laboratory, not the explosives building. "That's where all the visitors went to meet. I just don't know," he recalled.

Abdurahman became legendary in Khalden and the other camps he would attend as a rebel who seemed to get away with anything. He had little interest in learning what was being taught or of following the strict rules and often would try to run away. If he did escape, his father would always put him back in the car and sternly say, "Abdurahman, we're going back," and then drive in silence. One day, he called Abdurahman the "cancer of the family."

Abdullah was much more cautious and serious; he rarely spoke to the others. One evening, Abdullah was sent to the infirmary with a high fever and stomach pains and he met Abu Imam. They began to talk and Abdullah described an experience he had had a few years earlier. He had been traveling with his father in Khost where they witnessed one of the last battles before the fall of the Najibullah government. "Night after night, he saw the sky burning with mortar fire and rockets. Once, a bomb fell near where he and his father were standing on a public square. But it didn't explode. Everyone stood by for a few minutes waiting for something to happen, but nothing did. The bomb just lay there. He said that once it was clear the bomb wasn't going to explode, several Afghanis rushed forward to salvage the metal and explosive material inside. The people were desperately poor, and fed themselves by selling bits of ammunition and other material back to the mujahideen," Abu Imam recalled.

Then someone hit the bomb with a hammer and it did explode, sending body parts flying. "Isn't that stupid?" Abdullah asked Abu Imam after he finished telling the story, laughing and shaking his head. "The Afghans are so stupid."

"But I could tell from his eyes," Abu Imam wrote, "the story still upset him."

ON NOVEMBER 19, 1995, two men quietly approached the Egyptian embassy in downtown Islamabad. One carried a briefcase filled with the explosives and weapons needed to distract the guards. The other drove a Nissan pick-up truck packed with a 250-pound bomb.

Survivors would later describe the sound of two explosions but the truck that rammed into the front of the embassy caused the most damage. Most of the dead were Pakistani security guards, but one Egyptian diplomat died. The bomb left a ten-foot crater where the embassy's visa section once stood and when rescuers arrived to search for survivors, a shattered picture of Egyptian president Hosni Mubarak hung crookedly on the wall. "I was standing outside the gate and the body of a police officer came flying over the wall and landed beside me," Mohammed Iqbal, a security guard for the Egyptian Ambassador told Associated Press reporter Kathy Gannon after the bombing.

Sixteen people died and sixty were injured.

Three separate Egyptian Islamic groups claimed responsibility for the bombing, but authorities both in Pakistan and Egypt immediately suspected Zawahiri as the mastermind. Their suspicions were later confirmed in Zawahiri's memoir. "The bomb left the embassy's ruined building as an eloquent and clear message," he wrote.

It was Zawahiri's first major victory since vowing revenge for his imprisonment in Cairo in the early 1980s but it was not his first attack on the Egyptian government. Earlier that year, Zawahiri had held a meeting in Khartoum, Sudan's capital, with members of the Egyptian Jihad, a rival group to Zawahiri's al Jihad. The historic meeting ended with an agreement to put aside their differences and plot Mubarak's assassination.

On June 26, when Mubarak traveled to Ethiopia's capital, Addis Ababa, their plan was put in action. As Mubarak's motorcade traveled along the only route from the airport to the city, it came under fire from two cars waiting on the road. Two Ethiopian police officers were killed but so were five of the attackers and three others were captured. Mubarak escaped unharmed.

Once back in Cairo, Mubarak vowed to wipe out all Islamic loyalists in his country. His forces conducted a series of indiscriminate attacks, burning houses and seizing suspects who would never be heard from again. Women were stripped naked and humiliated for the suspected sins of their husbands and brothers. Soon after, Zawahiri's men bombed the Egyptian embassy in Islamabad.

Pakistan's Federal Investigative Agency, working with Egyptian authorities, quickly arrested twenty foreign suspects from Egypt and Sudan. Among the suspects named by Pakistani authorities, but not taken into custody, was an Egyptian named Khalid Abdullah. Abdullah, known by his *kunya* Abu Ubaydah, was a member of the Egyptian network that remained in Pakistan and Afghanistan after the Soviets' defeat.

IN THE SUMMER of 1995, a few months before the embassy bombing, Khadr had arranged a marriage between Abdullah and his daughter Zaynab. Zaynab was just fifteen and not pleased, as she had no interest in getting married or taking orders from a man she had just met, but she could not change her father's mind. A wedding contract was signed in July but the wedding ceremony was planned for December, the custom in traditional

Muslim marriages. Elsamnah had spent the fall preparing an apartment in their Hayatabad home where the newlyweds would live. By the time authorities came looking for Abdullah, he had already fled. It would take years before he finally married Zaynab, and even longer for the Egyptian authorities to find him.

Eight days after the bombing, police arrived at the Khadr home looking for Ahmed Said. He had been in Afghanistan at the time of the bombing and hadn't yet returned. Elsamnah did not know where her husband was and barricaded the door, refusing to allow the police in. When they finally got the door open, Zaynab ran to get one of her father's guns and held it over her head, screaming as loudly as she could. But she did not fire and was subdued. They took Elsamnah and all the children into custody. Omar and his two younger siblings tried to stay close to their mother who was also screaming and wailing. The police conducted a thorough search and seized boxes of papers and more than $10,000 in American currency.

Elsamnah and her children were detained only briefly.

On December 2, 1995, Khadr returned to Peshawar and was furious that his house had been raided and money, which he claimed was to pay the staff at HCI, had been seized. There are conflicting reports as to what happened next. Elsamnah said Khadr went to the police station a day after he came home to complain about the raid and didn't return. "Does a criminal go to the police station by himself?" a tearful Elsamnah asked a Reuters reporter ten days later. "They can fabricate any crime against him."

Pakistan's interior minister Naseerullah Babar told Parliament on December 3 that a suspected financier of the bombing had been arrested as he crossed the border. It was clear he was talking about Khadr, which meant Khadr had been picked up before he even crossed into Pakistan. But a report by an Ottawa lawyer hired by HCI after Khadr's arrest stated that Khadr had come into Pakistan on December 2 without incident and returned to his HCI office the next day. Seven police investigators arrived to talk with him and three other employees—the office manager, the assistant accountant and chauffeur. The investigators asked them to come to Islamabad for further questioning and when they arrived at the station they were taken into custody, Canadian lawyer Marc Duguay wrote in 1996. Khadr was interrogated for five days by both Egyptian and Pakistani authorities. "He was kept blindfolded and was forced to endure constant accusations, filthy language, threats associated with his family and various other forms of psychological and physical intimidation," Duguay wrote. "He was left to sleep on a chair during several nights. Fear tactics were also employed, such as the use of a shock stick, hair pulling and, in one instance, a threat was made that he would be taken to a laboratory, after which he would never sleep with a woman again."

On December 14, Pakistan officially confirmed Khadr's detention. By then, he was on a hunger strike and had been transferred to a hospital in Islamabad. In Canada, a group of supporters in Toronto and Ottawa's Muslim communities began to circulate a petition demanding his release.

Elsamnah left Peshawar and took her six children to Islamabad so they could visit Khadr at the prison hospital. A clearly traumatized nine-year-old Omar sometimes slept beside his father in the hospital bed as he had when his father had been injured. Elsamnah also took her children to the front lawn of the Canadian High Commission in Islamabad where she staged a protest and demanded that the Canadian government help one of its citizens.

The timing of their protest was perfect.

A PLANELOAD OF CANADA'S ELITE left Ottawa just after New Years 1996 on an eleven-day, four-country trade mission led by Canadian Prime Minister Jean Chrétien. On board were seven provincial premiers, many of the country's mayors, a smattering of university professors and more than 300 business professionals. There was also the requisite contingent of Canadian journalists who would document the prime minister's every step through India, Pakistan, Malaysia and Indonesia.

These international trade missions were seen as a way to secure foreign business deals and showcase what resources Canada had to offer other than wheat and wood. Top business professionals paid their own way to travel with the politicians, who brought publicity and clout. Chrétien called the trips Team Canada.

Chrétien's ascent through politics had been a classic Canadian rags-to-riches saga. Born January 11, 1934, in Shawinigan, Quebec, Chrétien was the second youngest of nineteen children, only nine of whom survived infancy. "Jean Chrétien in youth is small, skinny, deaf in one ear, deformed at the mouth, slightly dyslexic, poor of pocket and intellectually unadorned," Chrétien biographer Lawrence Martin wrote. Chrétien, who often called himself "*le petit gars de Shawinigan*," the little guy from Shawinigan, overcame his early shortcomings to attend law school and then talk his way into politics to become Canada's twentieth prime minister.

"The art of politics is learning to walk with your back to the wall, your elbows high, and a smile on your face," Chrétien wrote in his 1985 memoir *Straight From The Heart*. "It's a survival game played under the glare of lights. If you don't learn that you're quickly finished. It's damn tough and you can't complain; you just have to take it and give it back. The press wants to get you. The Opposition wants to get you. Even some of the bureaucrats want to get you."

Chrétien's first Team Canada trip in 1994 to China was a rousing success. Government estimates put the price of business contracts signed in the billions. There was also rare collegiality among the politicians. They called Chrétien "Captain Canada," and at the end of the tour, Ontario's New Democrat Premier, Bob Rae, presented Chrétien with a hockey jersey with a "C" emblazoned on the front.

But by 1996, Chrétien had been in power for three years and the political climate had changed. His stance on human rights had come under fire after he failed to condemn the Chinese government for arresting activists before the sixth anniversary of the Tiananmen massacre. The detentions of Tiananmen student leader Wang Dan and Ding Zilin, the mother of one of the students killed, particularly upset governments worldwide. "What, you might ask, does the government of Canada have to say about all this?" thundered an editorial in the Canadian national paper, the *Globe and Mail*. "Has the Department of Foreign Affairs issued a statement of concern? Has our ambassador registered a private protest? Have our representatives inquired about the health of Wang Dan or the status of Ding Zilin? The answer is: none of the above . . . This is typical of Canada's stand (or lack of it) on human rights in China."

Chrétien only angered his critics in trying to defend his actions. "China is a huge county and Canada is a small one. Canada does not have the power to force a change in China's human rights behavior," Chrétien told reporters.

There were serious domestic problems facing Chrétien, too, since Canada had narrowly survived a vote that could have torn the country apart. The October 30, 1995, referendum in the French-speaking province of Quebec asked voters if the province should secede from Canada. Only by a small margin did Quebecers vote against separating.

Some criticized Chrétien for forging ahead with the Team Canada trip barely two months after the vote. In an apparent snub, the premiers of Quebec, Alberta and Saskatchewan said they were opting out of the trip. Saskatchewan's Roy Romanow and Alberta's Ralph Klein both cited domestic commitments. One Maritime premier on the tour later said that the premiers "are implicitly suggesting that the rest of us don't care as much about what happens at home."

Against this negative backdrop, Chrétien's communications team was desperate to keep Team Canada '96 on message. They wanted to fill the papers with photo ops of smiling politicians locked in handshakes. Little did they know that more problems lay ahead. As Chrétien's communications director Peter Donolo later lamented, "There's always a problem with the sequel."

EVEN BEFORE TEAM CANADA arrived at its first stop, the trip's agenda changed. The delegation was met at Toronto's Pearson International Airport by a group of children with a message: Don't forget India's problem with child labor. "Today, there are millions of child laborers in South Asia, working in slave-like conditions," the children told the leaders and assembled press. "These include children working as carpet weavers, in brassware factories, in stone quarries, in textiles, in glass and bangle factories, in match and firework industries, in agriculture, as domestics and as child prostitutes." The children at the airport were members of a group called Free the Children, which had been started by Craig Kielburger, a savvy thirteen-year-old from Thornhill. Kielburger was already in Asia with his parents meeting various powerful figures, including Mother Theresa, as part of his campaign. Now he was setting the stage for Chrétien's arrival.

The media loved the story. Here was an articulate kid taking on the labor laws of India just as Canada was trying to strengthen business ties. But Chrétien did not try to sidestep the issue. Once in India, he met with Kielburger and raised the issue of child labor during his meetings with high-ranking officials, including one on January 11 with Prime Minister P.V. Narasimha Rao. In a speech in New Delhi, Chrétien told the business audience, "All of us must work to alleviate the poverty and underdevelopment that is at the root of this horrible problem."

The story may have diverted attention from the focus of the trip, but it had been managed well. But another story was brewing. On December 30, 1995, the *Toronto Star* had carried a story by a freelance journalist in Islamabad on Khadr's detention and hunger strike. "'I am a hostage,' said the Egyptian-born regional director of Ottawa-based Human Concern International," the story began. "'The last hope I have is Mr. Chrétien coming. Canada is one of Pakistan's biggest donors of aid, and with Chrétien's visit and the economic team coming, we have leverage.'" Khadr told the reporter he was a political pawn arrested because the Egyptian government was pressuring Pakistan to make quick arrests in the embassy bombing. "I want to go to Canada and have a rest," he said. "For ten years, I've been doing work for others, maybe now it's time to think of myself and my family for a while. I need a rest to think."

While still in New Delhi, a *Globe* reporter traveling with Team Canada spoke by phone with Elsamnah who implored Chrétien to mention her husband's case during his meeting with Pakistan's prime minister, Benazir Bhutto.

Canada's High Commissioner in Islamabad was Marie-Andrée Beauchemin, an outspoken diplomat with fiery red hair and a love for chunky gold jewelry. After her posting in Pakistan, she became Canada's first female ambassador to Egypt where she painted the Canadian embassy a soft shade of pink. The Canadian embassy was considered somewhat of a historic site since it had once been the home of Queen Farida, the beloved former wife of Egypt's King Farouk. In November 2000, the *Cairo Times* wrote about the controversy Beauchemin had caused, saying reaction to her color selection was mixed. "Opinions are divided down the middle: Those who describe the salmon-colored mansion as a 'droll pink wedding cake,' and those who applaud the new choice of colors as 'a welcome change from the traditional white which looks bland and dusty with the year.' The best comment yet came from the little girl who lives in a next-door building. 'Surely, anyone who lives in such a lovely house must be a princess!'"

The spectacle of the Khadr children sitting on the doorstep of the Canadian High Commission in Pakistan unnerved Beauchemin. She had met personally and often with Elsamnah and her children and believed they were receiving as much help and attention as officials could provide.

Consular officials had offered a lawyer to Khadr but Beauchemin said he refused, preferring to find his own counsel.

Beauchemin knew what the Canadian media didn't. Intelligence reports out of Pakistan had flagged Khadr's association with Zawahiri, the suspected instigator of the embassy bombing. The Egyptian and Saudi intelligence agencies had been following the activities of Zawahiri and bin Laden in Sudan but the West still didn't have a clear picture of their importance. Had Khadr financed the bombing and provided support in Pakistan for his friend Zawahiri? Beauchemin didn't know but didn't think Canada should stick its neck out any farther than it already had.

During a briefing with Canadian reporters in Islamabad, Beauchemin tried to steer the story away from Khadr. The informal meeting was a "backgrounder," meaning it was for information purposes only, and Beauchemin was not to be quoted. At times, the meeting got heated, Chrétien's media director recalled. "She was just apoplectic at the characterization of the situation about Khadr," Donolo said.

On January 15, the *Globe* ran its first interview with Khadr. "He lies in a hospital bed, wearing a windbreaker to warm himself from the damp chill of a northern Pakistani winter. There is nothing on the walls but fading paint. There is nothing on his table but a copy of the Quran and a deck of cards. Detained without charges, a hostage of the judicial system in a foreign land, Ahmed Said Khadr spends his days wondering if he will ever see Canada again. 'I feel very depressed,' he said, shifting to his side in the lumpy hospital bed. 'I feel saddened for so many things.'"

James Bartleman, who would become Ontario's lieutenant governor, was Chrétien's chief political advisor. When he wrote about the incident in one of his memoirs, he made no attempt to hide his disdain of the press. "The media contingent were in a bad mood as Team Canada flew into Pakistan. Some had disregarded the advice of the accompanying doctor not to drink the tap water in India and had contracted 'Delhi Belly,' the fierce local diarrhea familiar to travelers to the subcontinent. Others were tired of covering good news stories about happy business people concluding deals and describing colorful tourist outings by the prime minister, the premiers and their spouses. All hungered for a good juicy scandal to enliven their reporting. They had the scandal they had been searching for, complete with photogenic wife, cute children, and brave Canadian husband suffering in a prison hospital."

But Bartleman's scorn ignored the fact that Pakistan had an abysmal track record for justice—and that Khadr was being held without charges. Bhutto's government was dealing with a rise in militant fundamentalism that was threatening to engulf all of Pakistan. The struggle for control often played out in the courts, which were sometimes driven more by politics than credible evidence. The year before Chrétien's visit, Bhutto had come under intense international pressure in the case of a fourteen-year-old Christian boy who was sentenced to hang for blasphemy after allegedly writing slogans on a mosque wall. The evidence was flimsy and during an appeal it was revealed that the boy was barely literate and therefore unlikely to have written the offending words. When the judge asked the court to read aloud the five or six offensive words, the prosecutor refused, arguing that repeating the words would itself be blasphemous.

Human rights lawyer Asma Jahangir, whose father had been assassinated and had survived numerous attempts on her own life, won the appeal but took no comfort in her victory. "All it demonstrates is that people can get convictions, death sentences even, in Pakistani courts without an iota of evidence. They can rely on emotionalism and fear even within the courtroom," she told reporters.

Elsamnah was determined not to allow the press to overlook her husband's story. She followed the reporters constantly, showing up with her children at the hotel where the Team Canada delegation stayed and inviting them to her small hotel for a press conference.

On January 16, Chrétien met Elsamnah and her sons Abdullah, Omar and Kareem. The boys were quiet and polite, taking candy from a little dish in the hotel room upon Chrétien's insistence. Chrétien posed for pictures and shook Abdullah's hand. "Once, I was the son of a farmer and I became prime minister. Maybe one day you will become one," Abdullah recalled Chrétien saying.

That same day, the *Globe* quoted a Pakistani official on the role that Western media played in extremist propaganda. "This is a new tendency and trend among the staunch extremist terrorists that . . . when any of them is arrested, especially in Third World countries, there is this hue and cry about violation of human rights."

Chrétien said he had asked Bhutto to ensure that Khadr received a fair trial and told reporters he accepted her assurances. A few weeks after

Team Canada returned, Khadr was charged under Pakistan's Explosives Substances Act. Authorities moved him from the hospital to the Adiala prison in Rawalpindi. On Khadr's insistence, Elsamnah sent Omar, Abdullah and Kareem to live with her parents in Scarborough, for the duration of what he expected would be a lengthy detainment. Her parents didn't want the responsibility of looking after Abdurahman who stayed in Islamabad with his sisters.

Khadr's case was transferred to Pakistan's Special Courts which had heard all terrorism cases in the country since 1975. The Special Courts had a conviction rate of more than ninety percent.

Khadr faced the death penalty if convicted.

JACK HOOPER LOOKED INCREDULOUSLY at the picture of Chrétien shaking hands with Ahmed Said Khadr's eldest son, Abdullah. No one in the Canadian Security Intelligence Service (CSIS) knew that the prime minister was going to meet the Khadr family, or if someone had, they hadn't told Hooper.

Hooper was working at CSIS's headquarters in Ottawa as the Number Two man on the counterterrorism file. He would eventually take over CSIS's Toronto office before becoming the country's top spy during the chaotic years after 9/11.

Hooper had grown up the son of a firefighter but it wasn't fire trucks that had captivated him when he was young. From the time he could talk, Hooper told everyone he wanted to be a cop and not just any police officer but a Mountie. The picture of the Royal Canadian Mounted Police (RCMP) officer, in his red jacket and high brown boots sitting atop a well-groomed horse, is a cherished Canadian icon. "In the popular idea of the Mounties—foursquare, moral, conciliatory— many Canadians fancy that they see a reflection of their own identity," London's *Daily Telegraph* wrote in 2000. Canadians are "essentially Mounties at heart, and share with their celebrated law enforcers the old-fashioned virtues of honesty, modesty and endeavor."

But after university, Hooper took a job on a drilling rig in the frigid waters of the Beaufort Sea instead of joining the force. Hooper's mother had always tried to dissuade her son from joining the RCMP since her brother was a Mountie and had been beaten within an inch of his life while he tried to make an arrest in a tough mining camp in Flin Flon,

Manitoba, in the 1940s. The cold and the monotony of drilling, however, wore Hooper down, so over his mother's objections he joined the force. After moving from one small Canadian town to another for seven years, Hooper landed in Vancouver, British Columbia, in 1985.

By that time the federal police force was in the midst of an unprecedented scandal. Justice David Cargill McDonald, who presided over a federal inquiry that became known as the McDonald Commission, had just issued his report into allegations of thefts, break-ins and arson carried out by the RCMP's Security Service. An ugly picture of a police force run amok had emerged during the inquiry and evidence revealed the RCMP's use of illegal tactics. The Security Service, in an effort to quell the separatist movement, had even torched a barn in Montreal where Quebec intellectuals met to talk about their province's independence.

The McDonald Report left the police force's reputation in tatters. The judge recommended that the Security Service be disbanded and a separate, civilian security agency be created. The Canadian Security Intelligence Service rose from the RCMP's ashes.

Hooper had no intention of leaving the police force for CSIS, but he had little option. Hooper was a member of an RCMP tactical team in Vancouver that was called in to break up a group of protestors blocking the road to Simon Fraser University, where Hooper attended part-time for his master's degree in criminology. The situation quickly grew tense as panicked parents tried to press through the mass of protestors to pick up their children from the daycare on the campus. The RCMP team scuffled with the protestors. Hooper was in the middle of the fray and "had one of the guys upside down bouncing his head off the asphalt," he later admitted. A TV crew from the CBC captured Hooper's rough tactics on their nightly newscast. Hooper was called into his supervisor's office after a defense lawyer threatened to sue if the charges against his client weren't dropped. Hooper was told: "You can't work here anymore, find somewhere else to go." Hooper joined CSIS.

THE MAVERICK with an impish grin and a taste for expensive cowboy boots had finally found his home. Hooper may be politically incorrect and a self-professed redneck but he was also a charmer and in a business built on relationships, personality is everything. It didn't take long for everyone throughout the organization to know "Jack" and his lack of deference to his bosses became legendary. Friends started compiling lists of his "Jackisms," his blunt talk that would crudely explain the complicated world of spying or life in general. "If you're going to run with the big dogs, you better learn to piss in the high grass," was one expression of which he was particularly fond.

Hooper, once he rose through the ranks and moved to headquarters in Ottawa, got along famously with his FBI counterpart, John O'Neill. They had worked closely on the investigation into the 1996 Khobar Tower bombings in Dahran, Saudi Arabia, that injured hundreds and killed nineteen U.S. Air Force members. One of the bombers was arrested in Canada and sent to the United States.

O'Neill was a dark haired, tough-talking Atlanta native, with a weakness for women, fine cigars and Chivas Regal. During the 1990s, he was one of the few investigators who tried to warn the security and intelligence community of the danger posed by Osama bin Laden and his organization. After years of frustration at failing to deliver the message, he resigned from the FBI in 2001. In a twist of fate, O'Neill started a new career in August 2001 as head of security at the New York's World Trade Center. He died on 9/11 as he helped others to safety.

Hooper and O'Neill had a penchant for hard living. One night in Washington, they ended up in a cigar lounge, drinking Scotch before stumbling back to their hotel. O'Neill approached the reception desk. "We're going to need a 5:30 wake-up call," Hooper recalled him saying. The desk clerk, however, didn't look up and said instead, "Go stand up against the wall."

"I don't think you understand; we'll need a 5:30 wakeup call," insisted O'Neill.

"The guy didn't even look up, didn't budge and said 'Go stand against the wall,'" Hooper recalled. "And John can have a short temper, and he said, 'What is your problem? All I want is a 5:30 wakeup call.' The desk clerk looked at him and said, 'It's twenty-five after five. Go stand against the wall. I'll tell you when it's 5:30.'"

More than anything, O'Neill and Hooper were bound by a disdain of authority and protocol. And on that January morning when Chrétien's meeting with the Khadr family was the top news story, Hooper made it known he was pissed. "I was like, 'What the fuck is that all about? What's he doing?'"

Khadr was well known within CSIS who closely monitored his movements. In fact, Khadr was a subject in dozens of probes by CSIS's "Sunni Islamic Terrorism Section." Khadr may never have been charged in Canada but as far as CSIS was concerned, he was a terrorist. When Pakistani authorities arrested him for the bombing, many within CSIS were glad to see him finally behind bars. "We live in a very luxurious world compared to police because we can draw reasonable conclusions based on the information we have and what we do by way of analysis. Police have to provide a quality of evidence that passes muster," said Hooper. Hooper believed there was reasonable suspicion that Khadr was involved in the bombing. But he couldn't be sure that Pakistan had the evidence.

That wasn't of concern in Ottawa where Chrétien's intervention was seen as an appalling political error. Years later, a new term—"the Khadr effect"—entered Ottawa's lexicon as a phrase to explain why politicians were reluctant to intervene in cases that could become embarrassing. "It made government officials a little bit more careful about whom they talk to, whom they are seen with, and whom they have their picture taken with, and that's not a bad thing. That has to be a legitimate concern. There's nothing illegitimate about the Khadr effect," said Hooper. Others disagree, saying Ottawa's current reluctance to publicly condemn foreign governments for unlawfully holding Canadian citizens has unnecessarily prolonged the detention of innocents.

Three months after Chrétien's Team Canada visit, Khadr was granted bail after a judge ruled there was "no legal evidence" to justify his detention. Eventually, the charges were dropped.

Once free, Khadr and Elsamnah brought Abdurahman and their daughters to Canada. And despite Khadr having told a reporter he needed time in Canada to think and rest, the family didn't stay long.

HUMAN CONCERN INTERNATIONAL severed all ties with Khadr after his arrest. The charity's executive director, Kaleem Akhtar, doubted Khadr was guilty but knew the arrest had sullied the charity's name. Canadian lawyer Marc Duguay was dispatched to Pakistan to conduct an audit and although his report cleared the charity of any wrongdoing, HCI never fully recovered. "It was a horrible period for us both personally and professionally and for the life of the organization. We have always been focused in our work. We are not political and we do not want to participate in politics," a bitter Akhtar said a decade later. "All I can say is that it has been a sordid plight for us, a very sorrowful time it had and continues to have a very devastating impact."

In 1997, the Canadian government withdrew its funding from HCI, as did some private donors. As recently as 2006, HCI was still fighting for its reputation. CSIS was forced by its watchdog agency, the Security Intelligence Review Committee, to issue an apology to the charity for linking it to al Qaeda in a federal court document, claims that were cited in media reports.

While in Canada in the summer of 1996, Khadr seemed unsure of what to do next. Aly Hindy, the imam at Toronto's Salaheddin mosque, recalled that he had never seen Khadr so conflicted. "Stay here," Hindy told him. "You are an electrical engineer, I can help you get a job." Hindy had worked for two decades as an engineer with Ontario Hydro, helping design ways to protect the province's hydro-electric dams and nuclear plants. He thought it was time for Khadr to settle down in Canada. Khadr's younger children, especially Omar and Abdurahman, would have been delighted to remain. But Khadr decided if HCI would not work with him, he would run his own charity. "I have commitments," he told Hindy. "I need to go back." Khadr had already registered a company in Canada under the name Health and Education Project International, or HEP, with another friend, Helmy Elsharief.

Elsharief had also come to Canada from Egypt. Unlike most immigrants, Elsharief didn't come to Toronto or Ottawa, but settled his family in Winnipeg, Manitoba, in Canada's interior. In 1976, a Canadian consular official in Cairo had told Helmy that he had a good chance his immigration application would be approved if he chose Manitoba. "No one wants to go to Winnipeg," the official said. Elsharief spent two decades in Winnipeg operating a string of restaurants—Sara's Restaurant, Falafel Villa and the Princess Deli—enduring the harsh winters and endearing himself to a faithful clientele. In 1995, Elsharief volunteered briefly for HCI, but he didn't last long after a bout of malaria forced his return to Canada.

When Elsharief later moved to Toronto and prayed at the Salaheddin mosque, Hindy offered him a job as principal at the mosque's Islamic school. But Elsharief found running a school difficult and lasted only a few months. Instead, he settled on a job in the mosque's library and gift shop where he would sell honey and religious items to the men, while his wife would work in the adjoining shop for the women. Together they opened the mosque for daily prayers and soon everyone at Salaheddin knew Elsharief. He was a perfect fundraising partner for Khadr.

Khadr decided he would build orphanages with HEP and by late 1996 they were fundraising. Supporting one orphan would require an annual donation of $365, Khadr told the congregants at the Salaheddin mosque. "If you are willing to share the bounties, the price of one sheep is one hundred Canadian dollars, and the price for a share of a cow is forty-five Canadian dollars," the charity's website stated. Within a few years, the charity would claim to operate five schools and orphanages inside Afghanistan.

THE KHADR FAMILY returned to Pakistan in late 1996 to a very different life. Gone were the comforts of their rented Hayatabad home that they had lost when Khadr was arrested. They moved into one of Peshawar's poorer neighborhoods which the children disliked. Once again they were forced to make new friends and this time, with suspicion still surrounding the family and Pakistani authorities unhappy with their return, it wasn't easy. One day, Omar was hit by a car while riding his bike and he fell into one of the ditches filled with sewage. He stood briefly, covered in black muck, before fainting from the sheer stench. Elsamnah wanted her family out.

By now, the Taliban had control of much of Afghanistan and had support among a population weary of the warlords' fighting. Led by Mullah Mohammed Omar, a reclusive uneducated Pashtun, the Taliban drew its members from the religious schools and refugee camps along the border of Afghanistan and Pakistan. Wearing their trademark black turbans, they roared through cities in Japanese-built pickup trucks, enforcing a strict code of Sharia law. Women not completely covered by the burka were beaten as were men whose beards were not considered long enough.

Osama bin Laden and Zawahiri watched the rise of the Taliban closely since they needed a place to settle. Although Sudan had benefited greatly from bin Laden's fortunes, the government had been under intense pressure from Saudi Arabia, the United States and Egypt to expel him and his followers. Bin Laden had survived two assassination attempts and eventually Sudan did force him to leave.

On May 16, 1996, bin Laden flew with his bodyguards and close family members to Jalalabad. Other planes carrying the Arabs loyal to him soon followed. The Taliban had offered bin Laden's group sanctuary but the two groups remained wary of each other. Bin Laden didn't know whether to trust the Taliban and Mullah Omar was nervous about the international scrutiny the Saudi attracted. That relationship was tested on August 23, 1996, when bin Laden publicly declared war on the United States for the first time. Called the "Declaration of War Against the Americans Occupying the Land of the Two Holy Places" bin Laden's diatribe criticized the Saudi ruling family, the United States and Israel and lamented the loss of Muslim blood on the soil of Palestine and Iraq. "The presence of the USA Crusader military forces on land, sea and air in the states of the Islamic Gulf is the greatest danger threatening the largest oil reserve in the world. My Muslim Brothers: The money you pay to buy American goods will be transformed into bullets and used against our brothers in Palestine," he wrote. "The wall of oppression and humiliation cannot be demolished except in a rain of bullets."

JUST OUTSIDE OF JALALABAD, bin Laden established a compound for his followers and their families on a farm belonging to aging mujahideen commander Younis Khalis. Khalis had been a member of the Hizb-i-Islami run by Pashtun leader Gulbuddin Hekmatyar. Hekmatyar left Afghanistan once the Taliban took over, but Khalis, who was into his eighties, stayed and welcomed bin Laden back to Afghanistan. Bin Laden called the compound Najm al Jihad, "star of the holy war."

Khadr and his wife were delighted bin Laden and his followers were back in Afghanistan and in the winter of 1996 moved into a rented home in Jalalabad. Omar, who was ten, wasn't as enthused by the move. Peshawar may have been primitive but at least there was reliable electricity, and they didn't have to conform to the Taliban's rules. Zaynab also wasn't happy, since she had been happy to dress conservatively in Pakistan but in Afghanistan she had to wear the burka, which she abhorred.

The Khadr family made regular trips to Najm al Jihad, which the children nicknamed Star Wars.

There were about 250 people living in the compound, many of whom had come with bin Laden from Sudan. All the families had their own homes, each surrounded by a thick wall. Bin Laden had three homes within his compound, one for each of his wives, so the women and their children could live together without having to cover themselves each time they went outside. Bin Laden's wives were only allowed one day a week for visitors, but since the Khadr family didn't live in the compound, bin Laden made an exception and allowed Elsamnah and the children into his houses while Khadr met with the men.

Bin Laden's first wife, Umm Abdullah, was strikingly tall and beautiful. He had married her in 1974 when he was seventeen, she was fourteen, and they were in high school together in Saudi Arabia. In their youth, they made a handsome couple. Although polygamy was not common by the time bin Laden went to university, he married a second wife, an educated Saudi seven years his senior. Umm Hamza had taught at the women's college at King Abdul Aziz University and held a PhD in child psychology. Together they had one son. Umm Khaled, his third wife, was also educated and held a doctorate in Arabic grammar.

Like most women in the compound, Elsamnah and Zaynab were particularly fond of bin Laden's second wife, Umm Hamza, and liked to visit her house which was always scrubbed clean. "Anybody could talk to her, any age group, whatever your problem was and you didn't feel stupid," recalled Zaynab.

Although bin Laden pledged that he loved all his wives equally, it was clear Umm Hamza was also his favorite, which made the other wives jealous. Umm Khaled felt her intellect wasn't appreciated and became increasingly sullen. Umm Abdullah rebelled in her own way, obsessing about makeup, stories of shopping and dancing and begging Zaynab and Elsamnah to bring her back cosmetics from Canada. "When you wanted to have fun, you went to Umm Abdullah," Elsamnah recalled. "When you wanted advice, you went to Umm Hamza."

Not everyone in bin Laden's inner circle was pleased with the Khadr family's visits. Mohammed Atef was among them. Atef, known as Abu Hafs al Masri, was a former Egyptian police officer who would become one of bin Laden's closest advisors. Khadr had not pledged the *bayat* to bin Laden, and this infuriated Abu Hafs. "Osama is a very nice person but the people around him have a different opinion, they have different influence on him and some of the people there from the closed association were not very happy with our presence," Elsamnah recalled her husband telling her. "Maybe because we move more frequent, they thought it not very safe, you know, in and out. You don't know who watches you come in and leaving," she said.

Over Abu Hafs's objections, bin Laden eventually gave Khadr permission to build a house on the compound. As the construction started in the spring of 1997, Khadr went back to Canada to fundraise. Before he left, he asked bin Laden to allow Abdurahman to live on the compound until he returned.

While Khadr was abroad, the wife of one of bin Laden's followers approached Elsamnah with concerns about her husband. "He has been in jail [in Pakistan]," she said accusingly, asking if Khadr could be trusted. She wondered if he was a spy. Elsamnah was furious. She had sought her whole life for a place and people to call her own and felt she had finally arrived. Now her husband was again being called a spy as he had been a decade earlier by followers of Abdullah Azzam. She went directly to bin Laden's wife, Umm Hamza, with tears rolling down her cheeks and told her, "I don't want to be unwanted. If I'm unwanted come and tell me to my face." Bin Laden's wife assured her it was idle gossip and they trusted Khadr not to reveal the camp's location.

Shortly after, while Khadr was still in Canada, Elsamnah and her children moved into a house on the compound.

In March 1997, bin Laden invited a CNN crew to film his first television interview since returning to Afghanistan. Producer Peter Bergen and reporter Peter Arnett were taken on a secretive day-long journey, much of it spent in the back of a van with curtains drawn or being led blindfolded across rocky terrain by bin Laden's men, disoriented and unable to say where they had been. Shortly before midnight, inside a mud hut lined with blankets and lit by a flickering kerosene lamp, bin Laden appeared with a translator and several bodyguards. "Mr. bin Laden," began Arnett, "You've declared a jihad against the United States. Can you tell us why?"

In a rambling response, bin Laden lashed out against the U.S. and Saudi governments, saying even civilians share the blame since they had voted for their corrupt leaders. "We declared jihad against the U.S. government because the U.S. government . . . has committed acts that are extremely unjust, hideous, and criminal whether directly or through its support of the Israeli occupation [of Palestine]. And we believe the U.S. is directly responsible for those who were killed in Palestine, Lebanon and Iraq. This U.S. government abandoned humanitarian feelings by these hideous crimes."

Taliban leader Mullah Omar was not pleased with the interview and the attention it brought. There were also rumors that local leaders in Jalalabad were uncomfortable with bin Laden's presence and may have been talking to Pakistan's security service to reveal the location of the compound. Whether it was this threat or pressure from the Taliban, bin Laden suddenly decided to order the compound evacuated and move nearer to the Taliban's stronghold in Kandahar.

Elsamnah and the children had lived at Najm al Jihad for only two days. "Evacuate now means you move. You move means you leave everything and you carry what you need," Zaynab recalled. Within an hour, a convoy had lined up, ready to leave. Before the cars departed, Abdurahman and Abdullah had a heated argument over where they would sit in their car. Shouting led to shoving and shoving to weapons, and before long Abdurahman was running, with Abdullah in pursuit, pointing an AK-47 at his back. Behind them ran Elsamnah, hysterical, screaming for her sons to stop.

Bin Laden had told Elsamnah he did not want her family to come with him to Kandahar. He gave her the option of returning to Peshawar or Jalalabad and she chose to return to Pakistan because she felt it would be safer and easier for her husband to find them. But she was upset. How could they leave a woman and her children alone?

Before she left, Elsamnah begged the others to at least take Abdurahman until her husband returned since she could not control him. Bin Laden agreed, but after a night's rest in Kabul, he came to the guesthouse where Abdurahman was staying. "Do not come back until your father is with you," he said. One of bin Laden's disciples, an Egyptian named Saif al Adel, drove Abdurahman to the bus station. "Go to your family," he said before buying the fourteen-year-old a ticket for Peshawar.

EVER SINCE HE FLED PAKISTAN in 1995, Khalid Abdullah had tried to find Zaynab so they could finally have the wedding he had been promised. He phoned from Syria, he sent presents from Iran and he begged Khadr to bring his daughter to him.

In October 1997, over Zaynab's objections and those of Kareem and Omar who didn't want their sister to leave, Khadr finally agreed to take Zaynab to Tehran, where Abdullah had rented an apartment. But first, Khadr promised his children one last trip with Zaynab, so they took a circuitous route from Pakistan to Iran that involved stops in Jordan, Syria, Turkey and rides on planes, trains and buses. "It was the best trip ever," Zaynab recalled. It was also the only time the family could remember that Khadr vowed to focus exclusively on his family and not fundraising.

When the family arrived at the Iranian border on a bus from Turkey, they were stopped and ordered off the bus. They were traveling on their Canadian passports which should have granted them entry, but Elsamnah's visa did not list her children and the Iranian guards were suspicious. Unable to cross the border until the issue was sorted out, the family was held at a guard station that consisted of not much more than a roof and a couple of benches. Zaynab paced with her parents to try to keep warm as the younger children curled together on the suitcases to sleep. The next morning amid apologies and offers of food and drink, they were again on the move.

The kids loved Tehran and Zaynab's husband was a good host. He took Omar and the boys to the zoo and an arcade, in an attempt to win over his new brothers-in-law. Omar especially liked how clean Tehran was and the comforts of a bustling city. He didn't want to leave.

Khadr did meet with Pashtun warlord Gulbuddin Hekmatyar. Hekmatyar had enjoyed Pakistan's support throughout the war with the Soviets and during the civil war of the 1990s but after Pakistan endorsed the Taliban, Hekmatyar had been forced to flee. Tehran had given him refuge and freedom to continue his organization, Hizbi-i-Islami. Khadr hoped he could convince his friend to return to Afghanistan now that bin Laden was back. Hekmatyar was politically savvy and the Taliban could benefit from his help, Khadr argued. But Hekmatyar was content to stay where he was. (Hekmatyar did return to Afghanistan after Iranian officials expelled him in February 2002. A year later, the United States designated him a terrorist. His whereabouts are unknown.)

It was a teary goodbye as Zaynab's siblings left her. Zaynab made it clear to Abdullah that she was being forced into their marriage, but he believed she would learn to love and respect him after her family had gone. The bus ride home was long and miserable. Omar and Kareem cried and longed for Zaynab.

Zaynab was inconsolable in Tehran and Abdullah eventually grew impatient. Less than six months later, in the spring of 1998, Abdullah called Khadr to say Zaynab was returning. Khadr wasn't happy but it was clear the marriage wasn't working out.

Abdullah eventually left Tehran and began traveling again. He had evaded Egyptian authorities since the 1995 bombing of the embassy in

Islamabad but with the help of the CIA, the Egyptians finally caught up with him.

In 1999, Abdullah resurfaced in Cairo as one of 107 Islamists associated with Zawahiri's al Jihad and accused of plotting attacks for al Qaeda. The defendants became known as the "Albanian returnees" because the majority of them had been arrested a year before in Albania and rendered to Egypt. It's not clear, however, where Abdullah had been arrested since some of the suspects had also been captured in Azerbaijan, Bulgaria and neighboring countries. Abdullah was among the dozens convicted and sentenced to lengthy jail terms.

The CIA's involvement in the arrest of the cell had angered Zawahiri who issued a statement on August 6, 1998: "We are interested in briefly telling the Americans that their message has been received and that the response, which we hope they will read carefully, is being prepared, because, with God's help, we will write it in the language that they understand."

ON AUGUST 7, 1998, al Qaeda orchestrated a devastating attack that got the world's attention—the bombing of the American embassies in Kenya and Tanzania, the first major attack planned by Zawahiri and bin Laden that targeted the United States.

At 10:30 that morning, two men approached the American embassy in Nairobi. One threw a stun grenade that caused a small explosion and brought dozens of embassy workers to the window. Then came the massive explosion from the truck bomb that crashed into the front of the building. Frank Pressley, a long-time American bureaucrat, was propelled through the air, hitting a wall and landing on his back. Part of his jaw and arm were ripped off and he could see bone jutting out of his shoulder. When he finally got to his feet, he went to look for his friend and neighbor, Michelle O'Connor. "I heard a lot of noise, people crying, screaming. And I did see, I thought, Michelle O'Connor's body. But more than that, I saw some legs, a pair of just [a] man's legs with the pants on," he later testified.

George Mygit Mimba, a Kenyan information systems manager, was buried under bodies and debris. Choking, he prayed and fumbled with his identification badge, making sure it was still around his neck so that his father and brothers could identify his body because he was sure he was going to die. Mimba managed to extricate himself from the rubble and crawled to the front of the embassy where he watched the horror unfolding around him. "There was this man who was running and he didn't know that his intestine was out. His belly's been chopped off, so he's trying to hold on to his intestine at the same time he's running," Mimba told a U.S. court.

In total, 213 people died, including twelve Americans. Thousands were injured.

Nine minutes after the explosion in Kenya, the U.S. embassy in Dar es Salaam was attacked. A water tanker in front of the embassy stopped the truck bomber from directly hitting the building but the explosion still killed eleven Africans and injured another eighty-five.

Four days later, writing under the name the Islamic Liberation Army, al Qaeda tried to justify the deaths. "Before the Nairobi bombings, we warned Muslims not to visit anything that is American and we repeated this warning," they wrote. "We are forced to wage jihad anywhere in the world at any given moment."

WHEN THE EMBASSIES were bombed, Abdurahman was at another training camp where he had been sent by his father. He had visited all the camps that had been set up by the mujahideen—Khalden, Deronta, Khost. This time, he was at bin Laden's flagship camp, al Farouk, for the first time. Al Farouk was where al Qaeda recruits would hone the skills learned elsewhere. These recruits were watched carefully and a select few would be chosen for bin Laden's private army. Abdurahman would never be a bin Laden disciple but bin Laden accepted him, yet again, as a favor to his father.

Abdurahman was never happy at the camps, but at least at al Farouk he was able to spend time with a Canadian friend, a young man from British Columbia named Amer Ahmed. Ahmed had come from Vancouver with Essam Marzouk, an associate of Khadr's. Marzouk's relationship with Khadr went back to the days of the Red Crescent Society during the 1980s. When the Soviets withdrew, Marzouk flew to Vancouver on a false Saudi passport and was arrested by an immigration official who spotted inconsistencies in his story. He was eventually given refugee status in Canada, but Canada's spy service flagged him as a possible bin Laden associate, which prevented him from obtaining citizenship. Marzouk was visited often in Canada by an Egyptian-American named Ali Mohamed, an al Qaeda double agent who became a key witness in a U.S. terrorism case in 2000.

Amer Ahmed met Marzouk in Vancouver and decided he wanted the adventure of Afghanistan. All the Khadr children liked Ahmed because he understood what it was like to live both in the West and East. Omar also liked that Ahmed would insist on eating elaborate banana splits when he stayed with the Khadrs, which meant Elsamnah would stock the kitchen with ice cream and brownies and chocolate sauce. Ahmed was naïve and inexperienced but excited about his newfound life. One day, he showed Omar and Abdurahman a birthmark he had on his toe. "If I get killed," he said dramatically, "you can identify my body by that mark."

When the embassies in Africa were bombed, bin Laden's followers braced for American retaliation, which came two weeks later, on August 20, when U.S. president Bill Clinton ordered cruise missiles to target suspected al Qaeda camps. Abdurahman was returning from evening prayers at al Farouk when the sky lit up with fire. He dove for cover as the explosions erupted around him. When the bombing let up, Abdurahman ran toward voices, stumbling on body parts. He helped the injured into trucks, one of which he would drive to a Khost hospital. He was angry, angrier than he had ever been before. He hated the Americans and for the first time, he sympathized with his father's anti-Western politics.

One of the bodies was cut "into pieces," Abdurahman recalled. He quickly gathered them in his arms so the dead man could have a proper burial. When he picked up a severed foot, he stopped suddenly. There was Ahmed's birthmark on his toe. "It built rage in my heart," Abdurahman said. "So that day, I hated America."

4

Flight or Fight

By 8 A.M. ON SEPTEMBER 11, 2001, nineteen al Qaeda recruits were calmly sitting in their seats on four American planes about to change the course of history.

Mohamed Atta, the group's Egyptian leader, was on American Airlines Flight 11, a non-stop flight from Boston to Los Angeles. He sat in seat 8D in the business class section. Near him were four Saudis selected for the mission by Osama bin Laden.

Fifteen minutes after takeoff, the Boeing 767 hovered somewhere above 26,000 feet, the fasten-seat-belt sign chimed off and the hijacking began. Atta charged to the cockpit as the hijackers slit the throat of one passenger and stabbed two flight attendants. The air filled with a strange gas and passengers moved to the back of the plane. One of the hijackers tried to talk to passengers through the in-flight intercom: "Nobody move. Everything will be okay. If you try to make any moves, you'll endanger yourself and the airplane. Just stay quiet. Nobody move, please. We are going back to the airport. Don't try to make any stupid moves." He hadn't used the right channel, so the passengers didn't hear anything, but the Federal Aviation Agency in Boston determined that American Flight 11 was being hijacked.

Flight attendants Betty Ong and Amy Sweeney used emergency phones to call their airline's offices in North Carolina and Boston. "The cockpit's not answering. Somebody's stabbed in business class," Ong said in an 8:19 call to flight center employee Nydia Gonzalez. "I think there's Mace—that we can't breathe. I don't know, I think we're getting hijacked." Ong gave Gonzalez reports for almost thirty minutes, speaking in an unnaturally calm voice. Gonzalez tried to stay calm too. "What's going on, honey?" she asked at one point as Ong told her the plane was flying erratically.

At 8:44 the line went dead. "What's going on Betty? Betty, talk to me. Betty, are you there? Betty?"

Almost at the same time, Amy Sweeney was making her last call to the flight center in Boston. "We are flying low. We are flying very, very low. We are flying way too low," she said. "Oh my God, we are way too low." At 8:46, American Airlines Flight 11 crashed into the north tower of New York City's World Trade Center.

Some of those working on the floors of the tower directly hit began jumping from the burning building. Hundreds of 911 calls jammed the phone lines as police and fire trucks raced to the scene and New Yorkers filled the streets to stare at the smoking hole in the building. Most were still looking up when at 9:03, United Airlines Flight 175 crashed into the World Trade Center's south tower.

President George W. Bush was reading to a second-grade class at Emma E. Booker Elementary School in Sarasota, Florida, when at 9:05, the White House's chief of staff whispered in his ear, "America is under attack."

At 9:37, the third hijacked plane, American Airlines Flight 77, crashed into the west wall of the Pentagon. The flight had taken off from Dulles airport in Washington and was destined for Los Angeles but had circled back to hit its target.

Only one of the four planes was still in the air. The pilot of United Flight 93, which had left Newark bound for San Francisco, had managed to reach an air-traffic controller in Cleveland. "Mayday! Hey, get out of here!" he screamed. His message was followed by an unidentified voice: "Ladies and gentlemen, here the captain. Please sit down, keep remaining sitting. We have a bomb on board. So sit."

Passengers were trying to reach relatives. At 9:45 a.m., Mark Bingham got his mom on the line in Saratoga, California. "I want to let you know that I love you. I'm on a flight from Newark to San Francisco and there are three guys on board who have taken over the plane, and they say they have a bomb. You believe me, don't you, Mom?" the thirty-one-year-old public relations executive asked. "Yes, Mark, I believe you," Alice Hoglan replied.

Passenger Todd Beamer called from an in-flight phone and reached Lisa Jefferson, a supervisor at the Chicago office of GTE Airfone. "I understand your plane is being hijacked," Jefferson said.

"We're going down, we're going down. No, wait, we're coming back up. We're turning around . . . Lisa, Lisa?"

"I'm still here, Todd. I'm still here. I'm not going anywhere. I'll be here as long as you will."

"A few of the passengers are getting together. I think we're going to jump the guy with the bomb," Beamer said.

"Are you sure that's what you want to do?"

"At this point, I don't think we have much choice. I'm going to have to go out on faith."

"I stand behind you," Jefferson said as they recited the Lord's Prayer together.

"God help us. Help us, Jesus," said Beamer. Then yelled: "You ready? Okay. Let's roll."

Hoglan tried to call Mark's cell phone but only got his voice mail. "Mark, this is your mom. It's 9:54. It's a suicide mission and the hijackers are planning to use your plane."

At 10:03, United Flight 93 crashed in a field in Shanksville, Pennsylvania. It's believed the flight was destined for the White House or Capitol Hill.

The World Trade Center's south tower had collapsed by the time the United flight crashed. At 10:28, the World Trade Center's north tower also fell.

In total 2,992 people, including the nineteen hijackers, died.

AS THE SUN WAS RISING IN KABUL on September 12, 2001, Maha Elsamnah turned on the radio to listen to *Voice of America* as she did every morning. Days earlier, the radio had broadcast nothing but coverage of commander Ahmad Shah Masood's assassination. Two Arab men posing as journalists had visited Masood on September 9 with a powerful bomb hidden in their camera equipment. "It is difficult to overestimate how serious a blow it would be for the alliance if it transpires that he has been seriously injured or killed in the attack," a BBC correspondent wrote before it was confirmed that Masood had died as a result of the suicide mission. "Militarily, he is the lynchpin for anti-Taliban forces. But he is also the opposition leader whose reputation has come through twenty years of war the least scathed."

Masood had earned a reputation as a clever strategist during the Soviet occupation and then became the most important mujahideen leader to oppose the Taliban and al Qaeda in the late 1990s. By the summer of 2001, Masood's forces had control of northeastern Afghanistan, and although he was without the international support that helped conquer the Soviets a decade earlier, Masood still posed a serious threat to the Taliban.

Khadr had respected Masood so refrained from celebrating his death. But he didn't mourn it either. Masood had been an obstacle to Islamic governance in Afghanistan, which Khadr supported. The day after news broke about Masood's death, Khadr took a trip to Jalalabad with Abdurahman and was there when the United States was attacked.

As Elsamnah, Abdullah, Zaynab and Omar listened to the radio reports about New York and Washington, they wondered about their future. No one was surprised when a knock came on the door. "We're leaving. Time to go," said one of Khadr's friends. There was fear in Kabul. Everyone knew the hijackings were the work of al Qaeda and that the United States would strike as it had in 1998. Kandahar, Kabul and Jalalabad, where al Qaeda's followers congregated, were the most likely targets.

Abdurahman was alone in Jalalabad when he first heard the news about the attacks. "I remember listening to it and not understanding it. I remember listening to everything, there were two buildings, planes, the Pentagon and I just couldn't understand it," Abdurahman recalled. His father had been up in Najm al Jihad where some of bin Laden's men had returned after they had evacuated the compound in 1997. When Khadr returned to his charity office a couple of hours later, he excitedly told Abdurahman he had watched the attacks on television. He seemed surprised by the attacks too, but was quick to justify them.

"I just didn't know what to think because you live in a society which tells you to smile and laugh at something like this for so long, you know, and then you sit down and watch it and have conflicting thoughts and you don't know what to do anymore, you don't know what to think anymore. And I automatically go to what comforts me the most, asking questions and I just did that, I just started asking my dad so many questions. 'Why didn't you guys attack a nuclear site?' and his answer was, 'Oh, nuclear sites are outside cities.' And he's like, 'If we blow one up, everybody who's security there will die and that's it.' 'But why did you attack this? Is it right you killed so many people?' He's like, 'We didn't intend to target the people. We intended to target the economy.' One of the famous explanations of September 11 is these people pay taxes, the taxes go to the government, the government puts it into the army, the army gives it to the Israelis and they kill Muslims. You know, that long chain of explanation."

KHADR AND ELSAMNAH had been happier during their two years in Kabul than they had ever been. Khadr was delighted to finally be living in an Islamic state ruled by Sharia law, even if he did sometimes clash with the Taliban over such issues as wanting his daughters to get an education or that he allowed his sons to watch Hollywood movies. Elsamnah was content just to have a house and stay in one place.

They lived in a neighborhood called Karti Parwan, in an expansive home with nine bedrooms and five washrooms. The children spent their days playing with neighborhood children or watching action movies in the basement where they could get some reprieve from the heat. Omar was especially fond of the house's balcony where he could climb to the top of a fig tree, trying to avoid the leaves that irritated his arms, and collect handfuls of the fruit.

The children shared their home with many pets—two cats, hedgehogs and a lethargic turtle. The Taliban banned pets, believing dogs especially impure, but the Khadr children always managed to find stray puppies and sneak them home. Even when their father found them, he usually didn't have the heart to throw them back on the street. The only animal he ever turned away was a black dog found in Jalalabad, telling the children that a pure black animal was evil.

Zaynab lived in a separate wing of the house with her second husband, a Yemeni known as Yacoub al Bahr, whose real name is believed to be Sameer Saif. She had met al Bahr after her family relocated to Kabul. He had fought with the mujahideen in Bosnia but was just a few years older than Zaynab and not particularly hailed for his fighting skills. It was his voice that made him popular in Afghanistan and al Bahr was informally known as Kabul's wedding singer. Zaynab wasn't interested in him, but agreed to the marriage since she could remain with her family, living in a separate wing of the house. Khadr asked his sons what they thought of al Bahr and allowed them to vote before giving final consent to the marriage. Abdurahman, who had never been close with Zaynab, said he wanted al Bahr as part of the family. Kareem liked him, too. But Abdullah and Omar said they didn't want to vote and privately Omar told Zaynab he didn't want her to marry but didn't want to upset his father by saying so.

On the day of her wedding in 1999, Zaynab and the women celebrated separately while the men gathered in Kabul. The ceremony was huge and lasted well into the night. Khadr, the beaming father of the bride, basked in the attention from Afghanistan's elite which included Zawahiri and bin Laden.

Al Bahr sang one song after another until one of the guests snuck up behind him and fired an AK-47 into the air. The sound startled al Bahr and his voice cracked mid-song, sending the guests into fits of laughter.

Like Zaynab's previous marriage, this one was also fraught with problems. Her strong will irritated her Yemeni husband, who wasn't accustomed to having women talk back to him, let alone start loud and lengthy debates. Shortly after they married, Zaynab became pregnant with the first Khadr grandchild.

Zaynab returned to her grandparents' Scarborough home with her mother in 2000, so the baby could be born in Canada. Instead of letters, Khadr recorded messages on cassettes that he would send to his wife and daughter, talking about the children and saying how much he missed them. Omar, Khadr said, was looking after the entire family. "Omar is our mother and our father, our sister and our brother. He cooks our meals and does our laundry. Sometimes, I ask your mother, 'Are you sure he's ours? He's too good to be ours.' "

Zaynab gave birth to a daughter she named Safia, and a few months later returned to Kabul. But when Zaynab proudly introduced Safia to a neighbor who had trained as a nurse, she was told Safia's head wasn't forming correctly.

The neighbor was Australian Rabiyah Hutchinson, and among the foreigners in Kabul, Hutchinson's medical knowledge was revered. Hutchinson had taken a long and circuitous route to Kabul. A Muslim convert of Scottish heritage, Hutchinson, was on her third marriage. Her second marriage had been to a follower of the Jemaah Islamiyah, an Indonesian group tied to al Qaeda, which claimed responsibility for the 2003 Bali bombing that killed 202, including eighty-eight Australians. While living in Afghanistan, Hutchinson met her third husband, Egyptian Mustafa Hamid, also known as Abu al Walid al Masri.

At first, Zaynab dismissed Hutchinson's comments. "All the Khadrs have big heads," she replied, but she took Safia to a local doctor anyway.

Safia was eventually diagnosed with hydrocephalus, a condition commonly referred to as "water on the brain" and involves an abnormal accumulation of cerebrospinal fluid in the head's ventricles, causing pressure inside the skull that can lead to convulsions and mental retardation. Although the disease was rare, one of bin Laden's sons had also suffered from hydrocephalus and bin Laden had taken the boy to the United Kingdom in the late 1970s for treatment. Doctors told him the baby would need to have a shunt inserted to relieve the pressure, but bin Laden wouldn't let them operate. He took the boy home to Saudi Arabia where he tried to treat him by smearing honey on his head. The boy survived, but as he grew older was mentally delayed and had trouble interacting socially.

Zaynab did not object to having Safia treated but wanted to take her back to Canada to have an operation. Her husband insisted they go to a hospital in Lahore instead. Another fight followed. "He didn't like it because he felt we were imposing our opinion and our background on him," Elsamnah said. When they took six-month-old Safia to Canada over his objections, al Bahr moved out. After 9/11, Khadr ran into al Bahr in Kabul and gave him an ultimatum: "Divorce her, or stay married and come back, but don't leave her hanging." Al Bahr consented to a divorce on the condition that Zaynab write a statement saying she would never request anything from him. She quickly complied.

MOST OF AL QAEDA'S inner circle moved to a compound outside Kandahar in 1997, after leaving Najm al Jihad. Mullah Omar had offered bin Laden a housing complex that had been used for workers of an electrical company, but bin Laden instead chose an abandoned agricultural compound called Tarnak Farms. The conditions here were even more primitive.

The Khadr family was not invited to live in Kandahar, but they did visit to celebrate the engagement of Zawahiri's daughter, Umayma. Elsamnah and the children lived with Zawahiri's wife, Azza, and their five daughters during the week of celebrations.

Elsamnah had always respected Zawahiri's wife and was in awe of her serenity. "Azza is very, very patient, not like most Arab women who lose their temper and smack. We do this, I do this, when we lose our temper, smack or shout or swear, but Azza, I haven't seen somebody who is so diplomatic, from a very high class," Elsamnah recalled. Azza Nowair had come from a prominent and wealthy Egyptian family who were dismayed by her transformation during her years at Cairo University. The Nowair family wasn't devout but as a student Azza started wearing the hijab and eventually covered herself completely. Zawahiri was attracted to her piety and once the couple was married, Azza drifted farther from her family. Elsamnah had no idea of her friend's wealthy family when they first met but remembered once when living in Peshawar, Azza's relatives visited with Fisher-Price toys for Azza's children. "We were like, wow, because we couldn't even afford them in Canada and they got all these toys for the kids in Peshawar."

Azza was a petite and fine-featured woman who rarely complained, even when she suffered bouts of eczema that left her hands red and bleeding. She was also a doting mother, and Elsamnah trusted her enough to leave Omar in her care once when he was a baby and she traveled with her husband to an Afghan orphanage. "In her household, the girls were very spoiled, tender, you know, like toys we used to call them. Very tender and sweet. Sometimes the house would be a mess and there would be dishes, but she'd never yell or shout," recalled Elsamnah.

During the week in Kandahar with the Zawahiri family, the women talked continuously, carrying on well into one evening, not hearing Zawahiri's knocks at the door asking them to keep their voices down.

Those of bin Laden's followers who didn't live in Kandahar mainly congregated in the upscale Kabul neighborhood of Wazeer Akbar Khan. Khadr had his charity office there until the high rents pushed him to a more affordable location. A handful of al Qaeda's followers lived near the Khadr family in Kabul's Karti Parwan neighborhood. Saif al Adel, the Egyptian who had taken Abdurahman to the Kabul bus station in 1997, was among them. Al Adel had always been close to bin Laden and had followed him to Sudan. Al Adel, whose real name is not confirmed, had been indicted for the 1998 embassy bombings in Africa but like other al Qaeda members remained free in Afghanistan. After 9/11, he was named in some intelligence reports as al Qaeda's number three, ranked behind bin Laden and Zawahiri.

Al Adel was the son-in-law of Abu Walid, the Egyptian husband of Australian Rabiyah Hutchinson. Abu Walid's association with bin Laden also went back to the jihad against the Soviets. The mechanic-turned-journalist reported on the conflict for several Arabic publications and wrote books, including *The Afghan Arabs*, under his real name, Mustafa Hamid. Abu Walid's importance to al Qaeda is still unclear; he is often referred to as "al Qaeda's ideologue" but was also known to have written pieces critical of al Qaeda's extremist tactics.

Both al Adel and Abu Walid were reportedly captured after 9/11 in Iran, where they remain today.

Abu Faraj al Libi was also a neighbor in Karti Parwan. The Libyan, whose real name is believed to be Mustafa al Uzayti, was one of the men featured on Pakistan's most wanted poster in 2004. He had been a relative unknown but once his picture was released, few forgot his face. Al Libi had a skin disease called leucoderma, which meant his face was spotted with white patches where his skin was lacking the melanin pigment. He had come to Pakistan during the 1980s to fight the Soviets and then aligned himself with bin Laden and became an important figure in al Qaeda, Pakistani authorities alleged. When he was captured in May 2005, Bush described him as one of bin Laden's "top generals."

Al Libi disappeared into an undisclosed CIA jail until he was transferred to Guantanamo Bay in 2006. The Pentagon accuses him of leading an al Qaeda training camp in Khost and of creating an "urban warfare training camp" in Kabul. His job was to look after the families of al Qaeda fighters and his home doubled as a guesthouse and a "communication hub" for al Qaeda, the Pentagon stated in a press release.

In Kabul before the 9/11 attacks, most of the foreigners communicated by walkie-talkie since there were no phone lines and few had computers. The families were each given a number so they would know when someone was trying to reach them. The two-way radios only had range inside Kabul but sometimes they could hear reports from the front line where the Taliban fought Masood's forces. The soldiers were fond of singing and trying to keep their brothers awake or would play pranks when there were lulls in the fighting. "Listening to that thing was entertainment, especially if you were listening to the guys on the front line," Zaynab recalled. "They [made] so many jokes of each other. They would sit and mock each other." The Khadr family was known on the radio as "15," but at some point someone instead said "Kareem" and that code name seemed to stick. Saif al Adel was known in Kabul as Number 1.

AFTER THE 9/11 ATTACKS, the Khadrs moved to the province of Logar, southeast of Kabul, where they traveled between Khadr's orphanage and various safe houses. But they returned to Kabul often to collect their belongings, lulled into a sense of security in those first few weeks before the United States attacked. Even when the bombing began it was often predictable, at night, when no one would venture outdoors. On November 10, the day before Kabul would fall to the Northern Alliance's ground forces, Khadr and Elsamnah decided to spend one last night in their home.

Omar and Abdurahman had been in Kabul during the day but left before dark with the last load of furniture and belongings for Pol-e-Alam, the capital of Logar. Even though a war was being fought around them, the boys were in a mischievous spirit as they drove away, Abdurahman in the passenger's seat and Omar riding high on the top of the truck. If they passed someone on a bicycle they would wait until they were close and then blast the horn, looking back laughing as the startled cyclist tried to regain his balance. Omar and Abdurahman didn't always get along but on this ride they bonded as two teenaged brothers without any parents telling them what to do.

Once they got to Logar and unloaded the truck, Omar went to pray in his father's orphanage and Abdurahman went to find the director so he could pay the truck driver. Abdurahman hated Logar where there was no electricity, no music, movies or activity. For Abdurahman, boredom was worse than bombs. He wanted to go back to Kabul and more than anything he just wanted to come back to Canada. He was sick of the rules, the restrictions, the running. "I went and found Omar. He was praying. I just left him a message while he was praying. You're not supposed to talk to someone while they're praying, but I just told him, 'Oh, the directors don't have money and I'm going back to get money from mom,' and I didn't let him finish praying because he probably would have insisted, 'No, just stay here, just have the truck driver stay here and wait,' you know. I got into the truck and we left." Theirs was the only truck on the road going toward Kabul.

The next day, Abdurahman was arrested by the Northern Alliance, eventually handed over to the Americans and would not be seen again publicly for two years.

As KHADR AND ELSAMNAH were settling in for the last night in their Kabul home, the walkie-talkie sputtered to life. Kabul was about to fall to the U.S.-backed Northern Alliance. The Taliban were fleeing. When the couple emerged from their home, the walking wounded were already on the street. As Khadr and his wife raced to their car, one of the few that remained in the city, they came upon three men injured by a bomb. Elsamnah dumped a computer and a chair to make room in the back seat. They fled Kabul, Khadr driving fast, not looking in the rearview mirror.

At around 2 a.m., they reached a Logar hospital. Doctors took two of the men but the third, the most seriously injured, was turned away. It was clear he needed surgery and there just wasn't room. Khadr knew of another hospital, so off they drove again. "From the minute they put him in the car until we reached the next hospital, two or three hours, I didn't hear his voice, I didn't see his face. I didn't see that man's face from the minute they put him in, because it was dark, it was night, we were driving, driving," Elsamnah recalled. When they got to the second hospital the man, whom neither of them knew, had died from his wounds.

Zaynab had been awake all night with her daughter Safia and her siblings, praying her parents would return but ready to leave without them if they had to. Just after the sun came up, Elsamnah appeared at the door and collapsed. "She's crying and she's covered in blood and she's just in shock," Zaynab recalled. "Where's Abdurahman?" Elsamnah eventually asked, looking around.

"He went back," Omar said.

KHADR TRIED TO GET HIS WIFE to return to Canada with the younger children after Kabul fell. On January 25, 2001, the United Nations Security Council Committee listed Khadr as an individual associated with the Taliban or al Qaeda or Osama bin Laden. His assets were frozen and he would face questioning and possible arrest if he left Afghanistan.

But Elsamnah and the children had traveled to Canada in early 2001 without incident so Khadr believed they could again. "He kept reminding me, 'You know, Maha, you can leave,'" Elsamnah recalled. "But I said no. If he would leave with me, then okay. But to be honest with you, I was also so attached to the cause." For the Afghan-Arabs who were in Afghanistan, the veterans of the war with the Soviets, the U.S. invasion was the next jihad.

By the fall of 2001, the lines in the war had clearly been drawn. On September 20, Bush made his first major address to Congress. "Every nation, in every region, now has a decision to make. Either you are with us, or you are with the terrorists," he said to a standing ovation. In the audience sat Lisa Beamer, widow of United Flight 93 passenger Todd Beamer, whose last recorded words before his flight crashed into a Pennsylvania field were, "Let's roll."

A pre-recorded video of Osama bin Laden aired on al Jazeera two weeks later on October 7. "There is America, full of fear from its north to its south, from its west to its east. Thank God for that," bin Laden gloated. "These events have divided the whole world into two sides—the side of believers and the side of infidels."

Even before the 9/11 attacks, Khadr had chosen his side. "It looks like after we have removed the Russian empire we will have to be ending up removing also the American empire," he told CBS journalist George Crile who spent months documenting the Khadr family's story before his sudden death from cancer in 2006.

Once the Khadr family fled after 9/11, no one inquired about the whereabouts of others on the run. It was safer not knowing where people were, Khadr would tell Elsamnah and the children. Elsamnah would sometimes not see her husband for weeks.

In Logar, soon after bombs fell on Kabul, there was a knock at the door of the home where Elsamnah was hiding. She opened it to find Zawahiri's wife and children. Azza was disheveled and barely recognizable as she clung to her youngest child, four-year-old Aisha, who had been born in 1997 with Down's syndrome. The children were all barefoot, dirty and freezing. Like Khadr and Elsamnah, they had been in Kabul when it was taken over and narrowly escaped. No one asked where Zawahiri was.

After they helped care for Azza, the families moved from Logar to Gardez. Elsamnah and the children went to stay at the home of a gas station owner whom Abdullah knew and who had offered them sanctuary. Azza Zawahiri and her family spent the night in the home of Taliban leader Jalaluddin Haqqani, about a fifteen-minute drive away. That night there was an explosion so powerful that Elsamnah thought a bomb had landed outside the front door. But it was Haqqani's house, where U.S. forces believed Zawahiri was hiding, that was hit.

The next morning, Abdullah went to look at the remains and found his father, who had not stayed with the family the night before but who was already combing through the rubble. Azza and her daughters had been pinned under the collapsed cement roof and died before rescuers could get them out. Aisha had frozen to death. Zawahiri was not with them. Abdullah came back to the house breathless, dreading having to tell his mother that her friend was dead. He handed her Azza's purse and Elsamnah collapsed in tears.

BY NOW, ALL THE KHADR CHILDREN knew how to fire a gun and they were told to shoot if they ever felt threatened. From Gardez, they traveled without their father again, to the city of Zormat, a small village in Paktika province near the border of Pakistan. Abdullah was behind the wheel on the stretch of dangerous road, with an AK-47 at his side. Omar was hanging out the back of the car with his weapon. Zaynab, who sat in the back seat with the children, was also armed. "The order was if anyone stopped, if anyone stopped the car, you shoot. If anyone asked us to stop, you shoot. You don't think, you shoot," Zaynab recalled. "So you're sitting there going, 'I can do it, I can do it. I hope I don't have to do it. I can do it. I hope I don't have to do it.' "

It was the end of Ramadan and many of the families they had not seen since 9/11 showed up in Zormat. One evening, Zaynab and Rabiyah Hutchinson were listening to the radio while her father and a group of men talked and slept in a nearby room. They listened as the broadcaster read out the names of men wanted by the United States; rewards were being offered. Saif al Adel, their former neighbor, was worth $25 million. There were other familiar names. And they were all in the room next door.

The Khadr family managed to stay one step ahead of the fighting. They left Zormat in December at the end of Ramadan and after celebrating Eid. Three months later, Afghan and allied forces, including Canadian troops, launched Operation Anaconda in the Shah-i-Kot Valley, southeast of Zormat.

From Zormat, the Khadrs traveled to Bermel in the Paktika province. It was January 2002, and Zaynab's daughter Safia was almost two and required more medical care. Zaynab decided she would take her to a hospital in Lahore, and Kareem went with her. Abdullah needed an operation to remove cartilage from his nose, so he later joined them. Elsamnah stayed behind to be near her husband and kept her youngest daughter Maryam with her. Omar, who was fifteen, also stayed behind.

A little more than a month later, Elsamnah moved once more, settling in South Waziristan, just across the border in Pakistan, where villagers were sympathetic to their plight. Life was difficult and lonely. Khadr visited less and less, sometimes not showing up for a month, while Elsamnah, Maryam and Omar moved from one primitive shelter in the mountains to the next. Omar was at a difficult age. He didn't want to stay with the women but since he was the only male left, he had the responsibility to look after his mother when Khadr was away. One day, he was forced to don a burka so he could travel unnoticed with the women. He was furious.

Days would pass during which the three would huddle in a home with blankets covering the window. Elsamnah acquired thread and needles and tried to keep Maryam entertained by making her a doll. She used a sock Abdullah had left behind for the doll's body and Omar's gloves became the hands. Little green beads were sewn on for eyes and red ones became lips. The plump wool doll looked deranged, with a tight smile and enormous hands, but Maryam loved it and dragged it everywhere. On one of Khadr's rare visits, he hung a swing inside the house but it did little to cheer Maryam up. "She would sit there on her swing with her dolly and cry and cry," Elsamnah recalled.

Omar would spend most of his days drawing or making bead necklaces and bracelets for his mother and little sister. One day, he started sewing beads onto clothes and in no time, most of the clothes his mother wore were adorned with Omar's handiwork.

But Omar was growing restless and wanted to travel with the other boys and men, often begging his father to tag along. By that summer, Khadr allowed his son to live with some men his father knew as long as he checked in regularly on his mother and sister. By June, Elsamnah saw Omar less and less. In July, she didn't see him at all.

Khadr didn't tell his wife that one of his friends, Abu Laith al Libi, had been asking about Omar. Al Libi, who later became an al Qaeda spokesperson, was planning on traveling into Afghanistan, near the town of Khost, with a group of men. They wanted Omar to come along because he spoke Pashto. Omar was also familiar with the Khost region and its people since his father had once operated an orphanage there. Khadr allowed his son to go and Omar was delighted to finally be away from the women.

One day in August, a friend of Khadr's brought Elsamnah a bag with some of Omar's clothes. By the time Khadr arrived a few days later, Elsamnah was inconsolable. "What happened?" she demanded of Khadr. "Where's Omar?"

Khadr tried to calm his wife but he was angry too. "It wasn't supposed to happen like this," he told her. Khadr was suffering from malaria at the time and as he sat with his wife he looked much older than fifty-four.

"Omar's not dead," Khadr told her, explaining that Omar had been captured by U.S. forces.

Elsamnah had never met al Libi but Khadr knew him well, as did Abdurahman and Abdullah. Abdurahman first encountered al Libi in 1997 when the family was living in Jalalabad and the local Taliban leaders relied on al Libi to help mediate a fight between Abdurahman and Abdullah. "He was one of those cool characters. He knew a lot about Dubai. He knew about cameras. He knew about planes, laptops and stuff that's cool. He traveled a lot," recalled Abdurahman. "He knew about all these gadgets and that made him pretty cool. We'd talk about them and Abdullah knew about all these gadgets, so they'd be discussing and me sitting there saying 'Wow.' And cars, he knew a lot about Ferraris and Lamborghinis and stuff."

The Pentagon would allege that fifteen-year-old Omar had spent the month of June receiving "one-on-one, private al Qaeda basic training, consisting of training in the use of rocket-propelled grenades, rifles, pistols, grenades and explosives." The Pentagon's report continued: "After completing his training, Khadr joined a team of other al Qaeda operatives and converted landmines into remotely detonated improvised explosive devices, ultimately planting them at a point where U.S. forces were known to travel."

The Pentagon alleged that on July 27, 2002, when Special Forces soldiers attacked the compound where he was hiding, fifteen-year-old Omar donned an "ammunition vest and took a position by a window in the compound," with an AK-47 in hand. He did not want to surrender and "vowed to die fighting."

Khadr was upset the favorite son had been captured and furious with al Libi, who was not with Omar when the compound was attacked. Elsamnah said al Libi tried to later send food as a peace offering, but Khadr wouldn't accept it.

After Omar's capture, Zaynab, Abdullah and Kareem joined their parents and the community of foreigners hiding in Waziristan. Living near the Khadr family was an Egyptian named Hamza al Jowfi, whom Khadr had met years earlier in Khost. When Jowfi lived in Khost, he was an unfailingly gracious host, but in the rough terrain of Waziristan, he was an often cantankerous and demanding guest. Zaynab recalled that he would visit their makeshift home in the mountains and she would serve him tea. He would keep sending it back, saying it wasn't strong enough or hot enough or it was too thick or too thin. Kareem had smuggled movies and if there was enough electricity, the kids would huddle to watch bootleg copies of Harry Potter films on a laptop. But when Jowfi discovered their stash, he snapped each DVD in half as the children looked on miserably.

Jowfi had four children and in September 2001, his wife Umm Hamza went into labor with their fifth. Elsamnah went with her to the Kabul hospital where, as soon as she arrived, doctors discovered the baby was in distress. By the time they performed a Caesarean section, the baby was dead. A little over a year later when they lived together in the mountains, Umm Hamza was again pregnant and ready to give birth. Elsamnah was worried. The conditions were harsh. When the newborn began to cry, a wave of relief washed over the group of assembled women. They were so overjoyed by the arrival of the little girl they didn't notice how weak Umm Hamza had become. Within an hour, Umm Hamza died as her four older children looked on.

By 2003, Khadr had assumed more responsibility in Waziristan and was appointed the head of the local shura council, an advisory group that would coordinate the fighting of the Afghans, Taliban and al Qaeda.

The most detailed account of Khadr's whereabouts at that time was given by his son Abdullah during his interrogation with Canadian and American agents in 2005. Abdullah was captured by Pakistani forces in late 2004, held for fourteen months without charges and questioned by investigators with the RCMP, CSIS and the FBI. In December 2005, he was released and returned to Canada, but two weeks later he was arrested by the RCMP on a Boston court indictment for terrorism. U.S. prosecutors allege he was buying weapons for al Qaeda while in hiding.

According to transcripts of his interrogation, Abdullah said that in 2003 his father had been given operational responsibility for organizing attacks against Coalition Forces in Waziristan. During this time, he was in contact with Abd al Hadi al Iraqi, a suspected bin Laden advisor. Al Iraqi, whose real name was Nashwan Abd al Razzaq Abd al Baqi, was born in Mosul, Iraq, in 1961 and had been a major in the Iraqi army before arriving in Afghanistan to fight the Soviets. The Pentagon alleged he was part of bin Laden's own shura council before the 9/11 attacks and an important link between al Qaeda and the Taliban. When he was captured in Iran in 2006, authorities alleged that al Iraqi was working as a liaison between al Qaeda and Iraqi insurgents. He was kept in CIA custody until his transfer to Guantanamo Bay in 2007.

According to Abdullah, his father liked al Jowfi, who he says was responsible for procuring most of al Qaeda's weapons; however, he disagreed often with al Iraqi. He was especially opposed to al Iraqi's insistence that they fight a frontline war, since Khadr believed that guerilla tactics would be more effective, Abdullah said.

In early October 2003, Khadr traveled to a small town called Angorada, with his youngest son Kareem. Abdullah was not with him but later told American and Canadian agents what happened to his father and brother. "The night before the raid happened, almost the entire leadership of al Qaeda was in the house," Abdullah said. In addition to al Iraqi and al Jowfi, there was also Khalid Habib and Egyptian Sheik Essa, also known as Qari Ismail.

Abdullah said that while Pakistan's army was responsible for securing Waziristan, there were many sympathizers within their ranks and among Pakistan's intelligence service, so there were ways to avoid capture. "The arrangement between the army and locals is if there had to be a raid the army would inform the locals, this way it saved trouble for both sides," Zaynab later explained. "The locals would hide the foreigners. The army would come, they would search, they'd find no one, they'd leave. So, it would save face to the army and at the same time, they wouldn't have to fight with the locals because it was a known fact that the locals didn't give up their guests, so there would have to be a fight and to save all that, they would have this arrangement. So, what happened was whenever there was a raid, which happened a couple times while we were there, two or three days ahead or a week ahead, the locals would be informed and they would tell us that we needed to move."

The day the Khadr patriarch was killed, the warning came too late.

After morning prayers on October 3, 2003, Khadr told Kareem he had received word that a raid was going to take place. "Go ahead, I'll be right behind you," he said to his thirteen-year-old son. The shooting started moments after Kareem had left their safe house. He dove into a ditch and felt a burning sensation in his back and his legs went numb. A bullet had punctured his spine and for three hours, as the fighting raged around him, he waited for help, unable to move.

Khadr only made it steps away from the house when the aerial bombing started. His body had to be identified through DNA testing.

5

"Don't Forgat Me"

WITH THE MAJESTIC, SNOW-DRIPPED Hindu Kush mountain range as a backdrop, the U.S. military base in Bagram rises up from the dusty earth, an eyesore on an otherwise picturesque scene. It's not surprising that after 9/11 the Americans used Bagram's flat, elevated land, about thirty miles north of Kabul, for their northern base. The area has a history of providing sanctuary for the country's interlopers and the crumbling architecture is a testament to the battles they had.

A haunted-looking building in one corner of the U.S. base is a former Soviet aircraft machine shop that the Americans converted to a prison when they arrived in 2001. The low-slung, concrete-and-sheet-metal building with blown-out windows boarded up with plywood is large enough to cover a city block. Inside, the soldiers divided the floor into cages separated by concertina wire. Prisoners would use foam mats as beds, and, until the facility was renovated in 2005, sawed-off barrels as toilets. The second floor was reserved for interrogations in individual wooden booths. Every clank of leg irons, every step of a military-issued boot echoed loudly in the cavernous building. The soldiers called the prison the Bagram Collection Point or BCP; detainees called it The Barn.

Detainees were not supposed to be held at Bagram long but there were exceptions. Moazzam Begg was one. The thirty-four-year-old was different from the other prisoners, many of whom had never left their small villages, let alone Afghanistan. Begg had been born and raised in Britain, the son of immigrant Muslim parents who wanted their children to reap the benefits of life in the West.

Education had always been very important to Begg's father and as a child, Begg was sent to a Jewish primary school, sporting a Star of David on his blazer, because it was considered the best school in the working-class

Birmingham suburb where he grew up. During the 1980s, Begg attended a public school as a teenager and fell in with a South Asian gang called the Lynx that battled the skinheads, punk rockers and other anti-immigrant bigots.

Begg began to practice Islam in his late teens during a trip with relatives to Pakistan and Saudi Arabia. When he heard about the plight of Muslims in Bosnia, he traveled to the Balkans to work with an aid organization. Although he was fit and muscular, at five-foot-three, neither the street gang nor the mujahideen in Bosnia considered Begg a fighter. More philosophical in his outlook, Begg had always gravitated to the arts, acquiring his father's love of poetry and literature.

During his twenties, Begg decided to open an Islamic bookshop in London, which caught the attention of Britain's intelligence service that had been tracking the mujahideen returning from Afghanistan and Bosnia. Britain's domestic security service, MI5, raided the shop in 1999 and accused Begg of inciting Islamic extremism. He was charged under the Prevention of Terrorism Act, but the charges were dropped due to lack of evidence.

In July 2001, Begg moved with his wife Zaynab and their three children from Britain to Afghanistan, in search of a life true to Islam, uncorrupted by Western comforts or conveniences. He worked to build a girls' school in Kabul, a rare exception for the Taliban who had outlawed the education of females. When the American bombs began to fall in Afghanistan three months later, Begg moved his family to Islamabad. But authorities came looking for him. Just after midnight on January 31, 2002, Pakistani and CIA agents burst into his house and threw a hood over his head. He was accused of having high-level al Qaeda connections and taken to Afghanistan, where he disappeared into American custody. He wouldn't see his family again for three years.

Begg was held at the American prison in Kandahar before being transferred to Bagram. He was considered a high-priority captive and every security agency wanted to talk with him about Bosnia, Pakistan and Afghanistan. For the most part, Begg was compliant. In fact, one British interrogator described Begg to *New York Times* reporter Tim Golden as "devastatingly reasonable."

After a year in custody, however, the detention was taking a toll. "I have not seen the sun, sky, moon, etc. for nearly a year," he wrote to his father. "I am beginning to lose the fight against depression and hopelessness."

Begg's only advantage was that he spoke English and for guards who were battling the endless boredom of long days away from home talking to Begg was a welcome break. Some even became friends and questioned Begg about his culture and Islam. In turn, they allowed Begg privileges, such as delivering the food packages known as MREs (meals ready to eat) to the other prisoners. As he sat with the guards one day in late July 2002, he was told that a dangerous detainee was on his way. Within hours, the prison was abuzz with the news.

WHEN OMAR KHADR arrived at Bagram after the firefight in July 2002, his reputation had preceded him. "The guards told me they've just brought in this young kid who was extremely belligerent, extremely hostile; that a vehicle load of Americans just happened to be going past him delivering aid and he just lobbed a grenade at them," Begg recalled.

Omar was first taken to the base hospital so his injuries could be assessed and treated. Not long after, he was taken into The Barn. Begg couldn't take his eyes off the skinny, stooped-shouldered Omar as he was led past the other prisoners, up the stairs and into an interrogation booth. There had been other teenagers at Bagram, most of them inadvertently scooped up with their relatives and held until the military could figure out what to do with them. But Omar looked young, even for fifteen, and his injuries were some of the worst Begg had seen.

A few weeks after arriving, much of which he spent in interrogation, Omar was transferred to Begg's cell. The dozen or so Muslim men who shared the cell had no privacy, and using the sawed-off crates as toilets was especially humiliating for the detainees, many of whom had stomach ailments. Blankets had once been used as curtains but guards had seized them after a prisoner had used a blanket to hide a hole he was digging. Talking wasn't allowed but detainees tried to risk whispered conversations. If they were caught, they were brought to the front of the cell and forced to stand with their arms outstretched, a hood often placed over their head.

Omar retreated immediately to the back of the cell and sat down. Begg said he heard one of the guards say to him, "I hope you pay for what you've done," but Omar didn't look up. There were raw scars on his chest where there had once been two deep holes. Shrapnel had punctured the skin along his arms and legs. While the nicks and scrapes can sometimes look minor, they have a cruel habit of causing pain for years to come. Doctors will often not remove embedded shrapnel, preferring to allow the body to work on its own to eject foreign objects. While considered safer than extraction, it is incredibly painful as the shrapnel works its way to the surface, eventually bursting through like blood blisters.

Omar's introduction to Bagram was harsher than that of most detainees. Begg said the guards singled him out for the worst treatment, payback for allegedly killing one of their own. They would make him perform Sisyphean tasks, such as stacking heavy boxes and crates that the guards would knock over when he had finished and then force him to start again. Each time, they walked past his cell they would yell: *Murderer! Killer! Butcher!* "It was very, very hard to hear that because it was evident he was just a kid. Not only that, he was terribly wounded," said Begg.

The guards referred to the detainees as BOB, the Bad Odor Boys. "Every little operation was given the suffix 'Bob.' 'Operation Wash-Bob' would be to take prisoners out to shower," Begg wrote in his memoir, *Enemy Combatant*. "Operation Sun-Bob was getting everybody in The Barn out into the sun for a certain amount of time."

Omar, with his scarred body, became known as Buckshot Bob. After a month in detention, the guards no longer called him by his name or number. He was just Buckshot.

BAGRAM WAS SUPPOSED to be a clearinghouse, a place to gather real-time intelligence, not a prison. Many of the detainees had been simply snatched off the streets in Pakistan or Afghanistan by local forces greedy for the generous bounties paid by the Americans. Skilled interrogators would quickly assess the farmers, business owners and villagers and release them. But for many innocents, it could take months or even years for the military to discover the mistake.

If a detainee was not cleared for release, there were a few places to send him. A select group of so-called "high-value" detainees disappeared into a labyrinth of secret CIA facilities—"ghost prisons" or "black sites." Some prisoners were handed over to the interim Afghan government and an uncertain future. Anyone with a suspected Taliban or al Qaeda connection, and this was the case for virtually all of the Arab and Western detainees, was automatically transferred to Guantanamo Bay. Before they left, they would be taken to "Cell Number One" where their heads would be shaved and they would be strip-searched and photographed. They would leave for the long journey to Cuba wearing an orange jumpsuit, goggles with lenses painted black, earphones, and their legs and wrists chained.

Omar's arrival at Bagram coincided with the arrival of a new team of military interrogators and guards. There was always a difficult time of adjustment for both detainees and new guards. But there would be other problems with the Cincinnati-based 377th Military Police Company who took over daily operations in August 2002. They weren't experienced in policing prisons, let alone one in Afghanistan. The new interrogators were rookies too. These "human intelligence collectors," as the army called them, hailed mostly from the 525th Military Intelligence Brigade based in North Carolina.

Some of Bagram's prisoners were fresh from battle and potentially carried valuable intelligence, including perhaps the whereabouts of al Qaeda's elusive leaders, making the interrogators jobs crucial. "Often the first task for interrogators is sorting out who's been caught, distinguishing the fighters from the farmers, the terrorists from the townspeople—to some, evil from good," wrote a former Bagram interrogator under the pseudonym Chris Mackey in his book *The Interrogators*. "Prisoners might be captured at gunpoint on the field of battle, rounded up in pre-dawn raids or safe houses, or turned over by warlords or foreign intelligence services with agendas of their own . . . But the main objective of interrogation, as the army's field manual on the subject states, 'is to obtain the maximum amount of usable information possible in the least amount of time.' That imperative meant one thing before September 11, when our training still focused on large-scale conventional conflicts. It has taken on another meaning since then."

Interrogators knew that detainees arrived scared, a condition which they could use to their advantage. Getting information quickly was vital because once word got out about someone's capture, plans could be changed and tracks covered. Both the interrogation and guarding of detainees took experience and self-restraint. Some of those stationed in Bagram lacked both.

BEFORE SEPTEMBER 11, 2001, army interrogators adhered to the rules set out in *Field Manual 32-54*, which describes psychological tactics, and, more importantly, sets limits on how far an interrogator can go. The manual follows the rules laid out in the Geneva Conventions, four international treaties that try to limit the barbarity of battle and establish a standard of care for prisoners of war. Although history shows there were disastrous exceptions, the U.S. government had vowed to respect the Conventions. Even during the Vietnam War when Hanoi refused to treat captured American pilots as prisoners of war, the U.S. administration said it would treat their captives as such. American soldiers had all been given cards titled "The Enemy in Your Hands," which stipulated that Viet Cong prisoners must be treated in accordance with the Geneva Prisoner of War Conventions. The card included key words translated into Vietnamese, such as "halt" and "lay down your gun," and a quote from President Lyndon B. Johnson: "The courage and skill of our men in battle will be matched by their magnanimity when the battle ends."

Begg doesn't remember the Geneva Conventions being cited in Afghanistan but he does recall a card he was handed when he first arrived in Kandahar. The card was titled *EPW: Enemy Prisoner of War* and listed some personal details such as his prisoner number, 558. But after two weeks, he said the guards collected the card from him. After that, he was never referred to as a "prisoner of war."

On February 7, 2002, President Bush signed an order that gave the first public indication of how the United States would treat al Qaeda and Taliban captives:

> Our recent extensive discussions regarding the status of al Qaeda and Taliban detainees confirm that the application of Geneva Convention Relative to the Treatment of Prisoners of War of August 12, 1949 (Geneva), to the conflict with al Qaeda and the Taliban involves complex legal questions. By its terms, Geneva applies to conflicts involving "High Contracting Parties," which can only be states. Moreover, it assumes the existence of "regular" armed forces fighting on behalf of states. However, the war against terrorism ushers in a new paradigm, one in which groups with broad, international reach commit horrific acts against innocent civilians, sometimes with the direct support of states. Our nation recognizes that this new paradigm—ushered in not by us, but by terrorists—requires new thinking in the law of war, but thinking that should nevertheless be consistent with the principles of Geneva.

Although Bush had coined the term "war on terror," he was laying down the argument that those captured in Afghanistan were not traditional "prisoners of war," and so not automatically afforded Geneva Conventions' protections. "Consistent with the principles of" meant the Conventions weren't binding. The message was clear, even if the rules weren't. This was a different kind of war. Interrogators were told the information they extracted from prisoners would save lives. MPs were told never to let their guard down since they were guarding the world's most dangerous men. Often, they were told to "soften up" the prisoners for interrogation by scaring them, not letting them sleep, giving them the odd kick or punch.

But how far should they go? U.S. Vice President Dick Cheney and his cadre of like-minded lawyers and advisors began lobbying almost immediately after 9/11 for harsher interrogation tactics. "We also have to work through sort of the dark side, if you will," Cheney told NBC News' *Meet The Press* on September 16, 2001. "We've got to spend time in the shadows in the intelligence world. A lot of what needs to be done here will have to be done quietly, without any discussion, using sources and methods that are available to our intelligence agencies, if we're going to be successful. That's the world these folks operate in, and so it's going to be vital for us to use any means at our disposal, basically, to achieve our objective."

Asked host Tim Russert: "There have been restrictions placed on the United States intelligence gathering, reluctance to use unsavory characters, those who violated human rights, to assist in intelligence gathering. Will we lift some of those restrictions?"

"Oh, I think so," Cheney replied. "One of the by-products, if you will, of this tragic set of circumstances is that we'll see a very thorough sort of reassessment of how we operate and the kinds of people we deal with . . . If you're going to deal only with sort of officially approved, certified good guys, you're not going to find out what the bad guys are doing. You need to be able to penetrate these organizations. You need to have on the payroll some very unsavory characters if, in fact, you're going to be able to learn all that needs to be learned in order to forestall these kinds of activities. It is a mean, nasty, dangerous dirty business out there, and we have to operate in that arena. I'm convinced we can do it; we can do it successfully. But we need to make certain that we have not tied the hands, if you will, of our intelligence communities in terms of accomplishing their mission."

During the first few months of debate, the "ticking time bomb" scenario was often cited. Could an interrogator, should an interrogator, torture a prisoner if the prisoner could tell where a "ticking time bomb" was hidden? Was the safety of the nation not more important than the rights of one individual? Could torture produce reliable information? The intelligence community seemed divided. Then came the question: What is torture?

The most common international definition is found in Article One of the UN Convention against Torture. It states: "The term 'torture' means any act by which severe pain or suffering, whether physical or mental, is intentionally inflicted on a person for such purposes as obtaining from him or a third person information or a confession, punishing him for an act he or a third person has committed or is suspected of having committed, or intimidating or coercing him or a third person, or for any reason based on discrimination of any kind, when such pain or suffering is inflicted by or at the instigation of or with the consent or acquiescence of a public official or other person acting in an official capacity. It does not include pain or suffering arising only from, inherent in or incidental to lawful sanctions."

But after 9/11, the Bush administration established a new standard. On August 1, 2002, White House lawyer Alberto Gonzales and Jay S. Bybee, the Assistant Attorney General for the White House Counsel, signed what has become known as the "torture memo." The memo was a legal interpretation of the UN Convention against Torture whereby the lawyers narrowed the definition significantly. Torture, they argued, could be defined as activities that result in: "death, organ failure or the permanent impairment of a significant body function." The memo also advises that criminal law prohibiting torture "may be unconstitutional if applied to interrogations undertaken of enemy combatants pursuant to the President's Commander-in-Chief powers."

BAGRAM CHANGED THE MONTH Omar arrived. Stress positions, during which prisoners would spend hours and sleepless nights handcuffed or shackled in painful positions to induce them to talk, became part of the routine, a *New York Times* investigation later uncovered. The guards also used the "common peroneal strike," a crippling blow to the thigh that wasn't to be used unless a guard's life was in danger but the new unit of MPs used it routinely. Some guards later said they were amused when one of the prisoners screamed out, "Allah, Allah" after each strike.

The prisoner was named Dilawar, a twenty-two-year-old taxi driver who was wrongly accused of a rocket attack on an American base. For four days in 2002, his outstretched arms were chained to the top of his cell. The soldiers used the technique to keep the prisoners awake and upright, the pressure on their wrists unbearably painful if they slumped down asleep. Five days after his capture, Dilawar was found dead in his cell—the second death in Bagram in two weeks. An autopsy found that his legs had been beaten so badly that it looked as if he had been run over by a bus. A military coroner determined that his death was a homicide due to "blunt force injuries to lower extremities complicating coronary artery disease." An exhaustive military investigation recommended that twenty-seven personnel be charged with criminal acts. By that time, many of those soldiers had moved to Abu Ghraib prison in Iraq. Few soldiers ended up in jail.

Damien Corsetti was one interrogator who started in Bagram and moved to Abu Ghraib. Like the others, he had been given little training and lots of responsibility. Corsetti weighed close to 300 pounds, stood more than six feet tall, had a thick neck, dark bushy eyebrows that hung heavily over his eyes and had a booming voice he used to shout at the prisoners when they first arrived. He was an intimidator and he was good at it. It didn't matter what he said to the detainees who didn't speak English. Sometimes he would pick up a box of Kellogg's Frosted Flakes and scream the ingredients at the prisoners who didn't realize ascorbic acid or hydrochloride were vitamins, not threats. During his seven months in Bagram, Corsetti logged more than 3,000 hours in the interrogation booths.

Corsetti had two nicknames at Bagram: "Monster" and "The King of Torture." He had the word "Monster" tattooed on his stomach after one of his best friends was killed in North Carolina in 2001. His friend always called him Monster because he was so big. The tattoo was to honor him. His superior in Afghanistan christened him the King of Torture, although Corsetti has said he doesn't remember that name being used.

Corsetti was eventually charged with beating and sexually humiliating a Saudi prisoner at Bagram who claimed that Corsetti had pulled out his penis during an interrogation and screamed: "This is your God." During the trial, his lawyer portrayed Corsetti as a foot soldier led by a commander who demanded results at any cost: "The President of the United States doesn't know what the rules are. The Secretary of Defense doesn't know what the rules are. But the government expects this Pfc [private first class] to know what the rules are?" lawyer Capt. Joseph Owens asked. On June 1, 2006, Corsetti was acquitted of all charges and five months later, he left the army with an honorable discharge.

Begg doesn't remember Corsetti as a monster. During his free time at Bagram, Corsetti had made a point of sitting with the English-speaking prisoners to try to understand why they were there. He spent long afternoons drinking tea and playing chess with a high-ranking Taliban official who would try to explain Sharia law to the North Carolina native. Corsetti was especially fond of talking with Begg who had been nicknamed "The Professor" by the guards. As a present he gave Begg a book, a coveted possession since the tedium was overwhelming. Begg had never heard of Joseph Heller's anti-war novel *Catch-22* but he grew to appreciate Corsetti's sense of irony.

Corsetti believed in his work as an interrogator but outside the booth he was a different man. He was sickened by the conditions in which the prisoners were kept and tried to befriend as many as possible. "To keep a hundred men in five or six cages where they're not allowed to move off a six-by-six blanket for twenty-three hours a day, that's not right," Corsetti said after he left the military. "I tried to give them a bit of humanity as much as possible and let them know not all Americans are assholes."

Corsetti vividly remembered Omar. He was part of a screening team who visited Omar when he first arrived at the base hospital. When Corsetti saw the hole on the top of Omar's back, he held a Coke can to the wound. "You could have fit that can of Coke in the back of his head. He was really messed up," Corsetti recalled. As Omar was questioned, Corsetti kept an eye on the machines that kept track of the teenager's vitals. "You could see his pulse elevating on the machine and his respiration increasing if he got nervous. We're taught to see the signs of it physically, but you can never really see it actually happening on the monitor in front of you," said Corsetti.

Corsetti made a point of talking to Omar as often as he could, bringing him chocolates or letting him watch movies on his laptop. They talked mainly about basketball but sometimes they would talk about Omar's family. "Honestly, he seemed like a young kid who got swept up into something because of his family ties and never got the opportunity to make a choice for himself whether it was right or wrong," Corsetti said.

Begg used to watch Corsetti and Omar talk, happy to see the teenager being shown some compassion. "He treated Omar very well after he got to speak to him, after he got to know him. I think that's indicative to how people reacted to Omar," Begg said. "There's Omar the myth, and there's Omar the person."

DURING THE WEEKS that Begg and Omar shared a cell, Begg negotiated a daily half-hour of physical activity for all the detainees. Begg delighted in the thirty minutes he was permitted to walk, stretch or do pushups.

Normally, any movement was forbidden. But the other detainees, mostly from rural Pakistan and Afghanistan, had never exercised in their lives. "One of the things I found very difficult was to motivate the people there to do things and I noticed when the Americans saw that nobody was doing anything they said 'Well, if nobody's going to do anything, there's no point in you guys having this time.'"

Omar's injuries still restricted his movement and he often winced performing simple tasks. But after the guards threatened to revoke the exercise time, Omar, noticing Begg's distress, started to stretch awkwardly alongside him during the allotted time each day. "It really moved me because he was terribly wounded and for him to have done that was again indicative of the kind of person he was, is."

While most detainees spoke about their parents, wives and children, Omar said little about his family to Begg. Omar had been told during an interrogation that his brother Abdurahman was now working for the Americans. He knew that Abdurahman had been captured by the Northern Alliance in November 2001 but he didn't know where he had been taken. Begg said this news depressed Omar but that he was not altogether surprised that his older brother, who had always rebelled against his father, was working with his father's enemy.

In late October as the nights began to cool and wind storms coated the airbase in a thick layer of dust, Omar's name was written in blue on a board outside his cell. Begg knew what this meant and went to wish his young Canadian friend luck.

"You know, you are fortunate, because there are people who actually are concerned about you," Omar told Begg. "I don't have anyone."

Omar was soon transferred to Cell Number One On October 28, 2002, he was flown out of Afghanistan.

THE U.S. NAVY BASE AT GUANTANAMO was built around a sapphire blue bay on a scrubby, cactus-strewn plot of land on Cuba's southeast coast. A century ago, a pre-revolutionary Cuban government signed a perpetual lease that allowed the United States to inhabit the geographically strategic land. Cuba's first president, Tomas Estrada Palma, signed the deal with U.S. president Theodore Roosevelt in 1903 in return for 2,000 gold coins a month. In 1934, the deal was renewed, the rent increased to $4,085 and a stipulation added requiring the consent of both countries to break the lease.

When Fidel Castro's revolution triumphed in 1959, U.S. soldiers were banned from crossing into Cuba and the seventeen miles of fence surrounding the base was heavily fortified with armed guards. The United States refused to break the lease and the base remained.

"The naval base is a dagger plunged into the Cuban soil," Castro thundered soon after taking power. That dagger has been twisting in his side since. During a rambling speech in Chile on December 3, 1971, Castro told a crowd: "That base is there just to humiliate Cuba." A decade later, he rejected military intervention but said Cuba had the "moral and legal right" to demand its return. "It is part of our territory being occupied by a U.S. military base. Never has anyone, a revolutionary cadre, a revolutionary leader, or a fellow citizen had the idea of recovering the piece of our territory by the use of force. If some day it will be ours, it will not be by the use of force, but the advance of the consciousness of justice in the world." In August 2007, an ailing Castro wrote in an essay that even though the United States continues to send the rent every month, only one check has ever been cashed, a mistake during the early days of the revolution.

Today, guards remain on both sides of the fence but the focus for the Americans has turned inward. Coast Guard boats patrol the waters and guard towers scan the horizon to prevent the escape or attempted rescue of the detainees. Sometimes, the sun catches the reflection of a Cuban guard's binoculars, one of the few reminders of the base's history and uneasy tenancy.

Guantanamo may have weighed heavily on the minds of Cubans for decades, but its name didn't gain worldwide recognition until the Bush administration decided it was a perfect place to detain prisoners who had been captured in Afghanistan. The base is not on American soil and so, the administration argued, the prison was outside the reach of the U.S. courts.

Since 2001, the base has grown both physically and metaphorically. For many, Guantanamo now symbolizes all that has gone wrong with the U.S.'s efforts to fight terrorism.

The base occupies forty-five-square miles, roughly the size of Manhattan, and is divided into three distinct areas where the soldiers work and reside. Visitors arrive on a small landing strip on the leeward side of the base. In addition to the airport, this area consists of a couple of housing units, a mess hall and the brightly lit Clipper Club, which offers greasy food, beer and pool tables.

Crossing the bay by ferry or on one of the Coast Guard's "fast boats" takes visitors to the main base on the windward side. Here, spread along either side of Sherman Avenue is a surreal suburban town. A McDonald's, a Subway sandwich shop, a Kentucky Fried Chicken outlet and a Starbucks provide alternatives to the mess hall. A small mall houses the requisite Navy Exchange, or NEX, that sells everything from groceries and wine to candles and iPods. There's even a gift shop for Guantanamo Bay memorabilia, such as snow globes, key chains and T-shirts. Until journalists started to write about the crass keepsakes, the shirt selection included a pink one for babies that read "Future Behavioral Modification Specialist." Now the merchandise is more standard tourist fare, although the words Guantanamo Bay under the picture of a dolphin rising from foaming waves seems equally disconcerting.

Not far from the NEX is a golf course and while it looks parched and pathetic, any distraction for bored soldiers is popular. Drinking is also a favorite pastime and the Tiki Bar, a thatched hut with plastic chairs on a patio that looks out to the ocean, is usually packed in the evenings.

At first blush, this Caribbean Pleasantville masks a general discontent. Gitmo is not a popular assignment. Some of the soldiers say privately they would rather be in Iraq or Afghanistan and those who don't seem to feel guilty.

About a ten-minute drive from Sherman Avenue, through rolling, dry terrain, and past a series of well-armed checkpoints, is what has become the world's most famous jail. The ocean-side prison, known as Camp Delta, consists of cell blocks surrounded by razor wire and under constant surveillance. A thick green mesh wrapping prevents detainees from seeing the ocean or the land beyond their cells.

Camp Delta didn't exist on January 11, 2002, when the first military cargo plane brought detainees from Afghanistan. Those prisoners were brought to a group of hastily erected wire pens called Camp X-Ray. "One by one, manacled and masked, the first twenty of up to perhaps 2,000 Taliban and al Qaeda prisoners arrived in this sweltering U.S. military outpost," wrote *Miami Herald* reporter Carol Rosenberg. "Some apparently struggled and Marines appeared to push them to their knees. Most, however, seemed to offer little resistance as they hobbled from the huge Air Force cargo plane that ferried them halfway across the world to a jail for terrorism suspects on the edge of the Caribbean."

The detainees wore orange jumpsuits and turquoise surgical masks, since there was a fear some might have been infected with tuberculosis. They wore blacked-out ski goggles and earphones to muffle the noise during the flight and to keep them completely disoriented. "These represent the worst elements of al Qaeda and the Taliban. We asked for the bad guys first," Marine Brig.-Gen. Michael Lehnert told the journalists who watched the detainees disembark.

Controversy soon erupted as the first pictures were published in media around the world. The pens at Camp X-Ray resembled animal kennels with chain-link walls and ceilings that exposed the prisoners to the punishing sun. Detainees were only allowed out for interrogations which meant each cell had two buckets—one for water and one for use as a toilet. "Horror of Camp X-Ray," trumpeted Britain's *Mail on Sunday*.

Weeks later, a photograph showed detainees being wheeled on gurneys along a dirt and gravel path to interrogation rooms, which again provoked outrage. The Pentagon initially tried to defend this policy, saying it was for the safety of the detainees and guards, but the gurneys were soon prohibited.

Among the first detainees was David Hicks, an Australian in his twenties who had searched most of his life for purpose. In the late 1990s, Hicks went to Albania to fight with the Kosovo Liberation Army. He converted to Islam and ended up in Pakistan with the Lashkar-e-Tabia, or LeT, a Pakistani group fighting India for control of the Kashmiri territory. He wrote his father Terry saying he was excited to be firing "hundreds of rounds" across the Pakistani border into India. "There are not many countries in the world where a tourist can go to stay with the army and shoot across the border at its enemy, legally," he gushed. Hicks was scooped up in late 2001 at the age of twenty-six while trying to flee Afghanistan.

Three British citizens the guards would nickname "The Beatles" were also among the early prisoners at Guantanamo. In Britain, they had become known as the Tipton Three, since they had grown up together in the Midlands neighborhood of Tipton, about a two-hour train ride from central London. Ruhal Ahmed and Asif Iqbal were both twenty and Shafiq Rasul was twenty-four when they were captured in Afghanistan in October 2001 and accused of links to the Taliban. They were released in

2004 and told harrowing stories about their twenty-six-month detention, eventually making an internationally acclaimed film titled *The Road to Guantanamo.*

Their story started with a trip to Pakistan for İqbal's wedding in August 2001. When the United States attacked Afghanistan, the trio decided to enter Afghanistan to help the victims of war. The decision seemed suicidal in hindsight, but the young men were struggling to become devout Muslims and believed this was their duty and a way to compensate for their wayward teenage years of drinking, drugs and more than one encounter with the police. When they realized what they were in for, they tried to leave but were captured by Northern Alliance forces led by Rashid Dostum, the brutal Uzbek commander who survived by shifting his loyalties.

In November 2001, when Dostum was on the side of the West, his forces packed the Tipton Three and hundreds more into closed trucks for their journey to U.S. custody. The truck doors were sealed and most of the prisoners lost consciousness during the long trip. Iqbal passed out and when he came to he was lying on top of dead bodies, breathing in the stench of their blood and urine. Realizing the prisoners were suffocating, Dostum's men fired holes into the trucks with their machine guns. But they hadn't taken the prisoners out and the bullets killed some survivors. The Tipton Three licked the condensation off the sides of the truck for water and were among a handful who were alive at the end of the journey.

The Pentagon claimed the three Britons had personal connections to Osama bin Laden and as evidence showed a training camp video taken in 2000 where they could be seen with the al Qaeda leader. Britain's MI5 were trying to build their own file on the three men but stumbled on evidence that proved their innocence. They discovered that the Tipton Three couldn't be the men in the video, since there was proof they were in Britain at the time. The discovery led to their release but they had spent almost two years in Guantanamo.

The conditions at Camp X-Ray had been horrendous, but it was temporary, giving prisoners hope that their detention might also be. When Camp X-Ray closed for good on April 29, 2002, the prisoners moved to Camp Delta, which had room for 612 prisoners and provided individual cells, each with a sink, toilet and steel cot. After the move, Ahmed began thinking suicide was his only way out. Some five years later, he reflected on those desperate days: "I realized, 'I'm not going home,' and it just broke me in bits."

OMAR ARRIVED LIKE THE OTHERS, stumbling out of the cargo plane after a twenty-seven-hour journey, disoriented and only able to take baby steps while chained in leg irons and handcuffs that were attached to a metal belt, a restraint known as the "three-piece suit."

Omar became Internee Serial Number, or ISN, 766. His "in-process weight" was recorded as 155 pounds, his height, 70 centimeters, or five-foot-seven. The blast of Cuban heat in late October was likely Omar's first welcome to his new home. He got another greeting when he was taken to the detainee hospital for assessment. "Welcome to Israel," someone said.

Omar had turned sixteen while in custody in Afghanistan and that would change how he was treated. It's believed there were more than a dozen prisoners under the age of sixteen who were brought to Guantanamo, including three Afghans aged between twelve and fifteen, whose detention sparked international outrage and led to their release.

Those boys were held in a separate seaside cabin known as Camp Iguana. They were allowed to watch videos, including *Castaway*, the Hollywood blockbuster starring Tom Hanks about life stranded on a tropical island. Naqib Ullah was only twelve when he was captured and had never seen a television set before. He left Guantanamo with an American football and letter from the military saying he was innocent. Omar had turned sixteen just thirty-nine days before arriving in Guantanamo, so in compliance with a post-9/11 Pentagon policy regarding detainees, he was treated as an adult from the day he arrived.

Army Chaplain James Yee recalled being surprised when he first saw Omar, with his scraggly wisps of facial hair, held among the heavily bearded adult detainees. "He definitely seemed out of place in the general population," Yee said.

Yee was a thirty-five-year-old West Point graduate with a spotless military record, a wife, young daughter and a solid reputation when he went to Guantanamo in November 2002. An American whose parents had emigrated to the United States from China, Yee had converted to Islam after graduating from the military academy at West Point in 1990. He traveled to Damascus to study Arabic before returning to become one of only a handful of Muslim army chaplains. After 9/11 his services were in high demand. But after ten months at Guantanamo, everything would change. In September 2003, he was arrested at an airport in Jacksonville, Florida, and charged with terrorism offenses, ruining what he hoped would be his first visit home since being deployed to Guantanamo. The

Pentagon alleged that Yee had smuggled classified information and letters written by the detainees out of Guantanamo. If convicted of aiding the enemy, he faced the death penalty. Yee spent seventy-six days in isolation in a military brig in Charleston, South Carolina, while the allegations against him made headlines worldwide. The charges were eventually dismissed for lack of evidence and Yee retired from the army a broken man.

When Yee first arrived at Guantanamo, full of hope and patriotism, he spent much of his day walking the corridors of the prison speaking to the detainees who sought counseling. One day, Yee stopped outside Omar's cell. Two things surprised him as he bent down to talk to the teenager. Omar could speak perfect English which was uncommon in the blocks. He was also reading a book that had pictures of Mickey Mouse, Goofy and Donald Duck that Yee knew wasn't one the library stocked. Omar told Yee the book was a gift from one of his interrogators. He expected Omar to be insulted but instead he appeared delighted.

When Yee came again to the teenager's cell later that day, Omar was curled up asleep on his steel cot clutching the Disney book to his chest.

OMAR WAS CONSIDERED an intelligence treasure trove because of his father's connections and his own travels since 9/11. He was only ten when he lived briefly on Osama bin Laden's compound but the Khadr children had been schooled in their father's politics and had met al Qaeda's hierarchy. When the Khadrs fled after 9/11, they crossed paths with many of the terrorist organization's leaders still being sought.

The interrogators also had a precious piece of evidence that the U.S. soldiers had retrieved after Omar was captured. Following the July 2002 firefight, the Special Forces soldiers had returned to the battle scene. A small group of soldiers was posted to guard the bombed-out compound but the locals had already pillaged it. It was rumored that the villagers had uncovered two more bodies and, following Islamic tradition, buried them immediately. The soldiers implored them to disclose where the men had been buried so they could be identified but the townspeople refused, so it remained uncertain how many had been in that compound during the fight.

Capt. Mike Silver was part of the team and watched as an excavator tore down the remaining walls. "We found some unexploded ordinance, there were some RPGs [rocket-propelled grenades] in there. A couple of them went off because the place was still smoking and burning while we were there." There was also a largely intact building where recently harvested straw was stored. Just as the building was about to be torn down, the soldiers made a curious find—a plastic bag with some wires, documents and a videocassette.

The tape featured a few frames of Omar. One had him in a room filled with landmines, winding wires around his hand as another man looked as if he was attaching them to the mines. In another shot, Omar's smiling face was illuminated by the green hue of night vision in what looked like a scouting mission. There were other men in the video, including Khadr's friend, Abu Laith al Libi. The interrogators at Guantanamo were keen to know more.

All the American intelligence agencies had a presence in Guantanamo; at one point, the FBI even had a yacht moored in the harbor. But most interrogations were conducted by the military's Joint Intelligence Group, or JIG. Like the interrogators at Bagram, many of these soldiers were new to the job. The closest most had come before was to question mock suspects at the army's intelligence school in Fort Huachuca, Arizona.

Some were veterans who had been called back to action, but this was a much different war than what many of them had trained for. During the 1980s and even into the 1990s, interrogators were schooled in Cold War tactics and Russian was the most common second language. Before being deployed to Guantanamo, these older interrogators received a three-week refresher course. One week featured an overview of Islamic terrorism networks. The following two weeks involved practical exercises, including mock interrogations.

On January 21, 2003, after Omar had been at Guantanamo for almost three months, the military interrogators received a new SOP, or Standard Operating Procedure. It began: "History is being made with the Interrogations Operations taking place at Guantanamo Bay." The interrogators were expected not just to do their jobs but also to "radically create new methods and methodologies that are needed to complete this mission in defense of our nation," the manual stated. "There is much that you will be asked to do which is not in any of your prior training. There are legal, political, strategic and moral issues that influence and affect how operations are conducted in this vital part of Operation Enduring Freedom. You must be aware that your activities and actions are often directed by or reported to the highest levels of government."

Number One of the new Code of Conduct included: "Treat detainees humanely" and "TORTURE is not authorized under any circumstances."

Although the tricks of interrogating are complex, there are underlying principles and common tactics. At Fort Huachuca, soldiers are taught about a dozen techniques. There are "Love Your Comrades" or "Hate Your Comrades" ploys, during which an interrogator tries to convince a prisoner that cooperation would help their fellow fighters, or, if they felt betrayed in their capture, could be a way to exact revenge. There's the "Mutt-and-Jeff" approach, the good-cop, bad-cop routine.

"Pride Ego Up" or "Ego Down" exploits the prisoner's insecurities, or conversely, their arrogance. A technique called "Establish Your Identity" involves concocting false and damning allegations to prompt a prisoner to refute them with the truth. Sometimes interrogators offer incentives or sympathy, trying to win trust.

The most popular tactic by far, however, is "Fear Up," and it works the way it sounds. Interrogators try to intimidate the prisoner and scare him into talking. "The most productive time you can have as an investigator is when people are shit scared," explained Jack Hooper, the former head of Canada's spy service. "You scare them, you intimidate them, you make them uncomfortable to the extent you can make them uncomfortable. Nobody talks to you because they want to if you're an authority figure, whether you're an intelligence officer, whether you're a military officer or a police officer. They don't talk to you because they want to. They talk to you because they're afraid of something and the whole purpose of an interrogation is to make them afraid, make them say things they ordinarily wouldn't. Now you stop short of beating them over the head with a baseball bat but to the extent you can, through your demeanor, your posture, your words, your tone, you can instill fear, that's what you have to do because otherwise nobody would talk to you."

Detainees who knew Omar said he spent many of his early days at Guantanamo in its interrogation booths. Guards would arrive at all hours and tell him he had a "reservation," which was code for interrogation. Omar would later allege that his interrogations were physically and mentally abusive. If his accounts are accurate, he appears to have had the whole Fort Huachuca playbook tried on him—with some improvisation.

ONE DAY DURING RAMADAN in the late fall of 2003, Omar was taken into an interrogation booth to meet a man who called himself Izmarai, he would later claim. The interrogator said he was from the government in Afghanistan, but on his pants he sported a little American flag. He spoke mainly Farsi, Pashto and some English, and asked questions with words from each. Omar was told if he did not cooperate, he would be sent to Afghanistan, where "they like small boys." Before Izmarai left, frustrated by Omar's responses, he wrote in Pashto on a piece of paper: "This detainee must be transferred to Bagram."

During another interrogation that year, Omar said he was threatened with rendition to Egypt, and, again, the threat of sexual violence was explicit. The interrogator spit in his face and pulled Omar's hair when he would not answer. In Egypt, the interviewers would not be so nice he was told. He would meet *Askri raqm tisa*, Soldier Number 9, the guard who raped uncooperative prisoners.

One evening in March 2003, Omar was taken from his cell and in no mood to cooperate. The guards left him in the interrogation booth for hours, short-shackled with his ankles and wrists bound together and secured to a bolt on the floor. Unable to move, he eventually urinated and was left in a pool of urine on the floor.

When the MPs returned and found the soiled teenager, they poured pine oil cleaner on Omar's chest and the floor. Keeping him short-shackled, the guards used Omar as a human mop to clean up the mess. Omar was returned to his cell and for two days the guards refused to give him fresh clothes.

Ruhal Ahmed's cell was directly beside Omar's for most of 2003 and he became a surrogate older brother to him. Ahmed would watch the teenager return from interrogations, saddened both by the times Omar would return smiling and those when it was clear he was disturbed. "Sometimes he'd be happy because some of the interrogators would treat him nicely," Ahmed recalled. "Sometimes he'd come back and he'd talk, 'Oh they gave me this, they gave me that, and this, I watched this film.' Sometimes he'd come back and he wouldn't be talking and we'd know, okay, we shouldn't ask him anything. It was quite difficult to ask somebody what happened to you. We'd just ask, 'Are you all right?' He'd say, 'Yeah, I'm fine.'"

But then Omar would retreat to the back of his cell, put a blanket over his head and sob quietly.

DURING HIS EARLY MONTHS AT GUANTANAMO, Omar was still recovering from his injuries and would spend days in the prison hospital. He would often get one of the best rooms, adjacent to the nursing station and separate from other wounded or ill.

Chaplain Yee went to the hospital every day and looked forward to his visits since it was the only facility that had reliable air conditioning. Often he would sit beside Omar's hospital bed and talk or sometimes just sit there and say nothing. Omar was in pain most of the time and did not seek Yee's spiritual guidance. Despite some awkward silences, though, they seemed to draw comfort from each other.

Omar was well-liked by others at Camp Three, whose population in 2003 included the Tipton Three, David Hicks and some of the other Western prisoners. Omar seemed to prefer the company of the English-speaking prisoners with whom he could talk about movies or the cartoons some of the interrogators let him watch. Ahmed spent hours telling Omar every scene and twist of every movie he could recall—*Braveheart, Die Hard* and of course, *Harry Potter*, which was a favorite among the prisoners. There was camaraderie among the detainees at Camp Three which Omar would miss when he was put in isolation.

Nothing bonded the prisoners more than their abuse of unpopular guards. Part of their arsenal was "cocktails"—a combination of feces, urine and sometimes semen. As the guards passed their cells, detainees would throw the concoction through the bars. One guard received a mouthful as he leaned down to talk to a detainee through the bean hole, the slot where food was passed, and the prisoners screamed wildly.

Ahmed recalled the day an MP, who was especially despised, was called into a cell to unclog a toilet that had been jammed with sheets. Omar, Ahmed and the other prisoners of Camp Three each watched through the bars as the MP donned elbow-high black gloves. As he pulled the sheet out of the toilet, the detainees began to chant in English, "plunger, plunger, plunger." It grew louder, "PLUNGER, PLUNGER, PLUNGER," as they banged on the bars until even the other guards were snickering and repeating the MP's new nickname.

From that day on, both guards and detainees took great pleasure yelling, "Plunger, Plunger, Plunger," as the MP walked the blocks. The taunting took its toll. The MP just ran from the blocks one day, never to return. One of the guards told Ahmed that Plunger had sought counseling from the Combat Stress Team, a group of psychologists who worked out of Building 3206 inside the residential military area called Camp America. "Walk-in consultations and triage, brief solution-focused therapy, crisis intervention, roommate contracting, anger management, command consultation, suicide awareness and prevention," was how they advertised their services in a base newsletter.

Although the Western detainees in Camp Three were considered to be the most valuable and dangerous captives, all but Omar have been released.

BY THE TIME Omar arrived in 2002, Guantanamo had already had two commanders. U.S. Marine Brig.-Gen. Michael Lehnert, an engineer by training, was Guantanamo's first leader. Lehnert was hands-on and often visited the detainees in Camp X-Ray. In early 2002, the prisoners waged their first hunger strike and Lehnert went right to the cells to talk with the prisoners. "The general came to our cell and this general seemed really nice, and seemed really honest," Ahmed recalled. "The general sat down, he sat on the floor, which to me was like, so what, he sat on the floor, on dirt. But for the other guards and like the colonel, and the lieutenant, they were just gobsmacked because this was a general who sat on the floor to speak to a detainee."

Army Brig.-Gen. Rick Baccus replaced Lehnert, but only stayed for seven months before he was replaced in November 2002. A report in the *Washington Times* quoted an unnamed government source who claimed Baccus was replaced because he had been considered too soft.

The camp's third commander arrived only days after Omar. Army Maj.-Gen. Geoffrey Miller was a two-star general who walked with a swagger, had a Texan drawl and had been handpicked by Defense Secretary Donald Rumsfeld for the job. The Bush administration believed the offshore prison needed a shakeup. Interrogations were not yielding enough information and Washington was worried that the prisoners were getting too comfortable. Miller was sent to instill discipline, order and, above all else, to gather intelligence.

With Miller's arrival, the procedures changed both inside the cellblocks and interrogation booths. Detainees were forced into stress positions both before and during interrogations. They were exposed to extreme temperatures and noise. AC/DC, Britney Spears and Christina Aguilera were blasted into isolation booths. One prisoner was left shackled and wrapped in an Israeli flag as he was bombarded with music. Another was left in heat so unbearable, he ripped out clumps of his hair, an FBI e-mail later revealed. Miller liked to call Guantanamo the "testing lab in the global war on terrorism."

"Every single time, Gen. Miller referred to the war, it was the *global* war on terrorism. I knew nobody else who so robotically attached the four words of the term together each time he mentioned it," wrote Erik Saar, an army sergeant who had worked as a linguist in Guantanamo, in his book *Inside the Wire*. Miller called interrogations a "young person's game" and tactics were rarely reviewed since Miller didn't encourage the taping of interrogations, even though the booths were equipped with cameras.

Saar writes of one interrogation of a twenty-one-year-old Saudi detainee who refused to answer questions and instead prayed continuously. In an attempt to stop his prayers, the female interrogator whom Saar was translating for got up from her chair and began rubbing her breasts against the detainee's back. When that didn't work, she walked in front of him and began running her hands over her body. He stopped praying just long enough to spit in her face.

Frustrated, she left the room and sought the advice of another interrogator, who was Muslim. "She had a high-priority uncooperative detainee, she explained, and she wanted to find a way to break him from his reliance on God, his source of strength. He suggested that she tell the Saudi that she was having her period and then touch him. That could make him feel too dirty and ashamed to go before God later, he said, adding that she should have the MPs turn off his water so he couldn't wash," Saar wrote. "She grabbed a red marker and disappeared into the ladies' room. 'Let's go,' she said when she returned. Before we entered, she warned the MPs again to stay close by and come in if they heard any screaming."

There was screaming, but it was the detainee as he sobbed and shrieked. The interrogator had reached into her pants and wiped what the detainee believed was menstrual blood on his face in an effort to get him to talk. But he didn't talk. He became hysterical. "We closed the door behind us and I leaned against the wall," wrote Saar. The interrogator began to sob. "I just looked at her. I knew she hadn't enjoyed this. She had done what she thought was best to get the information her bosses were asking for . . . But I hated myself when I walked out of that room, even though I was pretty sure we were talking to a piece of shit in there. I felt as if I had lost something. We lost something. We lost the high road. We cashed in our principles in the hope of obtaining a piece of information. And it didn't even fucking work."

The sexual humiliation of devout Muslim detainees started during Miller's tenure. Brig.-Gen. John T. Furlow later conducted an investigation into these interrogation techniques. He reported that on at least one occasion during a 2002 interrogation, a female soldier had rubbed perfume on the arm of a detainee. "The interrogator admitted to using this approach with a detainee. At the time of the event, the detainee responded by attempting to bite the interrogator and lost his balance, fell out of his chair, and chipped his tooth. He received immediate and appropriate medical attention and did not suffer permanent injury," Furlow wrote. This was considered "an authorized technique" so neither the soldier nor her supervisor was reprimanded.

Furlow also found that a female interrogator once took off her shirt, rubbed her chest against a detainee's back and ran her fingers through his hair, using a technique he called "futility." "The interrogator also approached the detainee from behind, touched him on his knee and shoulder, leaned over him, and placed her face near the side of his in an effort to create stress and break his concentration during interrogation," Furlow wrote. The interrogator's supervisor was given a letter of reprimand for "failure to document this technique." That discipline satisfied Furlow, although he did recommend the technique no longer be used.

NEWS HAD A STRANGE WAY of traveling through Guantanamo. Detainees were ingenious at spreading information from one cellblock to the next, even though they were not supposed to communicate and their movements were restricted. There were times the guards themselves would spread news such as the capture of a high-ranking al Qaeda figure. There was much celebration among the soldiers after Iraqi president Saddam Hussein had been found, even though his capture meant little to detainees from Afghanistan and Pakistan.

In the fall of 2003, there was one story that everyone talked about. Omar's father had been killed. The guards told the detainees that Ahmed Said Khadr had been part of bin Laden's inner circle and had been killed by Pakistani forces on October 3. Omar said little. "He used to hide his emotions away from people," recalled Ahmed. "You can just imagine a sixteen-year-old kid if something happens. They don't usually share their emotions, they just kind of keep it inside them and when they do show their emotions, it's usually to their moms or whatever, not going to be some stranger next door."

If Omar had felt alone in Bagram, his father's death only intensified this sense of isolation. He wrote often to his grandparents in Scarborough, the only address he had for his relatives, signing his name with a little heart in the corner. "I pray for you very much," he wrote in one letter, "don't forgat me from your pray'rs."

6

The Elephant and the Ant

THEY CAME WITH A BIG MAC, pictures and many questions. Smiling, sweaty and red-faced, the woman and two men walked into the room where Omar had been sitting with his ankle chained to the floor for hours. The one wielding the burger sat in front of Omar. Off in the corner, the older gentleman took his seat, placed a notebook in his lap and tried to blend into the wooden walls of the small building. The woman didn't say a word as she also settled in the background.

"Do you remember me?" asked the man named Greg as he pushed the Big Mac toward Omar. The sixteen-year-old hungrily unwrapped it and finished it off in only a few bites as he shook his head. "But I remember him," Omar said, pointing to the older man who just smiled but said nothing.

Greg explained that he was from Canada and had a few questions. Omar had questions of his own. *How were his grandparents? What about his parents? Where were they? Was his brother here in Guantanamo?* It was February 2003, the first time in the seven months since Omar had been captured that he had seen anyone from Canada and Omar, like the rest of his family, placed a great deal of trust in the country where he was born.

Canada had been the land of his summer vacations, where he could endlessly watch action movies, play with his cousin Bilal and enjoy running water and reliable electricity in the comfort of his grandparents' home. When the Khadrs were in trouble, Canada had been their savior. Canadian doctors had saved his father's life and his dad quite possibly owed his freedom to the prime minister. There was no doubt the gold-embossed, dark blue Canadian passport was the most coveted Khadr possession. It's not hard to imagine that the sight of a Canadian walking into the room with a bag of fast food signaled to Omar that help had arrived.

But Greg was not there for Omar's benefit. A senior and well-respected agent with the Canadian Security Intelligence Service (CSIS), Greg was one of Canada's most skilled spies. He was also the head of the "Islamic Extremist" desk in CSIS's Toronto office. Everyone at CSIS knew the Khadr family, but Greg knew them best. He had watched the Khadr children grow up, and while Omar may not have remembered him, the two had met in Toronto years earlier during an interview with one of Omar's older brothers. Greg had been waiting for months to talk with Ahmed Said Khadr's second youngest son.

For the next two hours, inside the small meeting room of one of the buildings in Camp Echo, Omar and Greg talked. Right from the start, a few facts about the Khadr family dynamics became clear. In terms of sibling relationships, Omar was closest to his sister Zaynab and had an acrimonious relationship with Abdurahman, his elder brother whom CSIS referred to by the initials ARK.

"My age kept going up but my maturity didn't. I was a troublemaker. Omar would try to make friends with me because I was his brother," Abdurahman later explained. "He was a politician in the way that he'd always try to make everybody happy. He would be friends with me when I was calm, when I was doing a good thing, when I was helping my mom and dad. When I was just being me, he wouldn't be nice to me."

Although seven years younger, Omar wasn't just close to Zaynab, he seemed protective of her. "He knows more about Zaynab than any of them," his mother Maha Elsamnah said. "I guess because he's a trusty boy. You can give him a secret and he'll keep it. No one can take a secret out of Omar."

But on that day, with a Big Mac in his belly and Greg asking the questions, Omar talked plenty. A government report later described Omar as being "relaxed and open." Greg led Omar through a series of questions about his parents and siblings, focusing at one point on Zaynab's ex-husbands. Omar didn't realize that Zaynab's second marriage had also ended in divorce but told Greg he wasn't surprised since Zaynab never liked her husbands. She only married to keep her father happy, he said. There was a lot the children did to keep their father happy. Abdullah and Abdurahman went to training camps in their teens, and when he was fifteen, Omar told Greg, his dad sent him to become a translator for family friend Abu Laith al Libi.

Greg also had questions about men CSIS were investigating in Canada. He had a stack of photos he wanted Omar to identify. Since most had some association with Omar's dad, he hoped Omar could remember details about them. One by one, he pushed the photos toward Omar: "Do you know him? What about him?" Some of them Omar recognized from Scarborough and he seemed almost happy to be looking down at familiar faces.

THE OTHER TWO PEOPLE in the room never spoke. The woman was a CIA agent who worked out of the U.S. embassy in Ottawa and acted as a warden during the trip to Gitmo. She had traveled with the group from Canada to Washington, where they took a jet chartered out of Dulles Airport to Cuba.

The older gentleman, whom Omar thought he recognized, was Canadian Foreign Affairs official Jim Gould. Gould had never met Omar but he did fit the stereotype of a Canadian bureaucrat, and perhaps Omar had confused him with someone his father had dealt with. White, middle-aged and bespectacled, Gould looked like he would be more comfortable in a suit than the summer casuals he wore. But while he might have looked like a government employee, he didn't always talk like one. Gould was not one to toe the government's line and preferred debating the politics of the Middle East in crowded coffee shops to attending strategy meetings in Ottawa.

Gould's thirty-year career with the Canadian government had taken him around the world and helped put more than one degree on his resumé, including a master's in Islamic history from Cairo's American University and PhD in Islamic history from the university of Edinburgh in Scotland. Although Gould worked for the Department of Foreign Affairs, he wasn't in Guantanamo to help Omar. Gould was the deputy director of a secretive intelligence division within Foreign Affairs called the International Security Branch.

The Pentagon had ruled out consular visits, only allowing intelligence officials access to Guantanamo in 2003. Gould was admitted as an intelligence officer but his presence still made the Americans wary. They told him he could only observe, a message that had been reiterated during a stopover at CIA's headquarters in Langley, Virginia. "One word," the female CIA agent had warned him, "and the visit's over."

When the guards came to retrieve Omar after their first meeting, Greg asked the MPs if Omar could be isolated overnight. They said they would try, but Omar was returned to his regular detention cell at Camp Three. The next interrogation would be dramatically different.

IT HADN'T BEEN EASY getting the Canadians to Guantanamo. The visit was the culmination of a six-month battle of memos, phone calls and meetings. It began as negotiations between governments do—with a letter between diplomats. The Dip Note, as it's known in bureaucratic parlance, was sent August 30, 2002. The Chrétien government asked that a consular official be allowed to see Omar at Bagram, requested that Omar's age be considered and that he not be transferred to Guantanamo.

The United States is a signatory to the Geneva Conventions and the Vienna Convention on Consular Access, which both stipulate that foreign captives cannot be held incommunicado. But two weeks later, the State Department issued a terse reply that stated consular visits with "enemy combatants" were not "practical or possible." "Should an enemy combatant claiming Canadian citizenship be transferred to the United States Naval Base at Guantanamo Bay, the Department of State will notify the Government of Canada and other appropriate parties," the letter stated. Guantanamo was already considered a legal black hole and Canada, at least at that time, wanted no part of it.

Foreign Affairs "press lines" drafted before Omar's transfer pushed issues that they would later abandon. Press lines are the scripts to be used by everyone from top government officials through to media spokespeople. They ensure that the politicians and bureaucrats "stay on message" or "speak with one voice," to use the language of Ottawa spin doctors. Most notable in these early press lines is the inclusion of Omar's age and comparisons of his case to that of child soldiers. "Is the department concerned that a person who is not yet sixteen years of age has been detained in this way?" reads an anticipated question in the government's September 2002 press lines.

"Yes, we are concerned," the suggested reply states. "However, we are also mindful of the fact that there is a need to establish with greater certainty the circumstances under which he was captured by the American authorities. We are attempting to obtain further information. It is an unfortunate reality that many groups and countries recruit and use children in armed conflicts and in terrorist activities. Canada is working hard to eliminate this practice, but child soldiers still exist, in Afghanistan, and in other parts of the world."

The official who wrote those lines left his initials at the top of the draft. HGP stands for Henry Garfield Pardy, a name he says he got because "my mother got carried away." In Ottawa, he was known as Gar, or sometimes jokingly referred to as "Mr. Consular." Pardy knew more about foreign relations than most politicians, but the field hadn't been his first calling. The native Newfoundlander began his working life with his head in the stars at the Meteorological Service of Canada. "They kept shipping me north until I thought, 'Christ, there's an easier way to get to Moscow than over the North Pole,'" Pardy said. In 1967, he joined the Foreign Service. Over the years, his work included a stint as Canada's Ambassador for Central America and a posting in Washington. In 1992, Pardy agreed to help with the transition in moving the responsibility of consular services from the immigration department to Foreign Affairs. A decade later, when he was offered early retirement, he was still there.

For Pardy, Omar's age was important. Canada had cultivated a reputation for protecting the rights of children and was bound by an international treaty called the Convention on the Rights of the Child, or CRC, which Canada had ratified in 2001. "Both legislators abroad and the international community have acknowledged the vulnerability of children and the resulting need to protect them. It is therefore not surprising that the Convention on the Rights of the Child has been ratified or acceded to by 191 states as of January 19, 2001, making it the most universally accepted human rights instrument in history," a Canadian Supreme Court ruling read. The United States has never ratified the CRC although their courts have also recognized the importance of upholding its principles.

Pardy noted that Omar was only fifteen in the press lines he drafted in 2002. But Colleen Swords, the Foreign Affairs Department's legal advisor, objected. (Swords would go on to become the head of the department's intelligence section). She e-mailed the department's communications director, Lillian Thomsen, asking that they "claw back on the fact that [Omar] is a minor." Politicians were no longer to publicly stress that Omar was a teenager or to criticize the Bush administration for holding a minor.

CANADA WAS UNIQUE among the U.S. allies after 9/11. The countries share more than 5,000 miles of largely unguarded border, which means they also share security. In 1999, after "Millennium bomber" Ahmed Ressam was arrested trying to cross into the United States, Canada was forced to defend itself against accusations that liberal immigration policies made the country a haven for terrorists. Even though none of the nineteen hijackers on September 11 had come through Canada (a claim that was made erroneously by some U.S. officials for years), Canada's ability to root out terrorists was of immediate concern.

The Canadian government was also worried about the billions of dollars in cross-border trade that could be affected if the Bush administration decided to close the border. The "Smart Border Declaration" was signed by Canada's Foreign Affairs Minister John Manley and Homeland Security Secretary Tom Ridge on December 12, 2001, outlining a plan for the countries to ensure security while maintaining the free flow of goods. Manley later defended Canada's concern about cross-border trade when other countries were questioning the legality of the U.S.'s post-9/11 security laws. "Should we have therefore said, 'Well, we are not going to negotiate something like the Smart Border Accord with the United States because they may be engaging in practices of which we would not directly approve?' And my answer to that is I had too much at stake for the people that I represent to say, 'You know, you may have had thousands of people killed in your jurisdiction and you may be going over the top'—that's for someone else to judge. But for me, I have got to get my citizens their right to have their employment, and therefore the fundamental thing that I was concerned with was making sure that we reached an understanding that was going to protect Canadian interests."

For the first months of the war, Canada managed to avoid engaging in the debate of how the U.S. would deal with prisoners captured in Afghanistan. But in January 2002, an Associated Press photo showed three heavily armed members of Canada's secretive Joint Task Force 2 (JTF2) commando unit with prisoners at Kandahar airport, revealing that Canadian troops were working to hand prisoners over to U.S. authorities. Until the photo appeared on the front pages of Canadian newspapers, Chrétien didn't know that Canadian soldiers were capturing al Qaeda and Taliban prisoners and the public didn't know JTF2 had been dispatched to Afghanistan. The revelation caused an uproar and sparked a parliamentary investigation into why Defence Minister Art Eggleton hadn't informed the prime minister about JTF2's actions.

It was later disclosed that during the first year in Afghanistan, JTF2 participated in several Special Forces operations, including Anaconda, during which JTF2 performed a daring mountain climb to an observation point, apparently using skills they had acquired training in northern Canada. They had killed at least 115 suspected Taliban and al Qaeda fighters and captured more than one hundred. At least three of those captives ended up in Guantanamo.

JTF2's involvement raised troubling legal questions. They had handed captured suspects over to the United States, so how was Canada obligated to ensure these prisoners would be treated in accordance with the Geneva Conventions once they were in American custody? Canada insisted it had received assurances that detainees at Guantanamo were being treated humanely and would take the United States at its word. Other countries were less accepting. Spain, for instance, refused to extradite eight men charged with complicity in the September 11 attacks unless the United States agreed they would be tried in civilian courts. Both the British media and government reacted quickly when the Pentagon released a photograph of shackled and blindfolded detainees in orange jumpsuits kneeling in the hot Guantanamo sun. Britain's conservative *Daily Mail* editorialized that, "Even the SS were treated better than this." British Foreign Minister Jack Straw demanded an explanation.

But Chrétien did not object and adopted some of Bush's "you're with us or you're with the terrorists" posturing. In 2002 during a House of Commons Question Period, he infuriated opposition members of Parliament by branding them al Qaeda sympathizers. Bloc Quebecois leader Gilles Duceppe argued there were no guarantees that al Qaeda and Taliban suspects were being treated lawfully in U.S. custody. "It was not imprudent on the part of the government, in the fight against terrorism, to take the side of those who were attacked, and not become defenders of the terrorists as the Bloc Quebecois is doing," Chrétien fired back. "We are over there to defend those who advocate freedom and respect of citizens. At this time, we are attacking the terrorists who killed Canadians and Americans in Washington, and particularly in New York. We are fighting the terrorists. In that type of war, it is normal to have agreements between the troops to see who will take charge of the prisoners. In this case, it was decided that the Americans would do that." At first, Chrétien refused to comment on Guantanamo specifically and said he would deal with the issue if Canadians were detained. "We don't have prisoners there," he told the Agence France-Presse. "We'll tell you when we have them."

But when Omar arrived in October 2002, Chrétien still did not have a clear public position. Most media reports focused on his intervention in the case of Omar's father—the case was seen as an embarrassment and fodder for the right-wing American talk show hosts who wagged their fingers at Canada.

Omar's transfer also coincided with the impending invasion of Iraq and Chrétien's decision not to send Canadian troops. The decision was unpopular with the White House, made worse by an embarrassing quip from Chrétien's communications director. A *National Post* reporter had overheard Francoise Ducros call Bush a "moron," during a conversation at a NATO summit in Prague and published the remark. The story became a national scandal despite Chrétien's attempt to downplay the incident. "I know her very well," he told reporters. "She may have used that word against me a few times and I am sure she used it against you." Eventually, Ducros resigned but the relationship between Chrétien and Bush remained icy.

Chrétien did not want any more bad press and Omar's case posed that possibility. Four days after Omar arrived in Guantanamo, a Canadian embassy official in Washington wrote an e-mail on C4, the Foreign Affairs protected internal system, outlining a meeting with U.S. officials. "We opened the discussion by noting the profile that the Khadr case had acquired in Canada, both at the political level and among various Canadian government agencies . . . and that we were eager to gain early access to Khadr as part of a plan to manage the issue in Canada," Canada's political attaché Francis Furtado wrote.

At the meeting, the Americans made it clear that if Canadian officials were permitted to see Omar the only purpose of the visit would be to collect and share intelligence. "Consular visits were a non-starter and applications that appeared to be consular visits by other means would be scrutinized very closely—which could lead to delays," Furtado wrote.

On November 14, 2003, Foreign Affairs Minister Bill Graham met with U.S. Secretary of State Colin Powell for more than two hours to discuss security-related topics, Omar's case among them. But the meeting coincided with the release of an Osama bin Laden recording that warned that Canada and five other countries were now targets. Although the authenticity of the recording was later challenged, the news changed the tone of the meeting.

"Canada is just as vulnerable to terrorist attacks as the United States and should regard tighter border controls not as harassment but as a way to protect Canadian and American citizens, says U.S. Secretary of State Colin Powell," a *Toronto Star* story began the next day. Only as a footnote did Graham tell reporters that the two had also discussed Omar and that Powell had assured him "that we'll have access to Mr. Khadr as quickly as is conceivably possible."

Three months passed before the Canadian delegation was given the go-ahead. During those months, the press lines concerning Omar were continually updated. By February 2003, they included an anticipated question about Canada's actions in the case, or lack thereof.

Question: What is the Canadian government doing in respect to Mr. Khadr?

Answer: In November, the Canadian government requested that the U.S. government arrange a visit to Guantanamo Bay and a meeting with Mr. Khadr. This visit is presently in progress, and we are awaiting the return of our representative before commenting further.

Question: Is Canada satisfied with the treatment U.S. authorities are according detainees in Guantanamo Bay?

Answer: International law requires, as a minimum, that detainees receive fair and humane treatment. The United States continues to acknowledge its willingness to treat all detainees humanely and in a manner consistent with principles of the Geneva Conventions. Given these statements, and our own observations, the Canadian Government is satisfied.

Problem was, Jim Gould had not returned from Guantanamo when those lines were written. Saying Canada was confident that Guantanamo was a humane facility, by its "own observations," couldn't have been true. Pardy picked up on this: "I think there is a 'bridge to (sic) far' in the answers under the third question. Have we in any way formalized 'our own observations' or is that just a throw-away line?" Pardy asked Jonathan Solomon of the ISI unit, in an e-mail sent February 18, 2003.

"The 'our own observations' line was mistakenly included," Solomon wrote back quickly, assuring him it would be struck from the record.

LIKE MOST COUNTRIES AFTER 9/11, Canada was trying to find cells within the country's borders that might be planning a second wave of attacks. There was tremendous pressure on the government from the United States, and countless references were being made to Ahmed Ressam. In the winter of 2001, Canadian parliamentarians quickly passed an omnibus Anti-Terrorism Act and invested billions to try to patch gaps in the country's security. The criminal code was amended to include terrorism as an offence and government agencies were given broader investigative powers. The most significant change concerned the RCMP. The police force that had been kicked out of the national security arena two decades earlier was back in the game. Four counterterrorism police task forces led by the Mounties were established in Toronto, Ottawa, Vancouver and Montreal.

Not surprisingly, the first massive investigation, dubbed Project A O Canada, involved Omar's father. "The Khadr effect" might have referred to the fallout of Chrétien's intervention in the arrest of Omar's father, but the term could also be applied to Canadian security investigations. Ahmed Said Khadr was, for intelligence purposes, a major player. According to Canada's former top spy, Jack Hooper, it didn't matter if Khadr pledged the *bayat* to Osama bin Laden or identified himself as a member of al Qaeda. "Ahmed Said was a ranking Canadian al Qaeda figure—the most senior Canadian al Qaeda figure. Leave the Canadian aside. Ahmed Said was a big hairy ass in al Qaeda," he said. Countless investigations began or ended with Khadr.

The main target of Project A O Canada was Ottawa's thirty-year-old Abdullah Almalki, who had worked briefly with Khadr in Peshawar at Human Concern International in the 1990s. For years, the FBI had tried to link Almalki's electronics company with radios found in Afghanistan. Almalki ran his business with Lebanese friends in Montreal and New York. They bought cheap American electronics and sold them in Pakistan. The FBI, and ultimately the RCMP, believed the business was a cover to send electronics to terrorist groups. In January 2002, the Mounties raided Almalki's home and seven other locations, including the Khartoum Avenue home of Omar's grandparents.

Police also knocked on the door of an Ottawa home belonging to an engineer named Maher Arar. Arar had become a "person of interest" after having lunch with Almalki at an Ottawa restaurant called Mangos. Arar had grown up in Syria not far from where Almalki's family lived, although the two men met only after they moved to Ottawa and were casual friends.

The RCMP was also interested in Ahmed Elmaati, a friend of Khadr's who had attended training camps in Afghanistan in the early 1990s. His brother Amer, known by the nickname "Wash Wash," had also gone to Afghanistan in the 1990s but had never returned. A letter from the Canadian government informing Amer Elmaati that his passport had been processed was unearthed in a suspected al Qaeda guesthouse in Afghanistan after 9/11, prompting the FBI to issue a BOLO (Be On the Look Out) bulletin stating that Elmaati was "being sought in connection with possible terrorist threats against the United States." His whereabouts remain unknown, but it's believed he may be hiding in Pakistan's Balochistan province.

Project A O Canada would end in scandal and Arar, Almaki and Elmaati detained, tortured and held without charges in Syria. Two federal inquiries investigated the role of Canadian officials in their detention. Arar was given an apology and an $11.5 million settlement from the Canadian government for his ordeal. But in 2003, the investigation was still underway and Omar was the son of a suspect.

THE SECOND DAY Jim Gould and Greg met with Omar started much the same way as the first. The guards removed Omar from his cell early and left him chained and waiting. Instead of a Big Mac, Greg arrived with candy.

Omar looked angry and did not speak. When Greg offered him the candy, Omar shook his head, "No, no, no." He wasn't going to take their bribes today he told them. He called Greg "evil" and vowed he would not say another word until they brought him back to Canada.

"Obviously, he had been spoken to by someone who said, 'You know you're selling the farm here, kid, you gotta hush up, your dad would not like you,'" Gould later surmised. As Greg prodded, Omar stood and ripped off his shirt revealing his chest still pockmarked with shrapnel wounds. He yelled that he was being tortured and demanded they do something. Gould sat impassively and sketched the injuries to Omar's chest as Greg tried to calm the sixteen-year-old.

After it became clear Omar would not cooperate, Greg tried the "Mutt and Jeff" technique but needed a bad cop, so he could be the good one. Gould technically wasn't allowed to be involved but he took his cue and stormed out in faux frustration. Gould recalled their ploy: "It had been set up. I was the bad guy. The interrogator's there saying, 'You're wasting Jim's time, you're wasting his time here. He's here to listen to you talk and you're wasting his time and he's not going to be able to help you. He's from the federal government and he's told you where he's from, and if you don't cooperate how the hell's he going to help you?' I blew out and [Greg] stays in the room and says, 'If you're prepared to talk, I'll try to get him to come back into the room but I'm not sure he will, I think we're out of here.'"

On the third day, Omar had softened slightly but Greg needed time he didn't have—their flight was scheduled to depart that afternoon. Omar maintained that he was happy to talk, but in Canada. If they could bring him back, he would tell them anything they wanted to know. He cried and begged them to take him home.

Greg told Omar he was in the hands of the United States and Canada was virtually powerless in obtaining his release. "The United States and Canada," Omar later recalled him saying, "are like an elephant and an ant sleeping in the same bed." That was the last time Omar saw Greg.

IN THE FALL OF 2003, two CSIS agents named Ian and Paul went to question Omar. Ian looked like a spy or, without the suit and tie he often wore, maybe a university student who split his time between the library and the frat house. Only Ian's receding blond hairline and the creases in his forehead hinted that he was in his thirties.

Ian did most of the talking but Omar wasn't interested in cooperating. He told Ian that everything Greg had reported was a lie. He had been tortured by the Americans so he told Greg what he wanted to hear. He again ripped off his shirt to show his scars. Then he asked Ian why he hadn't brought a Big Mac. He said the prison food was torture and encouraged Ian and Paul to try it.

By this point, Omar had been through so many interrogations he trusted no one. That wasn't uncommon among detainees. One was adamant that he was being held somewhere in Africa. Another believed that the arrows painted on the recreation grounds which pointed east toward Mecca actually pointed west. Omar said he didn't know if he believed Ian and Paul were Canadian agents and even if they were, he didn't seem to care. "Bring me back to Canada, and I'll talk."

Ian confronted Omar with the video the Americans had uncovered that showed him alongside Abu Laith al Libi. But Omar said the Americans had fabricated the video so they could charge him with murder. He was the sole survivor of the attack; the Americans were making him a scapegoat.

For the most part, Omar looked dejected and meek, although every so often he would straighten his shoulders and act tough. He only let his guard down briefly to tell Ian about the letter he had received from Pakistan from his sister Zaynab and his mother. Zaynab told him she had divorced Yacoub al Bahr and that their father was setting up another marriage. Omar seemed saddened. "He felt that every person whom his father set [Zaynab] up with ended up mistreating her," a CSIS report later stated.

JIM GOULD RETURNED TO GUANTANAMO in March 2004, alone but still as a Foreign Affairs intelligence officer, not a consular official. What he had hoped to learn from Omar was not specific intelligence but a broader understanding of how Omar had been indoctrinated into his father's war. Gould had spent time researching the jihad in Afghanistan and could cite passages from the Quran. "What I wanted to know is how his dad educated him. How his dad trained him. How did the dad corrupt the whole family because we've got the problem of other fathers and their sons and that's what I wanted to talk to him about," Gould later recalled.

But Omar wouldn't talk.

Gould immediately noticed the difference a year had made. Omar was leaner, taller and more confident. "I met him two days for an hour-and-a-half each time. He was just playing with me. 'You get me back to Canada and I'll tell you everything you want to know.' 'You give me this and I'll tell you everything you want to know.' 'You get me that and I'll tell you everything,' but always more confident and more honed, in his eyes, recognition that he was playing. I think he had been hardened in that year since I'd seen him."

"[Omar] does really not understand the gravity of his situation," Gould wrote in a report of his visit. "He recognized that he would be on trial and also said that he believed that Canada could have him brought home 'if we wanted.' He does not appear to have given much, if any, thought to what he might say to a lawyer, but he did allow—after some hesitation—that perhaps he would speak to a lawyer if one were to show up."

Gould described Omar as a "thoroughly screwed up young man" who had been used his whole life. "All those persons who have been in positions of authority over him have abused him and his trust for their own purposes."

ONE DAY IN LATE 2003, an Edmonton attorney, who spoke with a lilting Scottish accent and wore cufflinks that read "Old Lawyers Never Die," knocked on the door of Omar's grandparents. "I'm Dennis Edney," he said. "And I'll be representing your grandson." Fatmah Elsamnah had invited Edney and another Edmonton lawyer Nathan Whitling into their home. She was delighted that someone was taking interest in Omar but immediately told Edney she didn't have any money and wasn't interested in making him famous. "I don't need your money," Edney said, "and I don't need fame."

Edney knew the Khadr case wasn't glamorous. He knew that he would likely never be reimbursed for the dozens of flights and hotel bills he would incur, let alone the hours of unpaid legal work. But after a lucrative career representing thugs, drug dealers, bikers, and some innocents wrongly accused, what drew Edney to the case was what always brought him clients—the law. Someone he had once represented called his Edmonton office and suggested Edney look into the case of a Canadian held in Guantanamo. Edney hadn't heard of Omar, but once he did, he knew he was about to have the fight of his career.

When he started, Edney was woefully unprepared for what lay ahead. He had extensive trial experience but knew next to nothing about Islam, Afghanistan or al Qaeda, let alone U.S. military law or international laws of war. He would mix up names and pronunciations, calling Scarborough's imam Mr. Bindy, since he never seemed to remember Aly Hindy's name. During one particularly frustrating interview he had with Zaynab, he demanded that she take off the *niqab* that covered her mouth. "I can't talk to you with that on your face," he said, and surprisingly, Zaynab complied.

Edney was blunt and charming, with street smarts he had acquired growing up in a working-class neighborhood in Dundee, Scotland. His mother had come from a wealthy Catholic family that owned a profitable coal business, but when she fell in love with his father, a poor handsome Protestant, she was cut off from her family and its fortune. "She was five-foot-one and as fiery as the day was long, so from a very early age I learned the power of women," Edney said.

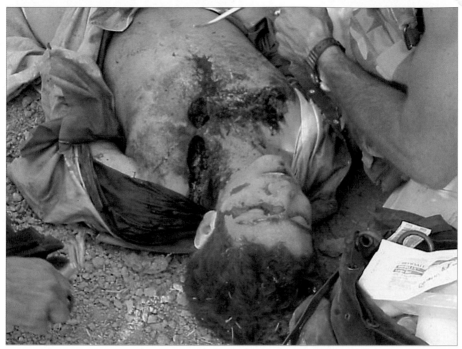

Omar at age fifteen, minutes after being shot by U.S. Forces and dragged from an Afghan compound following a firefight on July 27, 2002.

The remains of the Afghan compound that was bombed by U.S. Special Forces on July 27, 2002.

U.S. soldiers give Omar medical treatment after he was pulled from the compound and before his transfer to a U.S. prison in Bagram.

Soldiers and medical personnel take Delta Force soldier 1st Class Christopher Speer for treatment in Bagram after he was airlifted from Afghanistan.

Courtesy Tabitha Speer

Courtesy Layne Morris

Christopher Speer was fatally wounded by a grenade the Pentagon alleges Omar threw during a July 27, 2002, firefight in Afghanistan.

Special Forces soldier Layne Morris in Afghanistan before the July 27, 2002, firefight in which he was injured. Shrapnel blinded Morris in his right eye, forcing his retirement from the army.

Courtesy Maha Elsamnah

Omar (right) and his little brother Kareem in a family photo from the late 1980s.

Courtesy Maha Elsamnah

Courtesy Maha Elsamnah

Omar (front) and his brothers Kareem and Abdurahman in a family photo from the 1990s in Peshawar.

Omar in younger years in Peshawar in the 1990s.

Jean-Marc Carisse / Library and Archives Canada

Canadian prime minister Jean Chrétien shakes hands with Omar's sister Maryam during a visit to Islamabad in January 1986, as Omar's mother, Maha Elsamnah, looks on. His father, Ahmed Said Khadr, was protesting his arrest for the 1995 bombing of an Egyptian embassy during a visit by Chrétien to Islamabad. Omar is on the left, Abdullah in the background and Kareem on the right.

Peter Power / Toronto Star

Author interviews Khalid Khawaja, a former Pakistan intelligence agent and friend of the Khadr family, in May 2006 in Karachi. Omar's mother and sister lived with Khawaja's family for a period before they returned to Canada.

Canadian Press

Maha Elsamnah with her youngest son, Kareem, at her husband's bedside in Islamabad, Pakistan. Ahmed Said Khadr was on a hunger strike protesting his arrest for the November 1995 bombing of the Egyptian embassy in Islamabad.

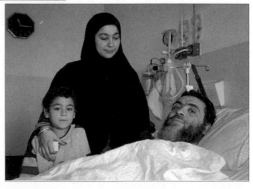

Lucas Oleniuk / Toronto Star

Abdullah Khadr, Omar's eldest brother, in his Toronto lawyer's office in December 2005. A week later he was arrested on an extradition order from the United States, where he had been indicted for terrorism offences.

Vince Talotta / Toronto Star

Abdurahman Khadr, Omar's older brother, shown in December 2005. Khadr was captured by the United States and worked for the CIA before his release and return to Canada.

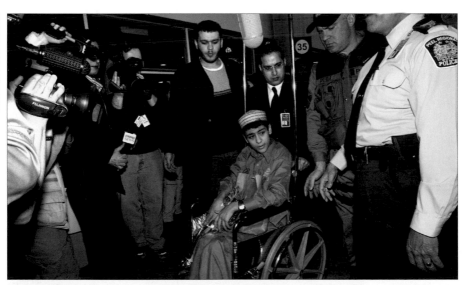

Ron Bull / Toronto Star

Kareem Khadr, Omar's younger brother, arrives at Toronto's Pearson International Airport on a flight from Pakistan in April 2004. Kareem was paralyzed in the October 2003 battle with Pakistani forces in which his father was killed.

Shane T. McCoy / U.S. Navy

A Department of Defense photo of the first detainees to arrive at Camp X-Ray in Guantanamo Bay in January 2002. The picture sparked an international outcry over the conditions at the offshore prison.

Peter Power / Toronto Star

A detainee peeks out of his cell at Guantanamo Bay's Camp 6, the most modern facility, where the prisoners are kept in isolation.

Rene Johnston / Toronto Star

Navy Lt.-Cmdr. Bill Kuebler addresses reporters following a military commission hearing in Guantanamo Bay in November 2007.

Gerald Burkhart / DRR.net

Lt.-Col. Colby Vokey in his office hallway in Camp Pendleton, California. The Marine defense lawyers called their office portable the "pirate's ship" because they commandeered the space and never gave it back.

Courtesy Muneer Ahmad

A photo taken in Toronto of Omar's grandmother, Fatmah Elsamnah; Canadian lawyer Dennis Edney; Omar's mother, Maha Elsamnah; Canadian lawyer Nate Whitling and Washington law professor and lawyer Muneer Ahmad. Omar used to keep this picture with him in his cell.

Louie Palu / Zuma Press

Marine Maj. Jeff Groharing, chief prosecutor in Omar's military trial, stands in front of Guantanamo's former Chief Prosecutor, Air Force Col. Moe Davis (left) and Groharing's co-counsel, Army Capt. Keith Petty at the Washington military commission prosecution office.

Janet Hamlin / Associated Press

An artist's rendition of a court hearing for Omar Khadr in June 2007. Omar (left) with his lawyers. The Pentagon will not allow photos to be taken of Guantanamo detainees that show their faces or can identify them.

It was a tough life, but his family managed and Edney survived more than one street brawl. After high school, Edney traveled with a semi-professional soccer team and worked a variety of odd jobs from digging ditches to making whiskey at a distillery in northern Scotland. By his thirties, he went in search of an intellectual challenge. The law program at Newcastle's Northumbria University looked good, although he wasn't really sure he wanted to be a lawyer; he just knew he wanted to be back at school.

Two life-altering experiences came before Edney turned forty. He met his future wife, Patricia Adams, during a trip to Canada to teach soccer. Six weeks later, he was back at school in Newcastle a married man. That's when he almost lost his life. Edney was riding his bike home from a soccer practice when a car going fifty-five-miles-an-hour struck him. Doctors weren't optimistic he would overcome the serious injuries to his head but Edney defied the doctors' predictions. He couldn't play soccer but he would learn again how to walk, talk and go on to practice law.

Edney settled in Patricia's hometown of Edmonton, became a Canadian citizen and set up a law practice. Soon after, his first son, Cameron, was born. Six years later came another son they named Duncan and Edney turned into the kind of father where almost every conversation came back to his sons. They fascinated him and he marveled at their different talents—Cameron's love of the arts and Duncan's ability to play any sport he tried. Sometimes, much to Patricia's annoyance, he would take one of the boys to a coffee shop to have long talks about life, letting him skip a class or two. His love for his wife and sons meant that now Edney had three passions in life: soccer, law and family. Many other things seemed to annoy him. He liked to quote what Patricia once told him. "Humanity, I love," he would say. "It's the people I hate."

Over the years, he tackled various constitutional cases in his law practice and, for the most part, Edney worked alone. While he may have been a team player on the soccer field, in law, he was fiercely independent and sometimes cantankerous with other attorneys. There was one lawyer, however, whom he knew he could work with, so when Omar's case arose, he went to Edmonton's Parlee McLaws firm and asked Nathan Whitling for help.

Whitling was Edney's opposite in almost every way. He was born and raised in Edmonton but went to Harvard to study for his master's in law. His wife, Kristen, was also a lawyer but stayed home to raise the four children they had within six years. Perhaps having four children under the age of six is what accounted for Whitling's incredible patience.

While Edney immediately makes an intimate connection with people, Whitling is hard to read. He talks and moves cautiously, only rarely revealing his wicked dry sense of humor and a laugh that sounds something like a teenager's giggle. Edney was a lawyer who liked to look at the big picture; Whitling liked the nitty-gritty details of the law. "I lay awake almost all night pondering the word 'or,'" he said on the eve of one of Omar's hearings.

Even their body language while arguing cases was different. Edney has difficulty keeping his legs still. He constantly shuffles in what amounts to an awkward four-step waltz. Whitling, on the other hand, stands perfectly erect when making his arguments. When sitting during the prosecution's turn, he will most often lean back in his chair as if contemplating his next move in a poker game.

Reporters would often point out the ying and yang nature of their relationship, to which Edney would reply, "I'm just a little guy from Edmonton, trying to find my way in the world. Nate's brilliant. I'm just hard-working." Whitling wouldn't say anything.

At first, neither lawyer knew much about Omar or his family but they were passionate about the principles of the case and excited about the legal history in the making. How could Omar be denied access to lawyers? Why couldn't he challenge the legality of his detention in the U.S. courts? How could the U.S. administration try a teenager as an adult?

And why was the Canadian government more interested in sending spies to interrogate Omar rather than in trying to get him out?

7

"We Are an al Qaeda Family"

IN A SECOND-FLOOR OFFICE in the heart of Toronto's Little Italy, Abdurahman Khadr sat behind a large wooden desk. The twenty-year-old leaned back in his chair and folded his meaty hands in his lap. It was early December 2003 and the thermometer hovered just above freezing but the law office, where a hastily called press conference was about to begin, was unbearably hot.

The expression on Abdurahman's face was hard to decipher. Most who watched the event live on the twenty-four-hour news stations described him as smug; the archetypal cat that ate the canary. But up close he seemed in awe of the cameras pointed at him. He smiled at reporters, some crammed on a black leather couch, others poking their heads through the doorway, trying to edge their way inside the small law office.

More than any of Ahmed Said Khadr's children, Abdurahman had always craved attention and managed to break all the rules. Now Abdurahman, the family's black sheep, the manipulator his father once called the cancer of the family, was going to get his fifteen minutes of fame. This would be the performance of a lifetime.

Beside him sat Rocco Galati, a short, frizzy-haired lawyer with a fiery temper and a reputation built on cases that most attorneys wouldn't touch. Galati had specialized in immigration issues during the 1990s, fighting for non-citizens the government wanted to expel. After 9/11, his popularity soared. As Canada's spy service increased its surveillance of Toronto's Muslim community and the RCMP came knocking, Galati's phone rang non-stop. His number was posted in mosques throughout Toronto next to a warning not to talk to authorities without a lawyer present.

Galati was legendary for his outbursts both inside and outside the courtroom. He once stormed dramatically out of one courtroom, telling the stunned judge that the law was rigged and the hearing to determine if a suspected terrorist should be deported was a "sham." It was more than theatrics. The cases had become personal for Galati and his clients had become friends. In the end, that involvement took its toll. Soon after the Khadr press conference Galati announced his semi-retirement. On the verge of tears, he told reporters he had received a death threat on his answering machine that ended with the words: "Now you a dead wop." Galati believed the security services—either in the United States or Canada—were out to get him. His departure left some of Canada's highest-profile terrorism cases hanging until new defense lawyers came on board.

A week before the press conference, Fatmah Elsamnah, Abdurahman's grandmother, had called Galati. She told him Abdurahman had called from Sarajevo, telling his family that he was trapped and that the Canadian government would not help him come home. Abdurahman had been missing since his capture in Kabul in November 2001 and his family had assumed he was in Guantanamo, like Omar, but there had been few details released about his case. He told his grandmother that the Americans had released him a couple of months earlier, but he was trapped in Eastern Europe. They should go to the media with his story, he said, and Abdurahman's grandmother turned to Galati for advice.

A day later, Galati held a press conference with Abdurahman's grandmother. In a shaky voice that started softly but quickly grew louder as she got angrier, she told reporters that Abdurahman was in Bosnia and could not get back to Canada. He had been released from Guantanamo Bay in October and taken to Afghanistan, and he had no identification or money. Abdurahman managed to cross the border into Pakistan and traveled on to Ankara, Turkey. In both countries, Canadian officials refused to help him, Fatmah Elsamnah said. Or so his story went.

The government was quick to refute the allegations. "We made it very clear to Mr. Khadr that he would be welcomed back to Canada and that the full level of consular services will be made available to him and, in fact, are being offered to him," soon-to-be prime minister Paul Martin told reporters. A Foreign Affairs spokesperson said Abdurahman chose to be released in Afghanistan instead of Canada—a curious comment that made Galati scoff. *Why would he choose Afghanistan?* Galati accused the government of abandoning one of its citizens. He charged that Canadian officials were "lying through their teeth or making stuff up on the fly. It's blatant racist treatment of people against whom they have no evidence and they detain without trial or protest . . . Canada, unfortunately, doesn't recognize the citizenship of brown-skinned Muslims and Arabs."

The government's answers may have been obtuse, but Abdurahman's story was full of holes. It was clear someone was lying. *But who?* The press was eager to get hold of Abdurahman Khadr himself.

Before Abdurahman and his lawyer walked into the office to face reporters on that chilly day in December 2003, Galati had told Abdurahman to talk freely but if he needed help to just tap him on his hand.

Abdurahman didn't think he would need any help.

ABDURAHMAN BEGAN HIS PRESS CONFERENCE by recounting the story his grandmother had told. In Ankara and Islamabad, his requests for help had been rebuffed. Canadian officials "wouldn't let me speak to anybody because I didn't have any documents, I didn't have any ID, nothing at all so I didn't want to insist because I was worried they might arrest me." With the help of smugglers and using money borrowed from some of his father's friends, he made his way out of Afghanistan, through Pakistan, Iran, Turkey, Bulgaria, and, finally, into Bosnia. Once his grandmother went to the press, he felt it safe to approach the Canadian embassy in Sarajevo. An embassy official accompanied him on his flight to Toronto's Pearson International Airport, he told reporters, and now he wanted to go about living his life, perhaps go to school.

When he finished his tale, questions flew fast and furious. For the most part, Abdurahman remained calm and confident, giving answers in a slightly condescending manner as if explaining something complicated to a young child. But about halfway through the press conference, a reporter asked Abdurahman if he had visited any training camps while living in Pakistan and Afghanistan. Abdurahman paused, and had he tapped Galati's hand, his lawyer would have likely steered reporters away from the Khadr family history. But instead Abdurahman smirked and admitted that as a teenager he went to Khalden, a training camp which he described as "al Qaeda-related."

To Western intelligence agencies, Khalden was more than just "related." Some of the most high-profile terrorism cases involved suspects who had trained at Khalden, including would-be Millennium Bomber Ahmed Ressam. But Abdurahman waved off the questions. He said he had never met Ressam and knew nothing of his plot to bomb the Los Angeles airport. He downplayed the significance of training at Khalden, saying it was a "very normal thing" for young boys in Afghanistan to learn how to fire Russian assault rifles.

"It's just training, not training to kill Americans, just training. In Afghanistan, you know, people just go to train. It's a common thing that every kid around fifteen, or that age, go and take training." He said his father had insisted. Then added a little darkly: "It was a waste of my life for three months."

Years later, Abdurahman said he had thought momentarily about denying that he had been to Khalden. "I was thinking, you know, that I could deny it all or admit it. If they're asking about it, they probably know about it, so I might as well admit it, and go around it. Oh, you know, 'We were too young to know anything about this and that.' You know, I think I played that whole thing okay." Or perhaps Abdurahman told the truth because there were just too many lies to remember.

After the press conference, Abdurahman walked into the cold December air, trailed by television cameras. Crossing College Street, he smiled when he noticed the parking ticket on his uncle's windshield. "Ha! Welcome home," he laughed.

He held that smile as he drove away. He was pleased with his performance. Maybe he got a little carried away with talk about the training camp but had stuck to the broad strokes of the script, and, as far as he was concerned, the media bought it.

SOMETHING JUST DIDN'T ADD UP. Why would the U.S. government return Abdurahman to Afghanistan? When Guantanamo detainees were released, the Pentagon always issued a media release, eager to show that prisoners were not being held indefinitely. When asked about Abdurahman's case, a Pentagon spokesperson insisted that there was no record of a detainee being released in October. Perhaps Abdurahman was mistaken and had been one of the twenty-seven detainees transferred that July or perhaps among those released in November? But then why Afghanistan? Abdurahman had been born in Bahrain and was a Canadian citizen. Other detainees had been sent to their countries of citizenship not returned to the country where they had been captured.

There were other questions. How did Abdurahman travel without a passport across four countries to reach Bosnia? Would Canadian officials really turn him away, knowing the scandal that would create, let alone their legal obligations to a stranded citizen?

Canada's Department of Foreign Affairs had a reputation for being secretive, staffed by press officers who never strayed from their dictated media lines. But spokesperson Reynald Doiron was especially cryptic when it came to Abdurahman's story. He often met questions with questions of his own, encouraging reporters to dig deeper.

Nazim Baksh was among those who did. Baksh had been a journalist since 1990, working mainly as a radio and television producer at the government-subsidized Canadian Broadcasting Corporation, the CBC. A dogged reporter, Baksh was also fluent in Arabic, making him even more highly valued after 9/11. One long-time CBC investigative reporter called Baksh the network's "secret weapon."

In 1993, a CBC reporter had wanted to investigate Ahmed Said Khadr and approached Baksh for help. There was suspicion that Khadr's fundraising was not going toward the HCI-directed orphanages but was financing the warring mujahideen factions. Baksh's family was very involved in Toronto's Muslim community; his brother was the vice-president of the Islamic Society of North America, ISNA, an offshoot of the Muslim Student Association. Baksh knew Khadr, had even prayed beside him at a mosque during one of Khadr's visits to Canada. He also knew that Khadr was revered and that he could be persuasive when making impassioned pleas for Afghanistan. "Women would literally take off gold bangles and throw them at him," Baksh recalled. "He was a hero."

Baksh traveled with a CBC crew to Afghanistan and Pakistan but Khadr would not meet with them. They did visit his orphanages, including Hope Village which impressed Baksh. "The more we filmed in Afghanistan, the more I was convinced we didn't have the smoking gun."

But while researching the documentary, Baksh discovered a much bigger story about an emerging threat. The story led him to Sudan, where bin Laden had been invited to live by the country's attorney general, Islamist Hassan al Turabi. With a crew from CBC, Baksh attended a conference whose participants included a who's who of terrorism's future. Large crowds of the assembled ended one evening with chants, "Down, down USA! Down, down CIA!"

One day, while leaving the hotel where the conference was being held, Baksh recognized the elusive Sheikh Mubarak Ali Shah Gilani. Gilani was the founder of the Jamaat al Fuqra whom *Wall Street Journal* reporter

Daniel Pearl would search for a decade later. "Sheikh," Baksh shouted, his heart pounding. "*Assalaam aliekum.*" No one was supposed to know Gilani was in Sudan and a man tried to stop Baksh from approaching. But Baksh ignored the man and continued talking directly to Gilani. An interview with Gilani would be an incredible feat, but for Baksh there was also an important Canadian angle. Five members of Jamaat al Fuqra had been arrested in Toronto for conspiring to blow up a Hindu temple and Indian movie theater and would be on trial that year.

Gilani told Baksh to meet him the next day and remarkably he agreed to an interview. Gilani admitted that one or two of the men charged in Toronto had studied with him in Lahore, but he denied that al Fuqra promoted violence. "[T]hey become real good citizens. They stop smoking, they stop stealing, they stop living on welfare. That is what I teach them."

Baksh had an award-winning and prescient piece that the CBC aired with the title "Seeds of Terror." The documentary didn't just focus on Gilani but told the story of rising Islamic fundamentalism born of the jihad against the Soviets in Afghanistan. The feature wasn't about Khadr, but Baksh never forgot him and remained suspicious. He had grown up with Islamists and didn't believe Khadr had devoted all his energy to this charity. He certainly didn't believe Abdurahman's story. A day after Abdurahman's press conference, Baksh aired his concerns on the CBC radio program, *Dispatches*. The segment was titled, "Abdurahman Khadr: Mischief or Terror?" Baksh reported:

> I've been aware of the Khadr family for many years. I interviewed the father, Ahmed Said, in the early 1990s, when he was deeply involved in the fight for control of post-Soviet Afghanistan. Today the Americans allege he is an al Qaeda financier. The father, friends told me, wanted to make fighters out of his four sons, committing them at an early age to holy war and sending them all to Afghan military camps for weapons training. People who knew the father say he was committed to creating a puritanical Islamic state in Afghanistan. And when a landmine crippled his arm and leg in the early 1990s, he attempted to turn his sons into instruments of his unfulfilled dream.

In early 2003, Baksh had tried to find the Khadrs. He called the Elsamnahs in Scarborough but they always said they didn't know. He traveled to Afghanistan where former friends and neighbors talked most about Abdurahman and characterized him the same way: He was committed to "fun, not fundamentalism." Stories emerged of a teenage rebel who openly defied the Taliban's rules. Abdurahman smoked in the streets of Kabul and watched bootleg DVDs on his father's computer. "He complained bitterly to friends that while other families were fleeing to the West to give their children a chance at a decent education, his father preferred the misery of Afghanistan to the comforts of Canada," Baksh said in his radio report, which continued:

> He didn't see himself in his father's circle of fundamentalist friends. He didn't even see himself as an Arab. To those he came in contact with, he insisted he was Canadian. In Afghanistan, that earned him a special status among ordinary people. As Abdurahman pledges now to get an education, the question is whether he is more likely to be an al Qaeda operative or just a kid who, to this point, has never really been in control of his life.

ON CHRISTMAS EVE 2003, Baksh was sitting at Toronto's Metro Convention Centre, talking to a friend on his cell phone. Baksh was an advisor to the organizers of a three-day conference called, "Reviving the Islamic Spirit" and he was enjoying a short break. He couldn't believe it when Abdurahman Khadr sat down beside him.

Baksh had planned on interviewing Abdurahman and getting at the truth, but had put the story off. "Abdurahman?" he said as he hung up the phone. Abdurahman was defensive, a little jumpy. "It's Nazim Baksh," he said as Abdurahman relaxed and grinned.

"My grandmother hates you," Abdurahman replied.

They decided to go for a walk. They talked as they went out on the street, then into lobbies of office buildings, up escalators, down stairs, through the downtown's maze of underground walkways until it was midnight and they realized they had been talking for five hours. They also had noticed that even though they were walking in nearly deserted buildings and standing in the freezing cold when Abdurahman wanted to smoke, there always seemed to be a lone white man following them. Baksh assumed they were Mounties or CSIS agents who would no doubt be keeping an eye on a Khadr son.

Abdurahman didn't tell his story that night but promised to meet Baksh again. Baksh called CBC senior correspondent Terence McKenna and told him to come to Toronto. He also booked a hotel room for Abdurahman, directly across from CBC's studio.

On December 31 the *Toronto Star* ran a front-page story that seemed far-fetched but explained some of the inconsistencies in Abdurahman's story.

Quoting a government official who spoke on the condition of anonymity, the story alleged that Abdurahman had been, in fact, a CIA mole hired to help the intelligence agency track down his father and al Qaeda members. Released from Guantanamo in the fall of 2003, Abdurahman had been quietly taken to Bosnia where he got cold feet. Abdurahman denied the story. Foreign Affairs officials refused to answer questions, as did U.S. authorities. Only a handful of CSIS agents and Department of Foreign Affairs officials knew the truth about Abdurahman. The *Star* article was circulated by e-mail among government officials with the subject heading: "What a mess."

AS ABDURAHMAN'S STORY started to fade from the headlines, Dennis Edney announced that he would represent Omar Khadr, even though Omar had no idea he had a lawyer and had never heard of a fifty-seven-year-old named Dennis from Edmonton. "We are in troublesome times," Edney told the *Edmonton Journal* in January 2004. "Under the banner of security, there is a real threat to the liberties of citizens, especially in the United States."

"I've always seen the law as a powerful tool," he said. "It is the ultimate form of reckoning. It can create remedies and set free the most abused."

A U.S. case concerning the rights of Guantanamo detainees, known as *Rasul v. Bush*, had been winding through the lower courts for two years and was headed to the Supreme Court. Edney and his co-counsel, Nate Whitling, joined dozens of lawyers across the United States and the United Kingdom in submitting arguments to the court.

The Rasul case asked one simple question: What role did the U.S. courts play in the detention of the men whom Bush called "enemy combatants?" Bush had issued a Presidential Executive Order in November 2001 that authorized the indefinite detention of foreign nationals at Guantanamo, revoking their right to challenge their detention in federal courts. A District Court had upheld the government's position.

Lawyers from the New York-based Center for Constitutional Rights, known as the CCR, argued that the president's order was unconstitutional, violated international law and ignored the fundamental legal principle known as *habeas corpus*. Translated from Latin to mean, "You have the body," *habeas corpus* entitles prisoners to challenge the legality of their detention. The writ of *habeas* is enshrined in the U.S. Constitution and revered as a crucial safeguard against arbitrary detentions. The constitution allows the suspension of that right only under narrow circumstances "of rebellion or invasion."

CCR had launched *habeas* petitions on behalf of British detainees Shafiq Rasul and Asif Iqbal and Australian David Hicks. But the Supreme Court's ruling would apply to all the Guantanamo captives.

Edney and Whitling's submission to the Supreme Court highlighted the unique factors in Omar's case, most notably, his age. The lawyers cited international and domestic law that protected children under the age of eighteen. Article 37 of the Convention for the Rights of the Child (CRC) states:

> No child shall be deprived of his or her liberty unlawfully or arbitrarily. The arrest, detention or imprisonment of a child shall be in conformity with the law and shall be used only as a measure of last resort for the shortest appropriate period of time.
>
> Every child deprived of his or her liberty shall have the right to prompt access to legal and other appropriate assistance, as well as the right to challenge the legality of the deprivation of his or her liberty before a court or other competent, independent and impartial authority, and to a prompt decision on such action.

Edney and Whitling also decided to launch their own constitutional challenge in the Edmonton federal court, going after the Canadian government. They argued that the visits by CSIS agents and Foreign Affairs' Jim Gould, violated Omar's right to a fair trial, since presumably what he told the Canadians could be used by the United States in a trial. The case confirmed for the first time that it had been CSIS, not consular officials, who had visited Omar in Guantanamo and it gave Canadians an important window into Canada's relations with the United States. But Omar's case didn't stay in the news for long.

IN EARLY MARCH 2004, the CBC's flagship nightly news program, *The National*, aired a two-part story titled "Al Qaeda Family" which featured Abdurahman Khadr. The documentary was co-produced by Baksh, and reported by McKenna, would forever cement the Khadrs in the country's conscience as "Canada's First Family of Terrorism."

"He was trained to be a terrorist," the announcer began, followed by a clip of Abdurahman. "Three times, my father himself tried to get me to become a suicide bomber. He was, like, 'You know, you be our pride. In this family, you be our pride.'"

"But he was different."

Most of the interview took place in a softly lit room at a downtown Toronto hotel where Baksh had taken him to meet McKenna:

Abdurahman: When the Americans started interrogating me, that's when I realized that there is no way out of this except to, like, you know, tell them, you know, okay, I'll cooperate with them because this is, this was their only way. They said, you know, "You work with us, or you know what? We can keep you here. We can take you to Cuba. We can do anything with you. Right now, no one in the world cares about this."

McKenna voiceover: Abdurahman says that he was interrogated extensively by two American agents, one from the FBI and one from the CIA. He says that they became much more interested in him when they realized how close he had been to the very center of al Qaeda.

Abdurahman: In a week or two, they started trusting me more. And you know, then they asked me, "Would you like to work for us? Would you like to go with the troops that are in Afghanistan to the front lines and work for us there?" And you know, to—you know, "tell us who the people we capture are." And you know, at the very beginning, it was my first time in, like, this situation, and I was scared of jail. And I said, "You know what? I'll do anything."

McKenna voiceover: For several months, Abdurahman says he traveled regularly around Kabul with American investigators.

Abdurahman: There was this tour. They called it the Abdurahman tour. I was famous for that. I took, like, the people from the—people from the CIA, the FBI, the military. We'd go around in a car in Kabul. I'd show them the houses of al Qaeda people, the guesthouses, the safe houses, where houses were. You know, this was the guesthouse they used before, this was the guesthouse they used later. This is the safe house they used after September 11, you know, just show them the houses. So there was that tour. And otherwise, I just told them what I knew.

McKenna voiceover: Abdurahman says he lived for nine months in a CIA safe house near the American embassy in Kabul. In the summer of 2002, he says, he received a financial offer from the CIA.

Abdurahman: They brought me a paper. They said, "A $5,000 bonus for you being very cooperative. And from now on just by, you know, working with us, just answering our questions, you get paid $3,000 a month until you stop working for us." The paper said I would get paid until someone found out about this. Now, the account was under my name. It was a CIA account somewhere. I don't know where. But the money went to my account. And whenever I want my money, I can ask for it.

McKenna on camera: Did the paper say that—say Central Intelligence Agency? Did it say who you'd deal with?

Abdurahman: Yes. You'd be working for the CIA.

McKenna voiceover: During the months that Abdurahman was in the CIA safe house, suspected al Qaeda members were being rounded up all over Afghanistan. Hundreds of the prisoners were put on planes and flown to Cuba, to Camp X-Ray at the U.S. Naval base at Guantanamo. The world could see that the prisoners were being treated harshly, but Abdurahman says he didn't know any of that when the CIA proposed a new plan to him. They would plant him as one of their spies in the prison population and he would funnel information to them. He says the plan was explained to him by his favorite CIA agent.

Abdurahman: [The agent] said, "Well, you'll go to Cuba. You'll be working for us there, talking to other detainees, you know, meeting other detainees and stuff, and telling us what they tell you and stuff." I said, you know, "How much— how long is it going to be?" She told me it would probably be from three to six months. I said, "Well, you know, faster." So I said okay.

McKenna voiceover: Abdurahman says he was told that he would have to be treated like any other prisoner on the way to Guantanamo to avoid suspicion. He was taken to Bagram air base near Kabul, where the Americans had built a processing center for suspected al Qaeda captives.

Here he began what he calls the longest and most painful ordeal of his life. He had no idea what he was getting into.

Abdurahman: They took off my clothes and everything. And they started taking pictures of me, pictures, like, of my face and then pictures of my—my private parts, like my—my back, you know, my—my penis, my—you know, just taking pictures of every part of my body. And they—you know, they check your—your—you know, your anus. They put their fingers inside to check it out. You know, all of that is humiliation to any person, you know? They put me in the orange suit, and then they took me into a room and they put me on the ground— again, hands, legs, everything cuffed, and my face covered. And I was kept on the concrete with nothing but that orange suit for twenty-four hours.

So I stayed in Bagram for ten days, and you could not move. You could not move your back, so you couldn't bend or straighten. There's one position, you stay in it. If you move, they hit you or they push you. So they tell you not to move. After that, they put us in a truck for an hour or two, the same position. Then they took us out of that to the plane. They tied us up in the plane, cuffed us up and everything in the plane.

McKenna voiceover: After ten days of captivity in Bagram, that plane trip to Cuba would last more than fifteen hours. By the time the aircraft landed, Abdurahman says, he was a broken man.

Abdurahman: There was points, you know, I just—in my heart, I just wished to God, I wished to God that one of these MPs would go crazy and then shoot me, just get up and shoot me. I was so depressed. I was so sick of everything. It was the only time in my life that I really wished for a bullet. You know, I was, like, "Please, God, do something, but just take away my life," you know?

McKenna voiceover: Like all other prisoners, Abdurahman spent his first month in Guantanamo in complete isolation. He says he was occasionally told by his jailers that they knew he was on a CIA mission. It was barely enough to restore his hope. And then he was moved into the prison's general population.

Abdurahman: Their hope was, when they take me into Cuba, they could put me next to anyone that was stubborn and that wouldn't talk, and you know, I would talk him into it. Well, it's not that easy, first thing, because lots of people won't talk to anyone because everybody in Cuba is scared of the person next to him.

McKenna voiceover: By this time, Camp X-Ray had been replaced by the newly constructed Camp Delta, which was designed to be more comfortable and secure. At one point, Abdurahman heard that his younger brother, Omar, was just fifty feet away in a neighboring yard. They could yell to each other in Arabic.

Abdurahman: So I asked him, "How are you? How is everything?" And he told me, you know, "Just stay with the original story. We have an organization and all." I said, "How is your health?" And he said, "It's okay. I'm just losing my left eye and all. They don't want to operate on it."

McKenna on camera: Omar said to you, "Stick to the original story." What does that mean?

Abdurahman: Original story, we have an organization. We don't have anything to do with al Qaeda. We don't have anything to do with al Qaeda members and all. We just stick with that story.

IN MANY WAYS, Abdurahman was the ideal informant. After being held by the Afghans, he was delighted to be handed over to the Americans in early 2002 and receive the attention of the FBI and CIA. His youth had been spent rebelling against an ideology he didn't believe in, and a pious, poor lifestyle he hated, and he was happy to finally have someone understand. And like all the Khadrs, Abdurahman loved to talk. He would spend hours in the safe house discussing al Qaeda's hierarchy as if he were simply bringing a neighbor up to speed on the local street gossip.

The first CIA agent he met told him his name was Sandy. Then came Jack, Scott and finally Jennifer, who told him she was the regional director in Kabul, and quickly became his favorite. Sometimes with Scott he would take the notepad and pen from him and say officiously, "Here, I'll write it out for you." He can't recall if it was Jack or Scott who had trouble with his name but he told one of them, "Just call me Ricky." He didn't tell them that he chose the name because he was especially fond of Puerto Rican pop star Ricky Martin.

Only one FBI agent gave Abdurahman his last name. Steve Bongardt was a tall, athletic former Top Gun Navy fighter pilot who had been tracking al Qaeda's movements well before 9/11. Bongardt had worked with John O'Neill on the U.S.S. *Cole* bombing investigation. The U.S. Navy guided-missile destroyer had been docked in Aden, Yemen when in October 2000 two men aboard a fiberglass boat filled with plastic explosives blasted a forty-by-forty-foot hole in the port side of the ship, killing seventeen sailors and injuring another thirty-nine. The investigation into what was thought to be al Qaeda's second attack after the embassy bombings in Africa, was marred by a lack of intelligence sharing between federal departments, often blamed on a U.S. Justice Department policy known as "the Wall." *New Yorker* writer Lawrence Wright wrote that just a month before 9/11, Bongardt wrote an angry e-mail to officials within the FBI, frustrated by the lack of communication. "Someday somebody will die—and, Wall or not, the public will not understand why we were not more effective."

Abdurahman liked talking with Bongardt, even if he did find him intimidating. As Abdurahman talked, he would watch Bongardt write with one hand and clench and release the fist of his free hand, flexing his forearm muscle. "He could just kill me," Abdurahman recalled thinking to himself.

It's unknown just how much, or if any of the information Abdurahman gave to the FBI and the CIA was used as intelligence for other terrorism cases. Abdurahman definitely knew tidbits about al Qaeda's most wanted. But was his information reliable?

As cooperative and knowledgeable as he was, Abdurahman was sometimes a dangerous ally. While he could be manipulated, he was also a manipulator. After his return to Canada, he admitted that he exaggerated some of what he told the CIA to try to appear important. He told his captors that his brother Abdullah had commanded a training camp, an allegation that came to be repeated as fact. But Abdullah was just a teenager when he attended the camps, making the claim that he was a leader unlikely.

Abdurahman, at twenty, also had the mentality and attention span of a teenager. He was like a caged animal when trapped inside the safe house and never would have been able to survive a lengthy detention at

Guantanamo. It is unlikely he would even have been able to get valuable intelligence at Gitmo, since his cover had been blown months before. Briton Moazzam Begg recalled that Omar knew while detained in 2002 at Bagram that Abdurahman was working for the Americans. "He told me that 'My brother is not a very good person.' That's how he explained it. He explained it in a very simple term. He didn't call him bad, he's a traitor or that, he just said 'My brother's not very nice,'" Begg said. Begg assumed one of Omar's interrogators had told him, either to taunt him or to try to get him to cooperate.

If Omar knew that his brother was an informant, there's a good chance, given how fast news was spread throughout the cells of Guantanamo, that as soon as Abdurahman arrived, everyone assumed he was a spy too.

Once the CIA's plan for Abdurahman at Guantanamo failed, they decided to send him to Bosnia. Sarajevo was seen as an important hub for insurgents on their way to the war in Iraq, much like Peshawar had been for Afghanistan during the 1980s. Abdurahman asked to be sent to Pakistan or Morocco, but his handlers were adamant that Sarajevo was where he could do the most good.

But Abdurahman hated Bosnia. He soon felt trapped and restless living alone in a town where he knew no one and found it difficult to infiltrate the mosques and befriend the targets the CIA had given him. "I was kind of getting frustrated and scared," Abdurahman recalled of that time. After he got his first paycheck, he went online to e-mail his uncle in Canada. He decided to blow his cover. He told his uncle he was in Sarajevo and couldn't get home. He told him to call his grandmother. "Go to the media," he wrote. "Tell them everything."

Scared the CIA would find out, Abdurahman went to a nearby bar and got drunk. He slapped down $500 of the money the CIA had just given him and told the bartender, with a grandiose sweep of his arms, that his friends would drink for free.

The next morning, he called "Tony," his CIA handler in Bosnia. He did not confess what he had done but told Tony that there was a chance his grandmother would go to the media with his story because somehow she had found out. The next morning, Galati held the press conference and the CIA quickly moved Abdurahman to a country home outside Sarajevo. Together they helped him concoct his false story, the one he would tell when he got back to Canada. "So we discussed everything, stick with the story, this and that, we'll get in touch with you in six months and I'm like,

'How?' and they're like 'Don't worry, we'll find you.' I'm like, 'Okay,' and I believed they would because if they wanted to they could," he recalled. The CIA never contacted him again and refused to comment on the CBC documentary. One anonymous government source told the *New York Times* that the "broad outlines" of Abdurahman's tale were true.

ABDURAHMAN'S ADMISSION that he spied was sensational but his description of bin Laden and the confession that he had been raised in an "al Qaeda" family made headlines. "Until now, everybody says that we're al Qaeda-connected family, but when I say this, just by me saying it, I just admitted that we are an al Qaeda family, you know? We had connections to al Qaeda. My family in Pakistan, they will never admit this at all. Why? Because they're totally, you know, they are what they are, and they deny it. They'll never admit this," Abdurahman told McKenna.

Abdurahman talked of bin Laden's love of volleyball and horses and his secret indulgence in his children. "I had seen this person that was the—America's most wanted, and then the next thing I know, he's in front of me, you know? So I'm—I'm amazed. I'm, like, 'Wow. This person, he's big,' you know? But I would say he's—he's a normal human being. He has issues with his wife and he has issues with his kids, financial issues, you know, the kids aren't listening, the kids aren't doing this and that. So it comes really down to he's a—you know, he's a father and he's a person."

Abdurahman also painted a dark picture of his father and his connection to al Qaeda. He related a fight he once had with his dad, who remonstrated: "'Why do you not act like the rest of the kids, so Osama can—you know, can, you know, always mention you, and you could be commander of a training camp or you can be something? Why are you different,' you know?

"And I would tell him, 'You know what? Being Osama is not going to heaven, okay, and being Osama is not being, you know, like a movie star, you know? It's not the top of the world, okay?'"

It was classic Khadr-speak. Somehow a fight about the world's most-wanted terrorist sounded like an argument between father and son about a high-school teacher. "Three times my father himself tried to get me to become a suicide bomber. He sat me down with the al Qaeda scholar. He sat me down with the—you know, the person to train people to become suicide bombers. He sat me down with these two people and tried to convince me to become a suicide bomber. He's, like, you know, 'You'd be our pride in this family, you'd be our pride,' you know, 'if you do this.' But I was totally against it. I was, like, 'I believe in fighting, you know, someone on the ground and he shoots me and I shoot him,' you know? But I don't believe in blowing myself up, killing innocent people. I don't— I just don't believe in that."

BAKSH AND MCKENNA HAD TRAVELED to Pakistan for the documentary to track down Abdurahman's mother, Maha Elsamnah, and twenty-five-year-old sister, Zaynab.

They had arranged a meeting through Elsamnah's lawyer, Hashmat Habib, who would not give them his office address but led them on what Baksh called "a cloak and dagger" journey to get there. When they finally arrived at Habib's law office, they were offered tea and told to wait for the women. There was no guarantee they would go on camera, but they had agreed at least to meet.

"Nazim, Nazim Baksh?" said a man who suddenly appeared. As Baksh stared blankly at the man standing before him, the man continued, "You don't know me?" Baksh started to panic, not wanting to offend this man who obviously knew Abdurahman's family, but he was unable to place him.

"I'm Khalid Khawaja, the man who was standing beside the Sheikh." All of a sudden, Baksh's mind drifted back a decade earlier and he realized the man before him was the one who had tried to stop him in Sudan from getting access to Sheikh Gilani, the leader of Jamaat al Fuqra. "My heart was pounding. I was spinning," Baksh recalled, thinking he had blown any chance of an interview with Elsamnah and Zaynab. But Baksh began talking quickly and his deferential nature seemed to win Khawaja over. The two went to say their nightly prayers together and when they came back, the women appeared. They agreed to do the interview right there and then, sending the CBC camera crew scrambling to set up lights and somehow illuminate the dark, cold room that smelled of stale books.

Elsamnah and Zaynab appeared on the CBC documentary with only their eyes visible above their black *niqabs*. They spoke to McKenna in their typical fashion—their voices rising as their words tumbled together in run-on sentences, the layers of black cloth unable to conceal their defiant body language.

McKenna, by way of introduction: Maha [Elsamnah] is proud of Omar.

Elsamnah: Of course. He defended himself. He just did not give any— you know, I thought they were very simple kids.

Zaynab: If you were in that situation what would you have done? I must ask everybody that.

Elsamnah: I hope you don't say, "I would bow down." No, no, no. Wouldn't you like your Canadian son to be so brave to stand up and fight for his right?

Zaynab: He'd been bombarded for hours. Three of his friends who were with him had been killed. He was the only sole survivor. What do you expect him to do, come up with his hands in the air? I mean, it's a war. They're shooting at him. Why can't he shoot at you? If you killed three, why can't he kill one? Why is it? Why does nobody say you killed three of his friends? Why does everybody say you killed an American soldier? Big deal.

Elsamnah: I like my son to be brave. I mean as I was telling you, if I was in Canada, I would like my son to be trained to protect himself, to protect his home, to protect his neighbor, to really fight to defend it. I would really love to do that and I would love my son to grow with this mentality.

Zaynab: So you should teach them to defend themselves and be able to fight for their rights and then to start to do everything else.

Elsamnah: You would like me to raise my child in Canada and by the time he's twelve or thirteen he'll be on drugs or having some homosexual relation or this and that? Is it better? For me, no. I would rather have my son as a strong man who knows right and wrong and stands for it even if it's against his parents. It's much better for me than to have my child walking on the streets in Canada taking drugs or doing all this nonsense.

McKenna: How did you react to the September 11th attacks when you saw them?

Elsamnah: To be honest with you, since I am Palestinian and I know the Americans are helping the Israelis so much, I said, let them have it. It's time that they—I don't want you I—maybe I am—maybe I am . . ."

Zaynab: Not the people themselves. You don't want to feel happy but you just sort of think, well, they deserve it. They've been doing it for such a long time, why shouldn't they feel it once in a while?

If there had been an audible reaction to the documentary in Canada, it would have sounded something like a collective, sharp intake of breath. The headlines the next day blared: "We are an al Qaeda family" and some politicians, columnists and bloggers demanded blood. Stockwell Day, who would become Canada's public safety minister once his Conservative party came to power in 2006, said the Khadr family should be barred from Canada. "We have to signal to our allies that we are serious about fighting the war against terrorism and we will not put political considerations first. We'll put safety and security first."

An online petition called "Deport the Khadr Family" demanded that the government revoke the family's Canadian citizenship. Within a month, it had more than 2,500 signatures. "Send them packing," one petitioner wrote. "Wake up Canada. Deport or pay later," added another.

Gar Pardy, the Ottawa bureaucrat dubbed "Mr. Consular," watched the documentary in disbelief. "For many Canadians, this was their worst nightmare," Pardy later said. "These two women, even Shakespeare couldn't come up with something like this."

Whenever Omar Khadr's case was debated thereafter, the comments from his mother and sister were replayed. Even the Canadian Muslim and Arab civil rights groups, who had been vigilant since 9/11 in highlighting cases of Muslims held without trial, would not utter Omar's name.

ABDURAHMAN HAD ASSUMED the documentary would clear his name. He had not only refused to follow his father and bin Laden and the most powerful terrorist organization in the world but he had also rejected the world's most powerful intelligence agency. With Baksh's help, he wrote a column for the *Globe and Mail* published on March 15, 2004, titled "I am the usual suspect."

> I didn't expect all the media attention I've received since the CBC aired my story. Perhaps I've been naïve in thinking that I could skip out after coming clean and telling the truth.
>
> To be honest, I feel safe in Canada, safer than I've been in any other country as far as I can remember. Canada is where I've always wanted

to be. Yet now I long for Pakistan and Afghanistan because that's where I've lived all my life. I often find myself in Little India on Toronto's Gerrard Street, getting my fill of kebabs and soaking up Bollywood movie songs. Every time I go there, it's like I am in Peshawar, Pakistan. For now, though, Gerrard Street will have to suffice because I don't think the folks down in [the Pakistani province of] Waziristan are likely to greet me with outstretched hands and wide smiles.

I was scared to go to Gerrard Street after the CBC documentary but a friend dragged me down to the Lahore Tikka House for dinner. The owner, a friendly man from Uganda, made sure I and my friends had enough to eat, and afterwards he asked me to take a few pictures with him. The fact that he understood what I had gone through made me feel relaxed and comfortable.

I needed a charger for my phone, and at the flea market, a Muslim man from South Africa gave it to me for free. He also recognized me from the documentary. But then a man my age from the Salaheddin mosque, the mosque I frequented after returning to Canada, told me in no uncertain terms that he didn't think I should have cooperated with the "enemy." Selling out was going to earn me a place in hell fire, he said. He was nice about damning me to the fire of hell; after I explained my opinions, we parted with a friendly handshake. That was a very Canadian experience.

In fact, many Muslims have accused me of selling out to the "enemy." For them, America is the enemy, and Muslims are the victims. I think the world is more complex than the simple black-and-white conclusions that Muslims and non-Muslims often seem to make.

I didn't sell out to anybody because there was nothing to sell. I was arrested in Kabul because I was an Arab in the wrong place at the wrong time. Still, I have to admit that there were perhaps solid reasons why a person like me would have been detained. I was finally handed over to the Americans. I didn't go up to them and say, "Hey, hire me, I have lots of juicy stuff to tell you about Osama bin Laden and al Qaeda." I was running from al Qaeda because I saw an opportunity to get out and I took it.

I always wanted out. I'd tried on several occasions before Sept. 11, 2001, to get out. In early 2001, I met with Canadian intelligence in Toronto and was met by MI5 on a stopover at Heathrow on my way back to Pakistan. They all knew I was not the least bit interested in military training, and that I was a rebel.

When I was interrogated by Canadian intelligence officers in Kabul in 2002, they asked me about a lot of people from Canada. Some of these people I had only heard about and I didn't even know their real names, let alone what they were up to, if anything. I had a bad reputation that prevented me from gaining access to al Qaeda's inner circles.

I told the Canadians, the Americans and the British all that I knew, because I believed it was the right thing to do. But I confess that I often made things up so that my captors would like me and give me courtesies and privileges, like watching movies. I also wanted to boost my credibility in their eyes so that they might start trusting me—and when they did, they would eventually let me go free, or provide an opportunity for me to skip and come back to Canada. The plan was foolproof.

In the months I spent in detention in Kabul, I became convinced that the Americans were doing the right thing and that al Qaeda was wrong in attacking the United States and killing innocent civilians. But when I was in Bosnia I came to realize that the CIA and al Qaeda agreed on one thing: I was expendable . . . an asset to be used in their global war against each other.

What finally motivated me to tell my story to the CBC was that I felt that at any moment, members of the intelligence community would leak information about me to make me look bad.

I don't want to spend the rest of my life denying or clarifying accusations from confidential sources.

A source told a reporter that I had traded information as to the whereabouts of my father to secure my release. That was false. I had no idea where my father was after the family split up in November 2001.

By making my story public, I wanted to make it known that I do not want to go back to the world of espionage. I am not a soldier. When I was attending training camps, I prayed every day that I would not end up with a bullet in my head. I feel the same way today. These are not my battles. I want a normal life. But I seriously doubt that I will ever have it. I still have no place to live, no income or documentation.

I am even a bit tentative about going back to Salaheddin mosque. Before the CBC documentary, people there were friendly towards me. I don't know what kind of reception I might get now. I like being around my Muslim brothers, and I hope that nothing will change.

I still haven't talked to my family, but I know my mother, sisters and brothers, as Canadian citizens, have a constitutional right to return to Canada. My mother and my sister have expressed views that are not consistent with my views or those of most Canadians—but I want to assure you that they are not crazy. Their views are not acceptable, but they are real. Canadians don't demand that everyone with strange views be put on a boat and sent to Guantanamo.

It has been reported that my brother Abdullah was a commander of an al Qaeda camp. I made that up when I was interrogated by the Americans. I don't know why. It sickens me every day that I said it. I worry now that if my brother remains in that part of the world, he will end up dead.

My father was held in high regard by a lot of Canadian Muslims. He gave up a good job in Ottawa and took his family to Peshawar to help destitute Afghans. He was always dedicated to his relief projects, even to the bitter end, but he was also a freedom fighter in the 1980s and early 1990s and people respected him for it. How my father got hooked up with the likes of al Qaeda is still something I am trying to work out in my mind. For now, I am trying to put as much distance as I can between his views and my own, and get on with my life.

AFTER PAKISTANI FORCES killed Ahmed Said Khadr and wounded Omar's younger brother Kareem in October 2003, the Khadr women moved into Khalid Khawaja's family home. Khawaja was a well-known figure in Pakistan and managed to walk that fine line between government friend and foe. He had once been an air force pilot for the Pakistani army and also served with the omnipresent Inter Services Intelligence, the ISI, from 1985 to 1987. Khawaja took credit for helping to unite warring mujahideen factions in 1993 and admitted he was once close to bin Laden, bragging he had a personal audience with the sheikh "more than 100 times." In short, Khawaja was connected.

This made him a favorite contact for journalists. When *Wall St. Journal* reporter Daniel Pearl tried to find the elusive Gilani in 2002, he approached Khawaja. Pearl was trying to uncover connections between the ISI and terrorist groups in Afghanistan, when one evening he disappeared on his way to an interview. Weeks later, his dismembered body was found and an Internet posting showed his beheading. Khawaja and Gilani had both been interviewed by Pakistani authorities after his disappearance, but were not among those eventually charged in his murder. Khawaja later explained his involvement with Pearl in an interview with CNN, saying the American reporter had been persistent in his quest.

Khawaja to reporter Christiane Amanpour: I said, "He will not be available, sorry." He was just requesting to me again and again. I said, "Look, Daniel, when I'm telling you something, just listen to it. He is not willing to come for an interview."

Amanpour: But Daniel Pearl is determined to get an interview with Sheikh Mubarek Gilani, whom he suspects of running al Qaeda's *hawala*, a grass-roots method for transferring money without bank records that may have helped fund the September 11 attacks.

Khawaja: He kept on calling me the whole day after every one hour. I said, "Danny, don't call me. I'll call you whenever I'm free." I called him at about nine o'clock. I said, "Okay, if you can come now to my office, you're welcome." He said, "Can I come in one-and-a-half hour?" I said, "No, I will sleep then." So next day, he again called me in the morning. He said, "Can I come?" "No," I said, "sorry, I'm busy now." This was the last call I received.

Khawaja, a graceful, articulate man who walks with his head bowed and hands clasped behind his back, is a committed Islamist who has never shied from the media spotlight. "I am what you in the West would stereotype as a terrorist, an extremist or an Islamist radical. But I wear none of these labels. I am a bridge—a voice of Muslim reason in a growing cacophony of disaffected voices, some of whom are irreparably damaging the message of a great religion and who must now be contained by people like me to insure we all survive the scourge of radicalism," he wrote in the *Financial Times* in August 2005.

"Do not fear us, because we are not your enemy. Our common enemies are fear and mistrust of each other's ways of life, systems of belief and the intense feelings of injustice that breed within ourselves as a result. We have failed in offering a path for our children. You have failed to understand our dilemma and how to help us correct the course from within. The time has now come to resolve this dangerous dilemma. We are ready, willing and able. Are you?"

Khawaja believed the Khadr family had been unfairly profiled both in Canada and Pakistan. When the Pakistani military refused to hand over Khadr's body, or confirm his death, Khawaja helped Elsamnah launch a lawsuit in Pakistan's High Court. On December 30, Maha Elsamnah and her daughters, Maryam and Zaynab, attempted to hold a press conference announcing the suit but Pakistan's security forces raided the conference, seizing the microphones and confiscating press releases already distributed to local journalists. "We have secret information that there is a link to al Qaeda," government official Asadullah Faiz told reporters, singling out their lawyer, Hashmat Habib, as an al Qaeda ally. If there was such information, authorities have yet to reveal it.

"These poor innocent ladies have suffered so much," Khawaja said. "They have to hide their identities. No one will rent a house to them here. They live in utter terror."

While the CBC documentary may have been causing waves in Canada, they did not seem to reach Pakistan's shores. Or if they did, the Khadr women didn't care.

In the spring of 2004, German journalist Bruno Schirra, who had been researching the Islamic movement in Pakistan and Afghanistan for the newspaper *die Welt,* went to Khawaja for help. "If you want to understand the holy power of our movement, if you want to know why we will win and you will lose this war, then speak to this family," Khawaja told him of the Khadr women.

Schirra had already met Khadr, twice; once as he fled Kabul and then, just a couple months before he was killed he interviewed him near Wana, in South Waziristan.

On Khawaja's invitation, Schirra met Elsamnah and Zaynab at their lawyer's house during a party one night. Habib was hosting almost 200 guests at his villa in an exclusive suburb of Islamabad when Schirra showed up looking for Zaynab and Elsamnah. The men and women were segregated, but the Khadr women, curiously, were allowed to sit with the men. "This was extraordinary," Schirra recalled. "All the men came to the ladies, said 'Hello, it's an honor, a pleasure to see you,' and then they walked away."

Many of the top Pakistani and Kashmiri Islamic party members from Jamaat-e-Islami to Jamiat-ul-Ansar were present, and Zaynab, surrounded by like-minded supporters, spoke freely about her views on the fight in Afghanistan. "You kill us with that, therefore we will kill you . . . Just like Daniel Pearl. He only got what he deserved. He was an American, he was a Jew, he was guilty."

Again, Elsamnah said she was proud of Omar. "He would have been so proud to die as a *shahid,* a martyr, as a soldier of Islam, as his father now is."

MAHA ELSAMNAH NEVER WANTED to return to Canada. But Kareem was languishing in a Pakistani hospital under guard and doctors said he would never walk again. Without the intervention of the Canadian High Commission, Pakistani authorities would not release Kareem.

The Canadian authorities would not give Elsamnah a passport since she had reported hers lost twice in the past. Instead, she was given emergency travel documents for herself and Kareem for one-way tickets home. Zaynab stayed behind with her daughter so as not to abandon Abdullah (Abdullah would be arrested later that year by Pakistani forces).

On April 9, 2004, Elsamnah and Kareem returned to Toronto, greeted at the airport by a swarm of reporters and cameras. As they came out of the arrivals gate, a media circle swallowed them, forcing photographers at the back of the pack to hold their cameras high over their heads and fire blindly into the slowly moving mob. Kareem was in a wheelchair and looked largely nonplussed. He flashed reporters a peace sign but did not say anything. His mother yelled out before climbing into an awaiting van: "I have no connections to al Qaeda."

Stockwell Day was again quick in his criticism. "Canadian citizenship is diminished when we allow it to be extended to people like the Khadrs," he told reporters. "They think they can prance back into Canada, recharge their batteries, and go back out into the field to do what they've been doing up until now. It's a stinging slap in the face to all law-abiding Canadians."

8

"It's Destroying Us Slowly"

THE TURBOPROP nineteen-seater plane glided down Guantanamo's airstrip as the sun set on a November evening in 2004, coming to a quick stop on the short runway. Muneer Ahmad, a slender young law professor from Washington, D.C., tentatively walked down the stairs to an uncertain fate. Behind him, his colleague Rick Wilson also walked gingerly, unsteady after more than three hours sitting with his knees crunched painfully against the seat in front of him. With the first blast of hot, humid air and the smell of sea, Wilson was transported back forty years to his days as a Peace Corps worker in Central America. The sparse island airport reminded him of one in Bocas del Toro, the first place he had landed in Panama as an idealistic peacenik in his twenties. He inhaled deeply.

Ahmad's journey to Guantanamo began more than three years earlier, on Tuesday, September 11, 2001, just eleven days into his career teaching at the American University Law College in Washington. He was on his way to the bank that morning when he ducked into a coffee shop close to his home. Everyone was staring with mouths open as the aftermath of the deadly hijackings unfolded live on the shop's television. Broadcasters warned more planes were on the way to the White House and the National Guard was taking to the streets of New York and Washington.

Ahmad instinctively pulled out his cell phone and called his mom, although he wasn't certain if it was to reassure her that he was safe or for her to reassure him. She told him not to bother with the bank and that sounded perfectly reasonable to Ahmad. *Yes, the banks will be bombed. I can't go there.*

Amid the chaos of that day, Ahmad didn't fully appreciate what it meant to be a thirty-year-old South Asian Muslim living in a country about to declare war. But it soon became clear in the panicked eyes of commuters as he boarded the subway or through the accusatory stares he received walking down the street. The day after the attacks, Ahmad's Pakistani neighbor hung an enormous American flag outside his house. "I don't think he did it purely out of patriotism," Ahmad recalled. "It was also a shield."

While thousands of Muslims living in the United States were being held accountable for the actions of nineteen murderers, Ahmad was asked to do so in public. Reporters, community groups and other universities called him with speaking or interview requests. He was a young lawyer and a human rights advocate and both telegenic and eloquent. Most especially, he was a Muslim American whose parents were from Pakistan and who was living in America's most powerful city.

On the first anniversary of the September 11 attacks, Ahmad's phone rang with another request: Would he represent a twenty-five-year-old Afghan-born Canadian citizen named Reza Zazai who the U.S. authorities alleged was a terrorist? Baltimore police, searching for someone else, stumbled on Zazai's apartment and arrested him. Police thought the fast-food clerk and his roommates who worked at the same fried chicken joint looked suspicious so they contacted the Immigration and Naturalization Service. Baltimore's police commissioner went on TV to say police might have stumbled on an al Qaeda cell.

Ahmad took the case *pro bono* and after a few months managed to get Zazai out of jail, exonerated of any terrorism accusations and deported to Canada since it was discovered he had overstayed his U.S. work visa. "It wasn't a big case but it really epitomized what was going on at the time," Ahmad said. "The threat of terrorism was so exaggerated that local police in Baltimore were calling in the INS because Muslim men were living together."

On June 28, 2004, the U.S. Supreme Court delivered its historic finding in the Rasul case—deciding whether Guantanamo prisoners had the legal right to challenge their detentions. In a stinging rebuke of the Bush administration, the high court ruled that Guantanamo prisoners had *habeas* rights. The ruling meant that, for the first time since Guantanamo had been established two-and-a-half years earlier, detainees would have access to lawyers.

Wilson, the founder of the American University law school's Human Rights Clinic where Ahmad worked, was teaching a summer course in England but he immediately thought to himself, *This is momentous*. He called a friend who worked at the Center for Constitutional Rights and offered his services.

Days after Rasul was handed down, Ahmad was on a train to New York to meet with the Center for Constitutional Rights lawyers who assigned them a case. Four months later, the two Washington professors arrived at Gitmo to meet Omar Khadr for the first time.

IF YOU'RE NOT TRANSPORTED in shackles, there are only a few ways to get to Guantanamo. Military flights most often leave from Jacksonville, Norfolk or Andrews Air Force base, a sprawling compound in Maryland where the President's Air Force One is parked. Two domestic airlines that specialize in short-haul island hops also run flights to Guantanamo out of the airport in Ft. Lauderdale, Florida. Lynx Airlines' website is adorned with pictures of seashells and white sand beaches. "Island Happy, People Friendly Fort Lauderdale Airline Flying People, Parcels and Mail to Hot Spots in the Caribbean." Lynx Air had certainly brought Ahmad and Wilson to one of the Caribbean's hotspots in November 2004. They were only the second or third group of lawyers permitted access to Guantanamo, and Ahmad recalled, "That first time it was scary as hell. The space Guantanamo occupied in the imagination was the hyper-militarized, very dark place and we were really concerned how we'd be treated." Ahmad was more worried than other lawyers. He had heard stories about how Muslims were viewed on the base and knew what had happened to Army Chaplain James Yee.

When the lawyers disembarked, they were met by heavily armed soldiers dressed in fatigues. The barren landing strip was bounded by barbed-wire fencing, with the ocean on one side and a single road on the other. The passengers were ushered through checkpoints on the tarmac and their luggage was searched before they boarded a small bus. They didn't talk much during the short drive along a dark road.

They spent the night at the CBQ, the Combined Bachelor Quarters, which has a sign out front boasting that it is the "Pearl of the Antilles," but with accommodations that resemble a college dorm. Each room has four single beds, a kitchen and shared bathroom. If all four beds are occupied the room costs $5 a night but if there are only two to the room, it's $10. In the morning, the lawyers would be ferried across the bay to watch the sunrise over the Windward side of the base then loaded into a van that would take them to the prison. It was cumbersome and time-consuming but the only way to get access to their client. The lawyers grew to hate it.

On the first visit, the lawyers, tired and tense, looked forward to going to sleep but as the bus slowed to turn into the circular driveway that led to the dormitory, they couldn't believe the sight. On a concrete patio in front of the CBQ, a group of a dozen men and women were milling about with beer bottles in hand. As they got off the bus, the smell of a barbecue and the music coming from a boom box on the patio washed over them. *Was someone dancing? This is Guantanamo?*

Ahmad and Wilson wouldn't realize it until months later but at that moment, the juxtaposition of the militarized airport and journalists and lawyers relaxing at the end of the day, typified the many contradictions found at Guantanamo.

Guantanamo was a paradox, which is hardly surprising since its architects were uncertain of what they were creating. The Bush administration had gone to great lengths not to call Guantanamo a prison. "Despite our persistent efforts to correct the record, many mainstream [media] outlets—print, voice and electronic—persist in referring to this facility as a 'prison camp.' This is not mere parsing of words or semantic folderol," Navy Rear Adm. Harry B. Harris wrote in a May 2006 editorial in the *Chicago Tribune.* "Prison is about punishment and rehabilitation; Guantanamo is about neither. What we are about is the detention of unlawful enemy combatants."

But Guantanamo did operate as a prison, as well as a place for interrogations and indefinite detention. That caused conflicts. For instance, interrogators would often try to make detainees feel hopeless about their future to get them to rely on them and cooperate. Once despondent, these detainees might come to the attention of the military psychologists who tried to keep the peace and prevent suicides. So someone who had been made to feel hopeless was now getting the attention of one of the military's psych teams and perhaps a prescription for Prozac.

Guantanamo could seem both frightening and laughable, sometimes at the same time. There was an international outcry when it was revealed that abuse tactics such as sexual humiliation or stress positions were used during interrogations. But while Washington debated what constituted torture, a law concerning the care of the island's other occupants, the native iguanas, remained undisputed. Striking an iguana was a crime, punishable by a $10,000 fine and possible jail sentence—and the soldiers knew it.

There was also the disconnect between the description of the detainees as the "worst of the worst" and the stories told by some of those who dealt with the prisoners. Gen. Richard B. Myers, chair of the Joint Chiefs of Staff, described the first detainees as ruthless killers. "These are people that would gnaw through hydraulic lines in the back of a C-17 to bring it down. So these are very, very dangerous people," he told journalists. While there was no doubt that some of the detainees were dangerous, there was also no question that the more than 775 detainees had to be judged individually.

Translator Erik Saar recalled one detainee he met in 2002, who asked if he could practice his English. "I want you to tell me if it's good," the detainee said. The prisoner then stood, looked Saar in the eye, and started to rap: "I like big butts and I cannot lie, you other brothers can't deny, that when a girl walks in with an itty-bitty waist . . . " It's unlikely that Sir Mix-A-Lot's raunchy 1992 song "Baby Got Back" would be approved for terrorist training camp curriculum or sung by someone who would chew through a hydraulic line.

AHMAD AND WILSON had reviewed the many scenarios they might encounter during their first visit with Omar. He had turned eighteen two months earlier and had been detained for more than two years. They had no idea what he had been told by interrogators, guards or other detainees. There was even a chance Omar would think they were interrogators posing as lawyers.

Language could also be an issue. Omar's family said he spoke English but his only full year of education in Canada had been Grade One. What if he had lost most of his English during his detention with mainly Arab detainees? The greatest concern, however, was his general mental state. *How did a teenager cope with Guantanamo?*

By the time Ahmad and Wilson arrived, most of the Western detainees Omar had befriended had been released and Omar had been transferred to a cell in the new Camp Five. Although the military didn't classify his detention as solitary confinement, effectively it was. Fluorescent light bulbs burned twenty-four hours a day and prisoners were punished if they tried to cover the lights.

Unlike Camp Three, the walls were solid so the prisoners couldn't talk to each other. They did manage to devise inventive ways to communicate, however, by shouting through plumbing pipes between floors or by using hardened toothpaste to attach written messages to long threads they had picked off their prison suits which they would cast into neighboring cells.

Camp Five was the first to be air-conditioned, something the guards in their full uniform loved and the detainees in their cotton jumpsuits hated. Detainees left their cells only if permitted recreation time in an outdoor pen or for interrogations. Sometimes, the only way they left was by force.

Three days before Ahmad and Wilson arrived, CBS aired a disturbing interview about the prison's enforcement team called the Immediate Reaction Force, or IRF. The IRF soldiers, wielding batons and dressed in riot gear, were only called to forcibly extract a prisoner or quell a disturbance. CBS's story, however, was not about a detainee but about an American soldier named Sean Baker. Baker had been assigned to Guantanamo in 2002 and was responsible for escorting prisoners along the causeways of the blocks, enduring taunts and the detainees' "cocktails" of urine and excrement.

On January 24, 2003, Baker offered to take part in an IRF training exercise. He was told by the lieutenant in charge of the IRF team: "We're going to put you in a cell and extract you, have their IRF team come in and extract you. And what I'd like you to do is go ahead and strip your uniform off and put on this orange suit."

"I'd never questioned an order before," Baker told CBS, "but, at first I said, my only remark was, 'Sir?' Just in the form of a question. And he said, 'You'll be fine.' I said, 'Well, you know what's gonna happen when they come in there on me?' And he said, 'Trust me, Baker. You will be fine.'"

The IRF team was not told that Baker was a soldier and the exercise a drill. They had been told a detainee was hiding under his cot and refusing to come out. *Thud thud thud thud.* The team arrived at the cell and grabbed Baker out from under the bed. They pushed Baker's head hard against the floor and applied pressure to his throat. Frightened, Baker yelled out "Red," the code word he had been given if he wanted the exercise to end. But the soldiers didn't stop and repeatedly slammed his head against the ground until finally one of them heard Baker groan: "I'm a U.S. soldier." Bloodied and disoriented, Baker began having seizures later that morning and was eventually airlifted to Virginia where he was diagnosed with a brain injury.

The morning Wilson and Ahmad set off for the prison, Omar had been taken out of his cell by a phalanx of guards and taken to an area called Camp Echo. Echo was outside the confines of Camp Delta, but still inside the wire. It consisted of more than a dozen wooden buildings around a yard. Each bungalow contained a steel cage, washroom and table and at least two MPs. The units were divided into two, one side where the prisoners would be detained, the other used for interrogations. High-priority detainees like Moazzam Begg had been detained in Camp Echo and said the isolation was even more mentally taxing than that of Camp Five. In a prison that already seemed small and cut off from the world, those who were kept at Echo felt they were part of a different universe.

By the time Ahmad and Wilson were allowed in, Omar had been sitting, chained by his ankle to the floor for more than an hour. At first no one said anything as Omar looked over the lawyers from head to toe. They were an odd couple. Ahmad looked young for thirty-three, especially when dressed casually as he was that day. Wilson, with his shock of white hair and gregarious smile, looked as if he had just stepped away from the backyard barbecue. He was wearing a traditional white Cuban *guayabera* that added to the impression that Wilson was a wayward American tourist who had somehow stumbled on Omar.

Whether it was the sight of this mismatched pair or just the thrill of leaving his cell and being able to interact with people, Omar began to smile, relieving the tension. In his quiet voice, the teenager began to talk.

For the next seven hours, the trio chatted. Omar told them his life story and they told him a bit about themselves and the world he hadn't seen for two years. For Wilson, who had two grown children of his own and a stepson just a couple years younger than Omar, it was hard not to feel paternal. "He was a charming kid. He had an engaging demeanor, with a winning smile. He didn't seem to me to be cynical or worn out at that point."

To try to build trust, they told him stories from his family. Wilson and Ahmad had traveled to Toronto before the visit and met Omar's Canadian lawyer Dennis Edney at Toronto's Royal York Hotel. They had spent a long day with Omar's mother and grandmother. The second day, they had talked with Omar's brother Abdurahman, collecting stories only a family member could know.

The lawyers were immediately struck by just how immature Omar was. He seemed a teenager not yet sure who he was; one moment Omar, the brave and defiant prisoner, the next, Omar, the ashamed and depressed captive. During the seven hours, humiliation turned into pride, resolve melted into insecurity.

Before the end of that visit, Omar lowered his voice even more and started talking about what had happened to him inside Guantanamo.

During the next few days, he would tell them about the interrogator who said he was from Afghanistan and the one who threatened to transfer him to Egypt where he would meet Soldier Number Nine. He told them about being used as a human mop after he had soiled himself. One of the interrogators had told Omar "Your life is in my hands," he said, and by then, Omar believed it.

Ahmad and Wilson scribbled furiously, the only record of the interviews they would have. When the MPs told them time was up, everyone rose. Ahmad stood just an inch or two taller than Omar, something he would chart during subsequent visits as Omar grew taller. They asked Omar if they could hug him. He agreed and hung on to them for a long time.

Before boarding the ferry back to their rooms, the lawyers asked their military escort if they could make a stop on Sherman Avenue. At a pay phone beside the NEX, they used their phone cards to call Omar's mother in Scarborough. Their military escort stood less than ten feet away and while they couldn't say much, they did tell her Omar appeared healthy and was in good spirits.

"When I look back at that first meeting, it is with sadness," Ahmad reflected. "I feel like it was the most optimistic moment Omar had, and it has been downhill since. We were the first people who came to see him and didn't interrogate him. There was a moment of hope that someone was there on his side."

BY THE END OF THE WEEK, Ahmad and Wilson were emotionally drained and had personalized the all-consuming legal battle ahead. "We'll be back," they told Omar but wondered, when? "One of the biggest problems representing Omar was that once we were starting to develop real rapport and get a trusting relationship we would up and leave and go back to the United States and he'd go back to his cage. The intervening four to six weeks for him was in an environment designed to build mistrust. Every single time, up until my last visit two years later, it was exactly the same problem. We'd start each visit from square one," said Ahmad.

That was one complaint all the Guantanamo lawyers shared. The military controlled every aspect of their visits and there was no other way to talk. Phone calls were not allowed and letters would take so long to be delivered and undergo such extensive censorship that they were ineffective.

Just getting to Guantanamo was an issue in itself. Some lawyers had their firms or human rights organizations supporting them financially but many of the lawyers took the cases *pro bono*, which meant they would not only have to pay for their flights to Guantanamo, they would also have to leave their practices for at least four days for what could amount to only a few hours of interviews.

Attorney-client privilege also didn't exist. All the notes the *habeas* lawyers took at Guantanamo were sealed in an envelope and sent to censors in Washington so the documents could be vetted for national security concerns. What documents the lawyers would receive back, sometimes months later, were often heavily blacked out. If they disclosed what Washington had redacted, they could go to jail. Not everything Omar had told Ahmad and Wilson made it past censors, but eventually the Washington lawyers had enough to go public with the bulk of his allegations.

In February 2005, Ahmad traveled to Toronto to meet with Dennis Edney. Together with Omar's mother and grandmother, they held a press conference in a second-floor room at the Royal York Hotel. The women wept as the allegation that Omar had been used as a human mop was read out but they would not speak to reporters, following their lawyer's instructions. Edney knew Canadians had not forgotten the damaging documentary and did not want his client's mother to divert the focus from the suffering of her son. Instead, Edney read a statement on behalf of Omar's mother, Maha Elsamnah. "As a mother, I beg every Canadian mother and father to help me get justice for my son and bring him home." But the effect was almost comical, especially when delivered in Edney's Scottish accent.

Omar's claims of abuse may have been horrendous but it didn't take long for questions to refer back to his family. "Why should Canadians care about Khadr's treatment?" one reporter called out. "Isn't there Khadr-family fatigue?" Edney paused before answering the reporter's question and chose his words carefully. "There is no doubt that there's a lack of sympathy towards the Khadr family. I've seen that from one end of Canada to the other," he said. "It's the principle you're fighting for and sometimes it's for clients who appear to be most untrustworthy."

Ten days after the press conference, Omar's sister Zaynab arrived in Toronto from Pakistan with her daughter Safia. RCMP officers met her at the airport with a search warrant for her belongings, which included her personal diary that would give police a detailed record of the Khadr family's travels after 9/11. Investigators also confiscated her laptop which contained downloaded al Qaeda propaganda, including a song titled "I am a terrorist."

Zaynab had returned to Canada on a one-way travel document since Canada had refused her a passport. She said the only reason she returned was out of concern for her mother and her brother Kareem. Since her brother Abdullah had gone missing in the fall of 2004 and was presumed to be in the custody of Pakistani forces, there was nothing to keep her in Islamabad. "I don't agree with the way culture's going on here, but I don't walk the street telling everyone who's not covered that you should cover, you must, and unless you do that you're bad. If you want to cover up, it's up to you, and if you don't want to cover up, it's up to you, and I can't judge you for that," Zaynab said in an interview soon after her arrival.

She disputed Abdurahman's claims that they had grown up in an "al Qaeda family," admitting that she respected the group's ideology but arguing that al Qaeda's leaders never fully accepted her family because they said they were too Western. "I respect its people for believing what they believe and sticking to what they believe. I mean, American soldiers in Iraq are fighting for something that I might think is worthless, truthfully, losing my life for petrol to me seems very stupid. But if that's what they believe and they're dying for it, I can't go and say 'They're stupid, they're dying for petrol.'" Zaynab described herself as a woman lost between her worlds—too Western for the East and not wanted in the West.

"I feel angry but I have a lot of reasons to feel angry. I feel angry about losing my house, the country that I thought was my home. When I was living in Afghanistan, it was more like a home to me. I feel angry that I lost my father. I don't think he's lost. We believe he's a martyr and he has the highest reward that ever can be granted to anyone. This is my belief. But he's my father. I miss him. I feel angry that I have a half-crippled brother who's only fifteen and can't walk on his feet. I feel angry I have two missing brothers. I had four brothers and I don't even know if I have one-and-a-half yet. I feel angry and any person would feel the same."

News of her return overshadowed Omar's story.

THE MORNING OF FEBRUARY 18, 2005, inside the Edmonton office of Parlee McLaws, Canada's top spy, Jack Hooper, filled a television screen. The video conference was part of Nate Whitling and Dennis Edney's federal court fight to prevent CSIS from visiting Omar in Guantanamo again. Although the case had received little attention in Canada, it was rare to have a senior CSIS official like Hooper publicly justify his agency's actions. He had filed an affidavit arguing the spy agency should maintain the right to visit Omar. This was Whitling's chance to cross-examine him.

"I take it that you are the same William Hooper who swore an affidavit," Whitling began formally.

"Yes."

"Referring to paragraph one of your affidavit, I understand that you're the assistant director of operations with CSIS, is that correct?"

"That's correct. That's correct."

For sixty-five minutes, Whitling, in his steady, methodical manner, led Hooper through a series of questions about CSIS's visits with Omar, trying to build a case that the federal agency had violated Omar's constitutional rights. The crux of his argument was that there was a good chance the Americans would be monitoring CSIS's interrogations and could use what the teenager said as evidence against him in any legal proceedings. Omar did not have a lawyer present during the interrogations nor did he fully appreciate that what he said could be used against him, his lawyers argued.

About halfway through his testimony, the normally reserved Whitling hit his stride. Why, he asked Hooper, does CSIS need to question Omar since they had already interrogated him extensively?

"We would like to reserve the right to speak to him when we believe he has information that is germane to the threat and the security of Canada," Hooper responded.

"Did anyone at CSIS advise Mr. Khadr that the answers he would give would be shared with the United States?" Whitling asked.

"I don't know that, sir."

"Did anyone at CSIS advise Mr. Khadr that he could be facing the death penalty?"

"I don't know that."

"Did anyone from CSIS advise Mr. Khadr that he could face other penalties such as life imprisonment?"

"I do not know that."

"You do not know that, I take it?"

"I do not know that."

"Did CSIS employees ever advise Mr. Khadr as to the reasons why he's being detained in Guantanamo Bay?"

"I don't know the answer to that."

"I believe it's CSIS policy to allow interviewees to have their counsel present at any interviews conducted by CSIS, is that correct?"

"That's correct."

"And did anyone at CSIS advise Mr. Khadr that he could have a lawyer present during these interviews?"

"My understanding of, of the protocols around permissible visits to Guantanamo Bay were . . ."

The government's lawyer cut Hooper off. "Mr. Hooper, I don't want to influence your answer, but just make sure you turn your mind to whether this is getting into an area that you objected to disclosing information in the past."

Hooper, not a man to be interrupted, continued. "My answer was going to be I think it would be virtually impossible for a lawyer to get into Guantanamo Bay."

"Are you aware," Whitling asked, "that since the dates of the CSIS interviews, two lawyers have, in fact, come in and consulted with Mr. Khadr?"

"No, I'm not."

It's hard to resist the temptation to compare legal proceedings about Guantanamo to the Hollywood blockbuster *A Few Good Men*. The 1992 film starring Jack Nicholson, Tom Cruise and Kevin Bacon was partially set in Guantanamo and involved the court martial of two Marines accused of murdering one of their own, Pfc. William Santiago. Cruise played the rookie defense lawyer who ended up exposing a cover-up that Nicholson was grilled about on the witness stand.

> "You want answers?" [Nicholson sneered.]
> "I think I'm entitled to them," [Cruise replied.]
> "You want answers?!"
> "I want the truth."
> "You can't handle the truth! [Nicholson shouted, in delivering the movie's most famous line.] Son, we live in a world that has walls. And those walls have to be guarded by men with guns. Who's gonna do it? You? [He thundered.] I have a greater responsibility than you can possibly fathom. You weep for Santiago and you curse the Marines. You have that luxury. You have the luxury of not knowing what I

know: That Santiago's death, while tragic, probably saved lives. And my existence, while grotesque and incomprehensible to you, saves lives."

Hooper was certainly a more charming, less snarling version of Nicholson's character, but he did share the Marine's contempt of lawyers and disdain for those who couldn't understand the sometimes ugly world of national security. After he retired in 2007 to the small picturesque town of Peachland in Western Canada's wine country, Hooper was unapologetic for his agency's role in Omar's case.

"I'll tell you what our choices are. We can talk to Omar Khadr in Guantanamo knowing that probably the Americans would be fools if they weren't taping our interview of Omar Khadr. So our presumption is yes, they're taping us, okay. Will they use that information that derives from our interview with Omar Khadr in the context of a prosecution? Possibly. Does Omar Khadr possess information for an investigation or that allows the prevention of an act of terrorism in Canada? Possibly. So we have the choice, talk to Omar, don't talk to Omar. Well, excuse me if my decision falls on the side of the greater good and the greater good is for the majority of Canadians. Omar has rights, he's entitled to certain rights, but so are the thirty-three million Canadians who are vulnerable. If I had to make the decision whose rights are likely to be offended, thirty-three million Canadians or Omar Khadr's, well, I'm going to go with thirty-three million Canadians and try to defend them every time."

Federal Justice Konrad von Finckenstein had a different view. In a decision released in Edmonton in the summer of 2005, the judge said he weighed the spy agency's right to gather intelligence against Omar's right to a fair trial. Since it was possible, even plausible, that information Omar told the Canadians could be entered as evidence at his trial, von Finckenstein said the visits had violated the Charter rights guaranteed to Omar as a Canadian citizen.

Edney and Whitling got what they sought—an interim injunction halting any more visits by CSIS to Guantanamo Bay. Von Finckenstein wrote that he was granting the injunction "to prevent a potential grave injustice." The "conditions at Guantanamo Bay do not meet Charter standards," he further stated in what remains the Canadian courts' most damning denouncement of the prison.

After the ruling, Edney issued a statement. "It's disgraceful the Canadian government won't come to his rescue but, thank goodness, the Canadian courts will."

By 2005, GUANTANAMO HAD REINVENTED itself again, as it did each time a new commander arrived. Gen. Miller was in Iraq, where he had been sent to streamline intelligence gathering at the Abu Ghraib prison. Miller reportedly wanted the military to "Gitmo-ize" the facility. When he was finished, dogs were being used during interrogations and naked detainees were humiliated and abused by MPs working the night shift, as revealed in a series of now notorious photographs. Seven low-ranking soldiers were charged for their conduct at Abu Ghraib. The most serious punishment was given to Pvt. Charles A. Graner, who was sentenced to ten years in jail. No senior commanders were reprimanded.

Maj.-Gen. Jay Hood, a no-nonsense hands-on commander who grew up in an army family, had replaced Miller at Guantanamo in 2004. Like all of Guantanamo's leaders, Hood was under intense pressure from Washington. His mission was to restore Guantanamo's badly damaged image, a task only exacerbated by the Abu Ghraib scandal that broke a week after he took command.

Hood soon faced another public relations disaster. The prisoners had stopped eating. There had been hunger strikes before but never as widespread or as well coordinated as the one that began in the summer of 2005.

Omar was among as many as fifty Camp Five prisoners who were protesting the conditions by accepting only water. According to what Omar told his lawyers, the prisoners had four main complaints. They wanted a trial. They wanted better medical care. They wanted conditions at Camp Five—the isolation, the temperature, the random system of punishment—improved. Omar said he would often curl up in a ball on his steel cot in an attempt to get warm. It got worse after guards seized his blanket as punishment. The last demand, and perhaps most important, was respect for their religion. Detainees had complained about the guards' reported abuse of the Quran and an allegation that a copy of one had been flushed down a toilet ignited riots in Muslim countries worldwide. Dozens of languages and dialects were spoken among the detainees, but religion united them all. The ritual of daily prayers brought them structure and comfort. Just before sunrise, the first of five calls to prayer would wake the prisoners and they would wash, unfurl their prayer mats, face east to Mecca and bow and kneel as they offered their praise to Allah.

The guards also started their day with praise, not to their God, but to their country. At 8 a.m. every morning, a siren sounded and soldiers across the base would stop in their tracks. They would turn to face the nearest American flag and stand perfectly still, one hand tipped to their forehead in a salute, as the *Star Spangled Banner* blared from speakers.

Neither group respected the other's devotion. Detainees would holler and bang their cages while the U.S. national anthem played; guards would talk loudly or jeer trying to disrupt the daily prayers. It caused a near riot if the call to prayer and the anthem would play at the same time.

Omar had memorized the Quran and was chosen by the other prisoners to lead a small group of detainees in Camp Five in their daily prayers. His melodic young voice called out to about seven or eight prisoners nearby, as the men knelt and bowed in perfect unison, alone in their cells. Omar told Ahmad and Wilson that he would not break his rhythm, even when the MPs would whistle or turn up the radio or the fans to try to drown out his voice.

When prisoners at Camp Delta heard about the Camp Five strike, they refused meals in solidarity which meant more than half of Guantanamo's prisoners were starving themselves. Sami Muhyideen al Hajj, the al Jazeera cameraman, was detained at the time in the Whisky Block of Camp Four, the camp with the most freedom. He kept a diary:

> On the 15th of July, there was an important group of visitors being shown around Camp Delta, people we believe to have been from the U.S. Congress. For reasons known only to the authorities here, these people were not given the normal tour of Camp IV, maybe because of the heightened tensions around the whole camp. But the tour did include the hospital, which is situated close to Whisky Block.
>
> Out of desperation, the prisoners started speaking out (actually, shouting) to the people on the tour, explaining our problems. Some of the detainees were shouting the word "Freedom!" Others, I am afraid, were shouting, "Bush is Hitler!" Others were shouting, "This is a Gulag!" Everyone was desperate for someone to listen from the outside world. Some of the visitors approached Whisky Block to get closer to the Detainees and hear them better (despite a warning not to from the escorting guards). Some of the visitors seemed to sincerely want to understand the situation, while others were looking at us in disgust.
>
> On the 17th of July at 5:00 p.m., the authorities at Camp Delta started to forcefully remove the prisoners from Whisky Block (we believe this was because of the incident with the tour two days before). They

took eighteen detainees back to Camps II and III (where the conditions are much harsher).

Washington was gravely concerned about the hunger strike and cognizant of the potential political fallout if someone died while in custody. History has shown that prisoners who died as a result of hunger strikes become powerful in death. The most famous example is that of twenty-seven-year-old Bobby Sands and nine other IRA members who died protesting in prison in 1981. Britain's prime minister, Margaret Thatcher, told the House of Commons at the time that, "Mr. Sands was a convicted criminal. He chose to take his own life. It was a choice that his organization did not allow to many of its victims." But more than 100,000 turned out for Sands's funeral and his death prompted a surge in the IRA's popularity and dramatic increases in donations. As one U.S. Department of Defense official said about Guantanamo's hunger strikes: "The worst case would be to have someone go from zero to hero. We don't want a Bobby Sands." The Bush administration was determined to prevent the transformation of a Guantanamo detainee to a political martyr and would go to dramatic lengths to keep detainees alive.

The striking prisoners quickly fell ill. On July 5, Omar fainted in one of the outdoor concrete recreation pens. He later described the incident to Ahmad and Wilson and said the MPs rushed him to the prison's air-conditioned hospital after he fell. He was kept there for four days as doctors tried to persuade him to eat, but he refused. Upon his release, guards forced him to wear blacked-out goggles and drove him in a van back to Camp Five. He told the guards he was too dizzy to walk and when he stepped from the van, he sat on the ground, his legs crossed. Furious, the guards lifted him and one MP, a specialist, kicked his legs repeatedly, Omar claimed. They screamed at him to walk. Eventually, three guards picked him up and carried him to his cell.

Omar Deghayes, a Libyan-born resident of Britain who had been arrested in Lahore following 9/11, was also a detainee who kept a diary. On July 9, after noting that at least one detainee had been found unconscious in his cell, Deghayes wrote: "In the morning before 11 a.m., several times doctor came around and asked questions. Some show concern. This is a new approach unseen in all previous strikes." He also wrote about Omar: "Omar Ramah is very sick in our Block. He is throwing [up] blood. They gave him cyrum when they found him on the floor of his cell."

On the tenth day of his hunger strike, Omar again suffered a dizzy spell. A doctor who was roaming the blocks called out, and when Omar didn't answer, the doctor looked through the cell window and saw Omar collapsed on the floor. This time he was taken to a room inside Camp Five. He was offered a can of the liquid meal-replacement, Ensure. Omar refused and also refused an IV. The guards then took him to the hospital and told him he must accept an IV, which he did.

WITH THE VERY REAL PROSPECT that detainees were going to die, Hood charged his second-in-command, Col. Mike Bumgarner, with ending the hunger strike. Bumgarner, a six-foot-two, 250-pound commander who spoke with a faint Carolina drawl, had been appointed just a month before to manage daily operations. Bumgarner didn't join the military to be a prison warden; he wanted to fight in Iraq. But he performed his job at Guantanamo with as much gusto as he devoted to all his work. He was determined to bring order and respect to the prison for the good of both the guards and the detainees. On his office desk sat a printout of the Geneva Conventions.

Bumgarner attempted to manage the crisis in a way that hadn't been tried at Guantanamo before. He struck an alliance with one of the most influential and dynamic detainees, a thirty-eight-year-old Saudi named Shaker Aamer. Aamer had spent much of his adult life living in London and the United States and spoke so eloquently that the guards nicknamed him "The Professor." He commanded respect among the detainees and Bumgarner knew this.

After a series of negotiations during which Bumgarner sat beside an unshackled Aamer and spoke to him with respect, the pair agreed that they would stop the strike. Aamer took the first step by accepting food himself; then, with Bumgarner and a translator, he traveled to the blocks and advised the prisoners to start eating. Bumgarner told Tim Golden, a reporter with the *New York Times*, that Aamer "was treated like a rock star, some of the places we would go in. I have never seen grown men—with beards, hardened men—crying at the sight of another man. It was like I was with Bon Jovi or something."

In return, Bumgarner promised change. He couldn't deal with the larger concerns such as bringing the men to trial but he could improve daily life. When prayers were being said five times a day, "prayer cones"—yellow pylons painted with a large "P"—were put outside the cells to warn the guards to stay quiet. The detainees were given bottled water instead of the yellow-tinged tap water they previously drank. Eventually, their diet would be increased from 2,800 calories a day to a whopping 4,200 calories, but the first improvement was the privilege of hot sauce and other condiments. "We all decided to end the strike—for one month," Deghayes wrote. "Because the General and officer promised to fulfill many conditions. [Shaker Aamer] is going round the camps and blocks to relay this message with General."

Buoyed by success, Bumgarner allowed a council of six detainees to meet with him so they could discuss how to continue to improve conditions and keep peace. Hood and many of the senior soldiers were wary but to Bumgarner it was simple. "This place isn't going away, so we might as well make the best of it," Bumgarner told Golden.

But on August 5, word went out among prisoners that a detainee named Hisham Sliti had been beaten during an interrogation and had his Quran abused. Around this time, Omar was also forcibly taken for a "reservation," al Hajj wrote in his diary.

The peace was broken. When the guards asked members of Bumgarner's prison council for the notes they had written during a meeting, they shoved them in their mouths in defiance. On August 8, Hood ended their meetings. Shaker Aamer was confined to the isolation of Camp Echo. In Camps Two and Three, riots broke out.

"Things are not going good," wrote Omar Deghayes. "They changed the food for two days and gave pepper and chili sauce, etc. Then they made sure now everyone has ended the strike they then went back as usual . . . It does seem very likely that the strike will restart again. I am very frustrated with these cunning officers and worthless men of no word."

By mid-August, the hunger strike was again in full swing although it is unclear if Omar still participated. On the fourth anniversary of the September 11 attacks, 131 prisoners were refusing meals.

Military doctors began force-feeding the hunger strikers by inserting tubes through their noses and snaking them down into their stomachs. When prisoners ripped out the tubes or vomited after the feedings, the guards confined them to stretchers. The military later acquired "restraint chairs" to which recalcitrant detainees would be strapped. The prisoners said it amounted to torture but the White House dismissed the concern.

"Well, yes, we know that al Qaeda is trained in trying to make wild accusations and so forth," spokesperson Scott McClellan told reporters.

Most doctors shun the practice of force-feeding, believing it violates the 1975 World Medical Tokyo Declaration which prohibits physicians from subjecting patients to inhumane treatment. In September 2007, more than 250 doctors from sixteen different countries wrote to the medical journal *The Lancet*, condemning force-feeding and other questionable medical practices at Guantanamo, such as using detainee's medical records to help in interrogations. Doctors who administer force-feeding should be referred to their professional bodies for breaching internationally recognized ethical standards, the physicians wrote. Access to the prisoners' medical records to exploit weaknesses was also considered unethical. "No health-care worker in the War on Terror has been charged or convicted of any significant offence despite numerous instances documented, including fraudulent recordkeeping on detainees who have died as a result of failed interrogations . . . The attitude of the U.S. military establishment appears to be one of 'See no evil, hear no evil, speak no evil.'"

A small handful of detainees, who have been on hunger strikes since 2005, continue to be force-fed today.

THE PENTAGON HAS REFUSED repeated requests by Omar's lawyers for an independent medical examination. In an attempt to assess his mental well being, Ahmad and Wilson administered two psychological tests themselves in late 2004 and in the spring of 2005. The first, the Mini Mental State Examination or the Folstein test, named after the doctors who created it, Marshal and Susan Folstein, was devised to screen for dementia. The brief exam includes questions that rely on memory, cognitive skills and the ability to perform such tasks as spelling the word "world" backwards.

After Washington's censors cleared the results, Omar's answers for the Folstein test were given to Dr. Eric Trupin who has extensively researched the effects of incarceration on teenagers. Trupin reported that there was a "high probability" that Omar was suffering from a "significant mental disorder, including but not limited to post-traumatic stress disorder and depression." Trupin concluded that Omar was experiencing symptoms "consistent with those exhibited by victims of torture and abuse."

"The impact on an adolescent such as [Omar Khadr] who has been isolated for over two-and-a-half years is potentially catastrophic to his future development. Long-term consequences of extended confinement are both more pronounced for adolescents and more difficult to remediate or treat even after solitary confinement is discontinued," Trupin wrote.

The second test was analyzed by Dr. Daryl Matthews, a professor of psychiatry at the University of Hawaii whom the Pentagon had invited to spend a week in May 2003 at Guantanamo investigating the detainees' mental health. Matthews interviewed many detainees and later concluded that there was a "huge cultural gulf" between prisoners and soldiers which made it difficult for the base's medical staff to properly assess psychiatric problems. Gitmo, he wrote, was "prison plus." "The stressors are incredible: never knowing if you'll get out, or when you'll get out; being sealed off from the community; not having access to legal counsel. In prison, relationships between inmates and guards are pretty affirming. Here, they come from two universes."

Dr. Matthews did not meet with Omar during his time at Guantanamo but later reviewed Omar's answers and concluded that they met the "full criteria for a diagnosis of Post-Traumatic Stress Disorder." Matthews confirmed what Ahmad and Wilson had feared and continued interrogations would surely only worsen Omar's fragile mental state. They used the documents in a bid for a court injunction to stop Omar's interrogations. Their request was denied.

WILSON AND AHMAD visited Omar as often as the Pentagon would permit. Sometimes they went together, sometimes alone, and Omar developed a different relationship with each of them. In many ways, he was closer to Ahmad because he was younger and they shared a religion. But this also caused friction.

Omar had always been devout, much more so than his brothers and his commitment to Islam had increased during his incarceration. He would often ask Ahmad about his devotion and Ahmad would answer him truthfully. He was Muslim but did not follow the traditions of his religion such as praying five times a day. Omar had trouble with this, and often, when Wilson wasn't around, tried to encourage Ahmad to pray more.

But most of their time together was spent discussing Omar's passions: cars, animals, movies and Harry Potter. Ahmad himself had been into cars as a teenager so they could talk for hours about different makes and models. Omar wanted to know what Ahmad drove in Washington. "I was supposed to be a human rights lawyer but drove a silver Audi TT. It was a bit embarrassing," Ahmad chuckled. But Omar seemed to approve of his selection. Wilson could talk about Harry Potter since he had read all of J.K. Rowling's books, as had Omar.

Everything the lawyers tried to bring to Omar had to pass through security. Automobile and *National Geographic* magazines usually made it past the guards, but many items didn't. For instance, a glossy coffee-table book of wild animals that Wilson's law students had bought especially for Omar was confiscated because it exceeded size limits. "They sent the book into the black hole of the military review process and it never came back out. Some guard or interrogator probably has it now on his coffee table," said Wilson.

These meetings were Omar's only chance for human interaction with people who didn't carry guns or interrogate him. The lawyers ended each session with a hug.

"He grew up before our eyes. He was really, really a kid when we saw him. He certainly passed through puberty. He grew taller, he broke out and I think he got more tired and more cynical, hardened as time passed. It felt like he was in a darker place. I think the isolation just took an immense toll," Wilson recalled.

"This place," Omar told Ahmad during one visit, "is destroying us slowly."

One day in mid-2005, Omar penned a note firing his American lawyers. He wanted to see his Canadian lawyers, but the Pentagon was still refusing them access. "I want you to witness that I'm withdrawing Mr. Richard J. Wilson and Mr. Muneer I. Ahmad, law professors at the American University who were my attorneys, from representing me, and from today, there is no relation between me and them," Omar wrote.

The letter marked the start of a tumultuous relationship with his lawyers that often left them disappointed, but not surprised. Ahmad and Wilson were U.S. citizens and paranoia about Americans was rampant in the prison. Besides, Ahmad and Wilson couldn't tell Omar that they were close to getting him released, so their efforts seemed fruitless. "Who could blame him?" Wilson said. "All we brought was bad news."

Omar had also grown frustrated with what he had to go through for their visits. It meant being shackled and taken by guards from his cell to another area where he was left for hours in isolation, sitting bolted to the floor.

And there was the issue of control. In a prison where you were told when to eat, sleep, shower, talk, go outside—where you weren't even allowed to starve yourself—the only power that detainees retained was whether to accept visits from lawyers.

LAYNE MORRIS, the Special Forces soldier who had lost sight in one eye during the battle where Omar was captured, had followed the Khadr family saga from his home in Utah. When PBS's popular documentary program *Frontline* picked up the CBC's documentary, Morris became enraged when he heard Zaynab say that Speer's death was no "big deal."

"It was when they pulled out the Canadian passports and started waving them around to come back and take advantage of their free everything because things hadn't gone well for them, that was the thing when I said, 'You know, there's something additionally I can do, and I think I need to do it,'" Morris recalled.

He approached two Salt Lake City lawyers to discuss launching a lawsuit against the Khadr family. Morris had always maintained that Omar was responsible for his actions and had made adult choices on the day of the fight, but he wanted to sue Ahmed Said Khadr's estate based on the argument that a parent has a duty to control the actions of his child. Khadr had been named by the UN as a terrorist financier in January 2001, so whatever assets the family possessed had been frozen. Morris wanted to make sure there was no way they would ever see that money again. "It was also important to send a message that it's not just combat. We don't fight this just on one level, the combat level in the field, but there are other ways you can fight it, financially and legally, to make it hard for them to operate and I thought that was worth doing all by itself. The chance to get some financial security for a buddy's wife and kids, that's huge. That would be great."

Tabitha Speer wrote a victim impact statement about her husband's death. "I sat in the middle of the living-room floor, explaining to Taryn what happened to Daddy. This was the hardest thing I have ever done. I need to be strong for Taryn and Tanner, but needed to grieve myself. Telling a little girl her Daddy would not be coming home was excruciating. While I was speaking to Taryn, I saw fear, abandonment and ultimately, overwhelming sadness in her eyes. Taryn became hysterical and began to cry. I explained to Taryn that Daddy had been injured and that his injuries had been too bad so he had gone to Heaven. I explained to Taryn that Daddy would always be with us now and that he would be an angel watching over us.

I explained that Daddy would never miss out on anything. Although I think my explanation helped a bit, I knew Taryn was crushed inside. That night, I could not sleep. I took some sleeping pills prescribed by my doctor to help me sleep. I was able to get a couple hours sleep, but awoke early the next morning. I needed some alone time and so I took Christopher's dog for a walk. While on the walk I told our dog what had happened to Christopher. I know this sounds crazy, but I think I did it in an effort to release some of the pain I was feeling."

In the end, the Morris and Speer families received a default victory since the Khadr family did not mount a defense. A Salt Lake City judge awarded them more than $102 million, but it was unlikely they would ever receive that money since Khadr's known assets amounted to no more than $30,000 and remained frozen.

But around the same time as the verdict, they received something else for which they had been waiting. Omar was finally going to trial. On November 7, 2005, less than two months after Omar turned nineteen, the Pentagon charged him with murder for Speer's death, as well as attempted murder, conspiracy and aiding the enemy.

The Bush administration had first announced the rules of the military commissions in March 2002, and the criticism had been immediate. "Even if you dress it up, a Kangaroo is still a Kangaroo," ran a headline in the *Los Angeles Times* over an opinion piece by Jonathan Turley, a professor of constitutional law at George Washington University. Turley and other critics said the military commission rules were written to ensure convictions and flouted international and domestic standards of justice. The commissions created the "mere pretense of a legal process," Turley wrote, but did not measure up to any standard of justice. Most egregious was the rule that allowed the prosecution to use hearsay evidence. Turley also objected to the administration's stipulation that government-appointed military lawyers must represent defendants. "Military defense counsel long have been criticized as inexperienced and often dominated by higher-ranking officers," Turley wrote. "Moreover, imposing uniformed counsel on these prisoners will inevitably chill attorney-client communications, given the defendants' alleged recent efforts to kill people wearing the same uniform."

Omar's case was further complicated by the fact that he had been a minor when arrested. "Omar Khadr is a child," Muneer Ahmad said after the charges were announced. "Since he was fifteen years old, he has been held in U.S. custody, first in Afghanistan and then at Guantanamo, under the worst conditions possible. Through torture, abuse and three years of illegal detention, this government has robbed Omar of his youth."

Through its silence, the Canadian government had given its blessing to the commission process. The only concession it managed to obtain from Washington concerned the question of a death penalty upon conviction. A day after Omar's charges were announced, the Pentagon stated that the death penalty was no longer an option, and if found guilty, Omar would receive a life sentence. Foreign Affairs officials in Ottawa said they were pleased capital punishment was no longer a possibility, but still did not condemn the military commission process as European and Middle Eastern governments had.

Omar's hearing was set for January 11, 2006.

9

"There Are No Rules"

A FEW MINUTES before 3:30 p.m. on January 11, 2006, the double doors of a makeshift courtroom opened to reveal a tall, skinny teenager flanked by four beefy soldiers. Spectators turned, some rising slightly from their chairs to get a better view of Omar Khadr as the soldiers led him to a table in the center of the room.

The public had by now been given two characterizations of Omar: the trained Canadian terrorist or the young, tortured victim of unjust laws. The night before the hearing, Guantanamo's chief prosecutor Col. Morris "Moe" Davis had chided the media for portraying Omar sympathetically, calling the coverage "nauseating." "You'll see evidence when we get into the courtroom of the smiling face of Omar Khadr as he builds bombs to kill Americans," he told about a dozen journalists. "When these guys went to camp, they weren't making s'mores and learning how to tie knots."

But as Omar walked into the room with gleaming white running shoes that seemed too big and clunky for his scrawny legs, he looked more like a teenager than part of Osama bin Laden's inner circle. A couple of Canadian reporters in the room snickered when they spotted the words "Roots Athletics" across Omar's chest, his lawyer's none-too-subtle effort to make Omar appear as the all-Canadian boy. Roots clothing and leather company, with its beaver logo and history of outfitting Canada's Olympic team, is about as Canadian as maple syrup and hockey, and lawyer Muneer Ahmad knew that when he ordered the shirt online.

Omar's hearing was the start of the first U.S. war crimes trial since the prosecution of Nazi commanders in the 1940s, but once the nineteen-year-old was seated, the defense team looked more like a high-school debating club than a team about to make legal history.

Beside Muneer Ahmad sat Captain John Merriam, an Army Judge Advocate General, or JAG, who was Omar's military counsel ordered to defend him. Merriam, whom everyone knew as J.J., had spent his military career as a prosecutor and had just returned from a tour in Iraq. This would be his first time leading the defense. It was also his first murder case, and Merriam was clearly nervous, his rosy cheeks turning a darker shade of red as he grew stressed. During the afternoon's proceedings, Merriam would repeatedly be asked to speak slower so the court reporter could keep up. "I understand," Merriam replied at one point. "I'm a little excited about this."

Omar had reluctantly resumed a relationship with his American lawyers after Rick Wilson had traveled to Guantanamo the previous fall and convinced him to accept their help. But Omar told the Washington professor he didn't have any faith in the trial process and believed, no matter what they did, he would remain in custody. That was certainly a possibility. Omar, like the other detainees, was classified as an "enemy combatant," which meant the U.S. government would hold him as long as he was considered a danger. Even if the military commission acquitted Omar, the Pentagon could decide he remained a threat and keep him locked up.

The prosecution in Omar's case was led by a Marine with cropped blond hair and a swimmer's physique. Maj. Jeff Groharing had joined the Marines in 1996 after graduating from law school at the University of Nebraska and a brief career in private practice. Groharing had asked to be assigned to the commission prosecution team. "I look forward to seeing how history will look at the commissions. I think everyone who goes and watches will be surprised at how fair they are, how open they are and how much of this is just like a regular trial," he said, after being assigned Omar's case.

In 2005, Groharing had personally delivered the commission charges to Omar in his cell. He had been researching the case for months so was eager to see what the Canadian looked like. The encounter lasted less than a minute. "He told me he didn't want me to be his lawyer," Groharing recalled. "I told him I'm not, far from it."

Before he began working with the prosecution's office in Washington in 2002, Groharing had been a Marine defense lawyer and had acquired a reputation as an unflappable attorney with a Marine's stamina. It probably didn't hurt his public image that he was married to Miss California 1999, which was noted on his online Wikipedia profile along with his Marine Corps marathon time of three hours and twenty-five minutes. Privately, the journalists covering the commission nicknamed Groharing "Kevin Bacon," not simply because he bore a slight resemblance to the Hollywood actor but also as another reference to the movie *A Few Good Men* in which Bacon played a Marine prosecutor.

Presiding over the hearing was Robert Chester, a Marine colonel who wore a gown and used a gavel but under military commission rules was called the presiding officer not the judge. Chester was only months from his retirement but had been asked to extend his stay for the commission cases.

"This military commission will come to order. Prosecutor?" Chester began with a crack of his gavel.

"Sir, this military commission is appointed by Appointing Order 05-0004, dated 23 November 2005. Copies of the appointing order have been furnished to the Presiding Officer, counsel and the accused. And they have been marked as Review Exhibit 6 and attached for the record," Groharing began.

The first issue to settle was if Omar needed a translator. Ahmad assured Chester that Omar could understand English and resisted the urge to say he wasn't sure how, in any language, he would be able to explain to Omar the rules of this court which he himself didn't understand.

"Mr. Khadr, do you understand what your defense counsel, Mr. Ahmad, just said?"

In a barely audible voice, Omar replied, "Yes, sir."

"I need you to please speak up so that I can hear you. All right?"

"Yes, sir."

Chester had a reputation of being gruff, even boorish, in court and it wasn't uncommon for him to roll his eyes during a lawyer's argument. But when he talked to Omar directly, he was polite.

"I consider it very important that you understand everything that we are doing today as well as throughout these proceedings. So again, I want to make sure you understand. If you do have a problem with the language, let me know. All right?"

"Yes, sir."

But as the hearing dragged on, Chester gradually lost his conciliatory tone and reacted to objections from Merriam or Ahmad like a colonel dismayed by a subordinate's challenge to his authority. A typical exchange would go like this:

"Sir, I can—if I could, I'd like to address that issue," Merriam said.

"Pardon me?"

"I'd like to address that issue."

"Well, I'll give you an opportunity to address it in a minute. Sit down, please."

It wasn't the only time Chester cut Merriam off by ordering him to sit.

Chester also took exception to Omar's appearance. "I consider his attire inappropriate. I consider any shirts with logos to better left [sic] for places other than a court of law and a commission," he said to Ahmad. "If possible, by tomorrow I would like that resolved; I think the trousers are fine but the shirt is not."

The pre-trial motions dragged on for hours but Omar didn't appear to follow much of the proceedings. He rarely took his eyes off the television that was broadcasting the hearing, including the occasional close-up shot of his face. Before the hearing broke for the day, Merriam told Chester that he needed help and requested that a senior military lawyer be detailed to the case. Lt.-Col. Colby Vokey, the forty-one-year-old head of defense counsel at Camp Pendleton, the same California Marine base where Chester was stationed, had agreed to take the case and was available for Omar's next hearing in April.

The hearing ended as it began with the whack of Chester's gavel. Outside the hearing room, a presiding officer from another case approached Ahmad. "I want to thank you for the quality of your arguments," he said to him. "You just elevated the process." Ahmad felt sick. "He really thought he had paid me a compliment," Ahmad recalled, "but his comment drove home the point that the price of being professional in that system, legitimized it."

THE COMMISSION ROOM was constructed inside a drab building on a hill with an expansive view of the bay. The U.S. Marines were the first Americans to land there in June 1898, during the Spanish-American War. After Cuba agreed to lease Guantanamo to the United States, the navy constructed an airfield on the windward side of the bay and a building on top of the hill served as a terminal. When the airfield was abandoned for a preferred site on the leeward side, the terminal became a public affairs office. It wasn't being used in 2003 when it was chosen as the site for the commission hearings.

To get inside the building, court observers had to undergo a series of searches, pass through metal and explosives detectors, climb a set of stairs and pass through another metal detector inside the building. Female observers who had the misfortune of wearing underwire bras were taken for a secondary search to assure the authorities that no contraband was being concealed. Visitors were allowed only a pad of paper and one pen. Wire-bound notebooks normally used by journalists were forbidden, which had forced a last-minute run to the NEX the night before the hearing in search of yellow legal pads.

The commission room itself looked like a movie set or a military portable that had been gussied up for the visit of some high-ranking official. A velvet curtain covered one wall and on it hung an American flag and the emblems of the five military forces represented at Guantanamo. A wooden rail separated the lawyers from the three rows of black-cushioned chairs where the spectators sat. Around the room, televisions broadcast the proceedings in real time and on a delayed feed to the media center down the hill.

Omar's case was the second hearing held that day in January. A thirty-eight-year-old Yemeni accused of being an al Qaeda propagandist had appeared before a different presiding officer earlier in the morning. Ali Hamza al Bahlul, a petite man with a confident air, had told the court he would not participate in the hearings. "This life will go on and will be gone at one point because you are going to be ruling in this life, this Earth, and God will be ruling based on justice," al Bahlul said, pausing, and smiling as the Arabic interpreter translated his words for the court. Al Bahlul was given time to read out nine points explaining why he would not participate. One was the fact that he could not represent himself since the commission rules forced him to be defended by a military lawyer. "It doesn't mean I hate all Americans. It means I am the enemy of all Americans who fight. I regard them as enemies," al Bahlul said.

When he was done, he calmly held a piece of paper over his head and turned to the spectators. He had written the Arabic word for "boycott" and made sure everyone in the room understood. "Boycott," he said in English to the reporters. "Boycott," he said again as he turned to the prosecutor. "Boycott," he said to the presiding officer and then settled back in his chair and removed his earphones that provided the Arabic translation.

Guantanamo's chief defense lawyer smiled as he watched al Bahlul's performance from the back of the commission room. Marine Col. Dwight

Sullivan believed the commission rules were stacked against his lawyers and there was no chance of fair trials. This meant the defense had to be political and work outside the courtroom at stoking public outrage so that foreign governments would demand the return of their citizens. The court of public opinion mattered. Sullivan later had black T-shirts made for his lawyers bearing the words, "The Office of Military Commissions Defense" written on the front, and "Boycott" in large Arabic script, across the back.

WHILE CANADA CONTINUED to give silent consent to Guantanamo, criticism in other countries was increasing. Britain, France, Germany and the United Nations were among those calling for the camp to be closed. Adding fuel to the debate was the Pentagon's release of thousands of pages of hearing transcripts about Guantanamo detainees. The U.S. federal court had ordered their release in response to a Freedom of Information lawsuit won by the Associated Press.

The documents provided the first detailed information of who was being held and why. High-profile cases such as Omar's were already known but the documents gave names and stories of dozens of others. One transcript quoted Pakistani prisoner Zia Ul Shah telling a military panel that he hated his American captors but had softened his views once shown photographs of 9/11. "I had never seen Americans. In the beginning when I came here, the interrogations were tough and I started hating them more, but then . . . someone showed me pictures from 9/11. Then I realized they have a right to be angry. My hate toward America was gone."

Another transcript quoted an unnamed military official asking a Yemeni detainee why he had a certain model Casio wristwatch that terrorists favor. "I didn't know that was for terrorists," the detainee replied. "I saw a lot of American people wearing the same watch. Does that mean we're all terrorists?"

The government had been forced to hold the hearings in 2004 after the Supreme Court ruled that prisoners have the right to challenge their detentions. Combatant Status Review Tribunals, or CSRTs, were established to determine if each detainee was a legitimate enemy combatant, which meant, by the government's definition, that they had fought against the United States or allied forces in support of the Taliban, al Qaeda or "associated forces." The Administrative Review Boards, or ARBs, were established to re-examine annually the facts presented at CSRTs to determine whether a detainee still posed a threat to the United States.

Critics said the tribunals were nothing more than show hearings since they permitted the use of hearsay evidence and information obtained by torture. Detainees were also not allowed to see classified evidence or to be represented by a lawyer. Some of the harshest criticism of the process came later from a lieutenant colonel who had worked with the CSRTs for six months in 2004 and 2005. U.S. Army Reserve Lt.-Col. Stephen Abrahams said the evidence used at the hearings was often incomplete, vague and prepared by inexperienced officers. "What were purported to be specific statements of fact lacked even the most fundamental earmarks of objectively credible evidence," Abrahams wrote in a June 2007 declaration for the Supreme Court. "Statements allegedly made by percipient witnesses lacked detail. Reports presented generalized statements in indirect and passive forms without stating the source of the information or providing a basis for establishing the reliability or the credibility of the source. Statements of interrogators presented to the panel offered inferences from which we were expected to draw conclusions favoring a finding of 'enemy combatant' but that, upon even limited questioning from the panel, yielded the response from the Recorder, 'We'll have to get back to you.' "

Omar's CSRT hearing was held without him on September 7, 2004. "The detainee chose not to participate in the tribunal process," the CSRT Decision Report stated. "Because the unclassified evidence only consisted of the Unclassified Summary of evidence and the FBI redacted information statement, the Tribunal relied exclusively on classified information in reaching its decision."

The panel unanimously declared Omar an enemy combatant and concluded that he was mentally and physically capable of participating in the proceedings but chose not to. "The detainee is properly classified as an enemy combatant because he is a member of, or affiliated with, al Qaeda," they ruled.

EVER SINCE THE PICTURE of kneeling, hooded detainees generated outcry in 2002, the physical construct of Guantanamo was debated worldwide. Some portrayed the offshore prison as a Caribbean gulag, while others highlighted the fact that prisoners were getting better food and health care than America's poor. "Detainees are permitted access to state-of-the-art medical care, healthy meals consistent with their cultural and religious requirements, and opportunities to observe their religious beliefs," U.S. Attorney General Alberto Gonzales told a gathering at London's International Institute for Strategic Studies. He said history would portray the United States as a great defender of human rights and rule of law.

In the years since it opened, hundreds of journalists, parliamentarians, dignitaries and other Pentagon-approved visitors have been given tours of Guantanamo. Most began in the vine-covered remains of Camp X-Ray, which had been closed four months after the iconic picture of detainees had been taken. Visitors would coat themselves in insect repellent and suntan lotion and stand inside the cages that once housed prisoners but where a family of banana rats, a possum-like creature indigenous to the area, now lived. The point of the tours was clear, even if the public affairs officers didn't reiterate it often, which they did. *That was then. This is now.* Nothing seemed to irk soldiers more than the media's continual use of the Camp X-Ray picture. Military escorts would show photographers the exact angle from where the 2002 picture was shot and encourage them to shoot the abandoned prison to document the change.

From X-Ray, the tour would move to Camp Delta, where guards had adopted a rather cumbersome greeting using the motto of the base: Honor-bound to Defend Freedom. As a superior would pass, a subordinate would salute and yell: "Honor-Bound, Sir!" The higher-ranking officer would answer: "To Defend Freedom, Soldier." On and on it would go, providing a singsong soundtrack to any walk through the prison.

But what was always lost during these tours was the bigger Guantanamo question. Was the prison itself lawful? And by 2006, there remained uncertainty and many legal challenges.

"I have been to Death Row in Texas, South Carolina, Missouri, Mississippi, Arkansas and Indiana. I have been to more maximum-security prisons than I can recall," wrote lawyer Joseph Margulies in his book *Guantanamo and the Abuse of Presidential Power.*

I have delivered some of the saddest news to men and women behind bars—parents have passed, children have been diagnosed, appeals have been denied. I have broken the news that a client's last chance for a reprieve has been turned down and his execution has been scheduled for a date in the near future. I have visited with clients late at night, in holding cells near execution chambers. Some paced nervously, others sat with a quiet dignity and peace. I have, only once, watched as a client of many years—a 62-year-old great-grandmother—was put to death. But I have never been to a more disturbing place than the military prison at Guantanamo Bay. It is a place of indescribable sadness, where the abstract enormity of "forever" becomes concrete: *this* windowless cell; *that* metal cot; *those* steel shackles.

ON THE MORNING OF APRIL 5, 2006, the double doors of Guantanamo's commission room opened again and Omar was escorted to his seat. His beard was fuller and his form bulkier, although he still looked like a teenager dressed in khaki pants and a checkered button-down. The defense table was more crowded than it had been three months earlier. Sitting behind Ahmad and Merriam was Rick Wilson and standing at the podium, in his Marine olive green dress uniform, was Lt.-Col. Colby Vokey.

It was clear from the moment the gavel came down that things would be different with Vokey in charge. The barrel-chested Texan, with the nickname Danger, had argued cases before Chester at Camp Pendleton and neither man appeared to have much respect for the other. Vokey had spent the last three months researching the rules of the military commissions and couldn't understand why the U.S. government had enacted new rules to try the detainees when the fifty-year-old Uniform Code of Military Justice or even more historic domestic criminal law could have been applied. Vokey was once a Bush-supporting Republican but by the time he came to Guantanamo, he was an Independent furious with the law his government had created.

He had decided he was not going to let Chester run the hearing as if it were a legitimate court. Even seemingly procedural issues—such as how to get Omar's Canadian lawyers appointed to the case as "foreign attorney consultants"—became loud debates between Chester and Vokey. The more they argued, the tighter Vokey clutched the podium before him.

"You have indicated that you want me to designate [the Canadian lawyer] an attorney or a special assistant to the defense. If that is what you want, then I need a brief from you and a motion," Chester told Vokey, his voice tight.

"Certainly, sir. That's—so am I to assume that you have the power to do that?"

"No, I would not assume that. You have asked me for some relief. If you want that relief then you need to file a motion, is what I am saying, and then I will take it up after the government has had an·opportunity to respond."

"I understand, sir," Vokey said. "But this is a little bit indicative of the kind of conundrum we are in all of the time. You are telling us we need to file a brief. We don't know who to request it from, the presiding officer, the appointing authority. There are no rules here!"

"Col. Vokey, there is . . ." Chester began.

But Vokey wouldn't let him finish: "The rules keep changing."

Chester lowered his voice and continued. ". . . a very simple rule. The defense has been reminded of it on at least two occasions through the appropriate review exhibits and in the form of e-mails where they have been reminded if they want relief from the presiding officer, they file a motion."

Vokey wouldn't let it drop. He noted that the Australian lawyers representing David Hicks had already been appointed through an agreement between their government and the U.S., not a court motion. "Now, we can come up with some kind of brief but it seems kind of crazy if the presiding officer does not have the power to act on it, to go to the presiding officer with that issue."

Chester countered, "And one way to learn whether or not I have the authority would be to brief it, argue it here in the courtroom and have me decide it."

"Sure, sir. Another way would be to have clear rules that told us exactly what . ."

"Col. Vokey . . ."

". . . to do before we start."

"If you want the relief," Chester snapped, "brief the issue, serve it on the government and we will take it up."

"Yes, sir."

There was a long pause as Chester tried to get the hearing back on track. Next on the schedule was the *voir dire* where the defense and prosecution had a chance to challenge Chester's impartiality and qualifications. But Vokey stopped him.

"Sir, before we take up *voir dire*, we have another matter to present to this hearing."

"What is that?"

"We have a statement that Omar Khadr wants to make at this time."

"In what—for what purpose?" Chester asked Vokey.

"Before we can go forward with any process with the hearing, he wants to have his say in what is going on here."

"What is it that he wants to address?"

"Sir," Vokey said, "it is a short statement. He is prepared to read it right now."

"Well, why don't you give me an idea what it is he wants to address, Col. Vokey?"

"Concerning the conduct and participation in this tribunal."

"Whose conduct and participation?"

"Mr. Khadr's."

"All right, Mr. Khadr. Do you want to address the tribunal?"

Omar stood and began reading softly from a sheet of paper: "Excuse me, Mr. Judge. I have been punished for—I have been punished for exercising my rights in being cooperative in participating in these military commissions. For that I say with respect to you, and everybody else here, that I am boycotting this procedures (sic) until I am being treated humanely and fair."

"Sir, I will have the statement that he read marked as a review exhibit," Vokey said.

"We can do it at recess," Chester said, then to Omar, "You have indicated that you are boycotting, Mr. Khadr?"

"Yes," he said.

"I need you to please speak up at the microphone so I can hear you."

"Yes," Omar said louder. "I am boycotting these military commissions until I am being treated fairly and humane."

"And for my information," Chester asked, "when you say, 'boycotting,' what do you mean by that?"

"I am not going forward on anything until I am being treated fairly. I am not proceeding. I am not going forward until I am being treated fairly."

"All right, and are you placing limitation on your counsel as to what they do?"

"No."

"Please have a seat. Thank you."

Omar did as directed. He was upset. A week before the hearing, he had been moved into isolation without explanation. For most of 2005, Omar had been held in solitary confinement in Camp Five, but late in the year he was transferred to Camp Four, the camp for "highly compliant" prisoners. Detainees were allowed to live eight to a room; they wore white, ate and prayed together. While still considered a maximum-security prison, the differences between Camps Four and Five were like those between a halfway house and Death Row. Omar would have happily skipped his hearing if it meant he could remain in Camp Four. Navy Cmdr. Robert Durand, director of public affairs for JTF Guantanamo, later told reporters that the transfer was consistent with regulations that stipulated detainees in pre-trial status were placed in isolation. "These measures are largely for the protection of the detainee," he said. But Vokey was livid when he arrived at Guantánamo and heard of Omar's transfer.

Chester was equally furious that Vokey had sprung Omar's statement on him and again asked Vokey to file a brief on Omar's transfer. The two argued back and forth, interrupting each other. It was just nineteen minutes into the proceedings and Chester and Vokey were practically shouting.

"If you want relief from me on that issue," Chester said, "then it is incumbent upon you to, number one, give me a head's up, which you could have done so . . ."

"No, sir," Vokey interrupted, "I could not have done that."

"You couldn't have approached . . ."

Vokey slammed his hand on the podium. *Whack*. "Sir, yesterday afternoon is what we discussed . . . *Whack* . . . all afternoon was that very same issue."

CRACK. Chester's gavel was down.

"We are in recess," he said before quickly storming from the room.

Lt.-col. Colby Vokey was born and raised in Texas and had never left his hometown of Dallas until he joined the Marines at the age of twenty-two. After receiving basic training in Virginia and graduating with honors from the U.S. army artillery school in Oklahoma, Vokey was posted with the 12th Marine Regiment in Okinawa, Japan. In 1991, he served as an executive officer leading a team in Saudi Arabia and Kuwait during Operation Desert Storm. During the mid-1990s, Vokey attended law school and moved with his wife Cindy and two young children to North Dakota. As a military lawyer, he prosecuted and defended dozens of Marines accused of murder, rape, drug charges and even bank fraud, while earning a master's degree in law.

Vokey was later stationed at Camp Pendleton, where he worked out of a dingy, faux-wood-paneled office inside a portable called the pirate's ship because the Marine defense lawyers had acquired the space from another unit and refused to give it back. On a typical day, a steady stream of younger lawyers would come in and out of his office seeking advice, which gave the portable the feeling of a college dorm. Leaning back in his chair, with his hands most often folded behind his head, Vokey would listen patiently to the stories, bending forward only occasionally to spit chewing tobacco into a Diet Dr Pepper can.

His office bookshelf contained the four volumes of the Geneva Conventions, *PowerPoint for Dummies* and *Vietnam—A History*, among other legal and historical books. On an adjacent table, he kept a twisted piece of rocket that had landed dangerously close to his head during the Gulf War.

Vokey was the chief defense counsel of the western region, meaning he oversaw all the Marine defense lawyers in the southwestern United States. It was a busy job that only got more hectic when two cases from Iraq were assigned to his lawyers later that year. The cases became known for the Iraqi towns where the alleged crimes occurred—Hamandiyah and Haditha—and both involved Marines charged in the deaths of civilian Iraqis. Vokey personally took on the defense of Staff Sgt. Frank Wuterich, a twenty-five-year-old Marine squad leader charged with unpremeditated murder in the deaths of twenty-four civilians in Haditha. Wuterich's Marine unit was accused of going on a murderous rampage to avenge the death of one of its own. The victims included men, women and children as young as two. Human rights groups had drawn comparisons between the Haditha killings and Vietnam's My Lai—the attack on hundreds of Vietnamese civilians in 1968 that sparked worldwide outrage and helped change the course of the Vietnam War.

Defending Omar and Wuterich at the same time seemed like a contradiction. Certainly for those who regard war in black-and-white terms, it was difficult to reconcile the case of a civilian charged with murdering a soldier and a soldier charged with murdering civilians. But for Vokey, the cases were both about the laws of war. "I don't have any conflict in my head where I have to switch gears and go from one side to the other, I don't think so at all," Vokey later said. But he was well aware that both cases were politically charged and there were times when that got uncomfortable—the evening, for instance, his daughter gave a speech at a veteran's association and mentioned her dad's role in defending Wuterich. "I didn't dare mention to them that I was doing something in Guantanamo as well," Vokey recalled.

To prepare for Omar's case, Vokey wanted to start in Afghanistan and arranged the trip through the Office of Military Commissions. Prosecutor Groharing decided to go as well, creating an unusual situation where the prosecutor and defense would travel, track down witnesses and take depositions together. By late May, a month after Omar's hearing, Vokey and Groharing landed in Islamabad. Vokey quickly acquired a *shalwar kameez,* the traditional loose-fitting clothing worn by many Pakistanis, and food poisoning that left him incapacitated for a week. Before leaving Islamabad though, Vokey managed to secure a couple of interviews without Groharing's knowledge that helped him understand Omar's history. One was with Khalid Khawaja, the former ISI agent with whom Omar's mother and sister had lived before returning to Canada.

Khawaja said he first met Omar's father in early 2001, although they had likely crossed paths in the late 1980s and 1990s. Ahmed Said Khadr had tried to come back to Canada around the time he was listed by the UN as a terrorist financier. When he crossed the border from Afghanistan, Pakistani officials seized his passport and would not give it back. Someone suggested he go to Khawaja for help. In the end, Khadr became too fearful to travel to Canada so went back to Afghanistan with Abdullah, while the rest of the family continued on to Canada. But by then, Khadr and Khawaja were friends.

Khawaja shared Khadr's vision for an Islamic government and said it was a quest that either man would be willing to die for—a sacrifice he said the West would never understand. "We play only a win-win game," he said in a March 2006 interview with the *Toronto Star.* "For this reason, you cannot win from us. You fight to live; live a comfortable life. We fight to die. You love to live. We love to die."

OVER THE SPAN OF THREE WEEKS, the military lawyers took a whirlwind tour from Islamabad to Peshawar to the U.S. air base in Bagram where they took a helicopter to Khost and on to Jalalabad before returning home. But researching a case in a war zone posed serious problems. Groharing and Vokey were expected to wear their Marine uniforms and full protective gear in Afghanistan and they traveled in a convoy of Humvees. There was nothing that distinguished them from the U.S. soldiers who were trying to take over the Taliban strongholds.

When they finally located the small town where Omar had been captured—the crime scene—almost nothing was as it had been on

July 27, 2002. A new building stood on the rubble of the compound where the battle had taken place. The owner had died and some villagers clearly remembered the battle, but a village elder warned against speaking to American soldiers.

After Khost, the team moved to Jalalabad where Vokey hoped to track down friends of Omar's father and information about the charity projects Khadr ran for the Health and Education Project International. Omar's mother and sister had given Vokey specific instructions on how to reach someone who could vouch for Khadr's charity work. But as the Humvees crept through Jalalabad's narrow streets, Vokey lost hope. "It was a bad idea. If I got out there myself in a *shalwar kameez* . . . maybe." When the convoy inched closer to their destination, something exploded nearby. Suddenly, the street was on fire. Vokey and Groharing were standing in the road as a crowd began to form. Behind them soldiers knelt and raised their rifles. The situation was tense and they needed out. "We're done," Vokey shouted and the soldiers scrambled back into their Humvees. "All it would have taken was someone yelling, 'Oh, the Americans were responsible for the fire' and we were done. With the number of people that were there, I don't care what kind of weapons we had, we were done and we weren't getting out of there," Vokey recalled.

They soon returned to Washington.

By the late spring of 2006, Guantanamo started to unravel both from the inside and out.

Col. Mike Bumgarner's initiatives to end the hunger strike the year before had failed and the mood inside Guantanamo had soured. But Brig-Gen. Jay Hood maintained his optimism as he turned his command over to Rear Adm. Harry B. Harris Jr. in April. "The American people would be proud of the discipline that is demonstrated here," Hood told reporters before leaving.

A month later, on May 18, a riot broke out in Camp Four, where the highly compliant detainees lived. The uprising began when guards saw what looked like a detainee hanging himself. Soldiers ran to stop him but they slipped on a mixture of feces, soapy water and urine that the prisoners had poured down. The prisoners then attacked the fallen guards with broken light fixtures and fan blades. Prisoners in two of the three remaining blocks in Camp Four went on a rampage, ripping down fans and security cameras until rubber bullets and tear gas were brought in. None of the guards or detainees were seriously injured but there was an immediate crackdown on security. There was fear that detainees were plotting other attacks.

A few weeks later, three detainees did execute a well-coordinated plan. Shortly before midnight on June 9, three prisoners—two Saudis and a Yemeni—who were detained in separate cells at Camp One, stuffed clothes under the blankets of their cots and retreated to the back of their cells. All three had been on hunger strikes and had been force-fed. That night the three men had to work quickly before the guards noticed their ruse. They slipped behind the blankets they had managed to hang from the ceilings, stepped up into the stainless-steel sinks in their cells, put their heads through nooses they had somehow woven together from ripped clothing and linens. Each then stepped off the sinks.

By the time the detainees were discovered, they had been without oxygen for more than twenty minutes.

The first deaths at Guantanamo drew international outrage, which was only fueled by the military's reaction. Adm. Harris told reporters the suicides were an act of war. "They have no regard for human life neither ours nor their own. I believe this was not an act of desperation but an act of asymmetric warfare against us." From Southern Command in Miami, General John Craddock told reporters: "They're determined, intelligent, committed and they continue to do everything they can to become martyrs in the jihad." All three men left suicide notes, but the contents have never been revealed.

The Camp Four riot and suicides changed conditions at the prison. Construction was underway for Camp Six, a two-storey indoor prison that could hold about 200 detainees and was modeled after a maximum-security penitentiary in Michigan. The $37-million facility was being assembled with prefabricated sections shipped from the United States. Detainees would live one to a cell but be allowed to interact at assigned times throughout the day.

But by the time detainees were transferred, plans had changed. The recreation area where prisoners were supposed to spend two hours a day had been fenced off into individual cages. The eating area with steel picnic tables was off limits indefinitely so meals were inserted through small slots in the cell doors. Plexiglas and other shields limited contact between the guards and detainees.

Camp Four's bustling population was reduced to little more than thirty as soon as Camp Six was completed. Among those shuffled to Camp Six were eighteen Uighurs—members of an ethnic minority in northwestern China—who had been detained after being sold for a bounty to the U.S. military in December 2001. Their cases had long attracted controversy since the men said they had nothing to do with al Qaeda but instead were opposed to the Chinese government's control of their homeland. The Pentagon had cleared some for transfer, which meant they could be returned to the care of the Chinese government, even though they were still designated enemy combatants. But because China viewed the Uighurs as members of a rebellious minority, the Americans couldn't return them to face torture or execution, so they were stuck. "They have never experienced anything like this at Guantanamo. They pass days of infinite tedium and loneliness," their lawyers wrote in a U.S. Court of Appeals case protesting the conditions of Camp Six. The court petition noted that one detainee's neighbor "is constantly hearing voices, shouting out and being punished. All describe a feeling of despair, crushing loneliness and abandonment by the world."

Omar Khadr was also transferred to Camp Six.

On JUNE 29, 2006, the U.S. Supreme Court issued its ruling in the case known as *Hamdan v. Rumsfeld*. Lawyers for detainee Salim Ahmed Hamdan had argued that the military commission which oversaw the cases of Hamdan, Omar and eight others was unconstitutional. The crux of their argument was that the Bush administration was making all the rules and enforcing them too, ignoring the U.S. government's long-established system of checks and balances.

In a five-to-three vote, the high court agreed, slapping down another administration policy and declaring the military commission illegal. Writing for the court, Supreme Court Justice John Paul Stevens stated that the Constitution gives Congress authority to make rules concerning the laws of war, not the president. Civil rights lawyers and those representing Guantanamo detainees were jubilant. But despite the significance of the decision and the fact that all the charges were now dismissed, the ruling meant little to Omar and the other detainees.

Vokey knew the decision would not end the military commission. He was certain the Pentagon would find another way to try to bring Omar to trial so he continued to build a defense. At the end of the summer, he traveled to Toronto with J.J. Merriam and Marine Sgt. Heather Cerveny, a twenty-four-year-old paralegal who had been assigned to help in Omar's defense. Vokey had met Omar's mother, sister and brother Abdurahman during a previous visit to Toronto, but this was the first time the soldiers would visit their home.

The Scarborough neighborhood where the Khadrs live is a hodgepodge of cultures, where women in tight jeans and tube tops live alongside traditional Muslim women who cover all but their eyes in public. But even with this range of cultures, the sight of the three Americans walking to the Khadr apartment must have turned heads. Vokey, a tall, pale, Marine and rugby player who bears a slight resemblance to actor Liam Neeson, had decided to wear his *shalwar kameez* to the meeting. Merriam was dressed like a preppy college student. Then there was Cerveny, with her blond hair pulled back off her face, in a miniskirt and wedge sandals that revealed her toenails painted with little flowers. But Omar's sister and mother appreciated that they didn't wear their uniforms and were gracious hosts. Over three hours and much food, they discussed Omar's case.

Vokey wanted to tell the family about his visit to Afghanistan and get more information to build a defense. He also wanted to tell the family to stop speaking publicly. He had watched the CBC documentary and read the various news reports and cringed every time he got news that someone in the family had been interviewed. "Every time you open your mouths," he told Omar's mother Maha Elsamnah and his sister Zaynab, "you hurt Omar's case."

Earlier in the summer, Zaynab and her brother Kareem were featured on the front pages of Canada's newspapers after they appeared at a court hearing for a high-profile terrorism case. On June 2, the RCMP conducted the country's largest terrorism sweep since 9/11, arresting seventeen Muslim men and teenagers (one more suspect was arrested later that summer). The group was accused of belonging to what police called a "homegrown" terrorist cell plotting to attack Toronto and southern Ontario targets, including a military base, the Toronto stock exchange and the Toronto headquarters of Canada's spy service. Police had intercepted what they said was a delivery of ammonium nitrate that the group had planned to use to create fertilizer bombs.

The arrests sparked worldwide attention and the parking lot of the courthouse where the accused had their bail hearings became an international newsroom filled with antennas, lights, television cameras and more than a hundred journalists. Many were still there ten days later when Zaynab arrived with Kareem in his wheelchair to support the families of the accused, many of whom they knew. Kareem wore a shirt from his favorite show, *The Family Guy*, an animated Fox series about a dysfunctional family. Kareem's shirt featured Stewie, the baby who speaks eloquently with an upper-class English accent and continually tries to kill his mother and dominate the world. Underneath his picture were the words, "Victory will be mine." Omar's siblings didn't talk to reporters but their presence was enough to make the news.

Kareem had been introduced to the suspects by the eldest accused, forty-three-year-old Qayyum Abdul Jamal. Jamal was a Canadian citizen who had emigrated from Pakistan and had met the younger accused through an Islamic Center where he sometimes led prayers or discussion groups. Jamal was married to Cheryfa MacAuley, a Canadian from Nova Scotia who had converted to Islam. The couple had met when Jamal's first wife was dying and MacAuley helped provide homecare.

When Elsamnah returned to Canada with Kareem, MacAuley phoned Elsamnah to offer support and homecare equipment Kareem might need for his wheelchair, which MacAuley had kept since Jamal's first wife passed away. Kareem liked talking with MacAuley, as did Elsamnah, since the family had largely been ostracized since their return to Toronto. Jamal introduced Kareem to a group of boys closer to Kareem's age—many who were subsequently arrested in the Toronto raid.

Vokey cringed when he saw the coverage of Kareem at the trial. During his visit, he made Zaynab and Elsamnah promise not to speak to the media for one year. "If by then you see it hasn't made a difference, then fine, but give me one year," Vokey said. Then they practiced how to deal with the media once Omar's trial started. Vokey pretended he was a reporter and he held mock interviews. "If the media asks you anything you say three things," Vokey told them. "You say you miss Omar, you say you want him back and you ask why Canada is doing nothing." At first, they stuck to the script, managing to keep on message. But when Vokey asked Zaynab about 9/11 and the arrests of the Toronto suspects, she began to talk quickly and loudly about the unfair targeting of Muslims and how the September 11 attacks were not the work of al Qaeda but of the U.S. government. "No," Vokey stopped her and they tried again.

When they left the apartment, Vokey made a bet. How long before the family spoke out? Merriam said a week. Cerveny gave them a couple. Vokey was most optimistic and said one month.

JUST AS OMAR'S FAMILY GOT TO KNOW his lawyers, he was firing them. In a July 13 letter that would not be delivered until months later, he wrote his mother in his typical penmanship:

> I hope you are not mad at me and am not and will not and dont thank because im not writing you often its because the situation down here thes days but will write when it gets better and please dear mom don't be mad . . . i have fired all my American lawyer i think i'm better with out them and Allah is our defender and helper.

Vokey and the Washington professors had been taking turns visiting Omar whenever the Pentagon would permit. But the cumbersome logistics meant Omar would be left alone for weeks with no word from the outside. The isolation of being held in Camps Five and Six seemed to be taking its toll. In a letter to Ruhal Ahmed, one of the Tipton Three, Omar wrote that he missed his old cellmates and their talks between the bars at Camp Three: "i miss you guys and theos nice day beside each other," he wrote. "any way take care of your self and be very careful in everything you do and feal all ways Allah and that he sees you. About me you know life down hear not the best day pass fast (same old same old) as they say i'm fine as moch as i can i this plase."

Sometimes Omar would refuse visits with his lawyers, but in September he agreed to meet with Vokey and Cerveny and they hoped they could convince him to accept their help. It turned out to be a visit neither Marine would forget; not just because it was the last time they would see Omar but because they were later disciplined for talking about what they saw.

It was a couple of days after Omar's twentieth birthday so Vokey and Cerveny arrived with a cake from the NEX. They had also brought a sketchpad and crayons as presents. Omar was an avid drawer but only had a dull pencil to work with so they hoped the brightly colored crayons would cheer him up. Vokey tried to talk to Omar about the case. Since the Supreme Court had dismissed the military commissions, the Bush administration had been drafting a new law. If the law received Congress's approval, there was a good chance Omar would be facing a murder charge again. Vokey wanted to tell Omar his legal strategy, but Omar had no interest in talking law. He would shake his head or stop talking every time Vokey tried.

Instead, they spent their visits eating the cake and other food they had brought and flipped through car magazines together. Cerveny had read the Harry Potter books, so conversations about the books and the upcoming movie helped fill the hours. Omar seemed to like her. Cerveny had a baby and toddler at home but she wasn't maternal with Omar. "He was more like my little brother," she later said. "We'd just try to joke around."

Vokey and Cerveny left Guantanamo more depressed than ever. They worried that Omar was suicidal. Omar wouldn't talk about the suicides that summer but it was clear they bothered him. The tougher security measures that followed meant that blankets, other "comfort items" and personal possessions were seized. All of Omar's possessions fit into a shoebox and he was upset with the temporary loss of the box of letters and pictures. His toothbrush had also been taken away. "This really, really upset him," Vokey recalled. "I made inquiries but who knows if they ever gave it back to him."

They were also disturbed by what they had heard outside the prison. Commission lawyers stayed on the windward side of the base, living among the other soldiers while visiting their clients. One evening, Cerveny joined a group of sailors at the base's bar. They didn't ask her what she did when she sat down and she didn't tell them. The guards all seemed to have a story of how they had abused detainees and got pleasure from punishing them. Finally, one of them asked Cerveny what she did on the base. When she answered, the conversation abruptly ended.

The next day, she told Vokey what she had heard. He encouraged her to write a formal complaint. On October 6, she did, including the names of the sailors that she could recall.

Steven was a Caucasian male, about 5′8″, 170 pounds, with brown hair and brown eyes. He stated that he used to work in Camp Five but now works in Camp Six. He works on one of the "blocks" as a guard. He told me that even when a detainee is being good, they will take their personal items away. He said they do this to anger the detainees so that they can punish them when they object or complain. I asked Steven why he treats the detainees this way. He said it is because he hates the detainees and that they are bad people. And he stated that he doesn't like having to take care of them or be nice to them. Steven added that his 'only job was to keep the detainees alive.' I understood this to mean that as long as the detainees were kept alive, he didn't care what happened to them . . . From the whole conversation, I understood that striking detainees was a common practice. Everyone in the group laughed at the others' stories of beating detainees.

Vokey had hoped the report would lead to the discipline of the guards, but instead it was Vokey and Cerveny who were punished. Both were told they were under a month-long gag order that forbade them from speaking to the media.

"Maybe I was a little naïve when I agreed to take one of these cases," Vokey later reflected. "I knew it would be political but I didn't realize it would be quite like this."

The U.S. Southern Command ordered Army Col. Richard Basset to conduct an investigation into Cerveny's allegations. He interviewed Cerveny in Camp Pendleton, and, according to Vokey, accused her of making a false claim. The results of his report have never been made public. Vokey and Cerveny would never see Omar again.

MUNEER AHMAD AND RICK WILSON would have their last visits with Omar in the fall of 2006. Before Omar was brought into a room in Camp Five to see Wilson, a guard came and said, "The detainee has requested that you do not touch him during the visit." Omar barely spoke and long moments of silence passed. Even Harry Potter conversations didn't seem to interest him. Wilson, like Vokey, worried about Omar's mental state. When Omar stood to go, Wilson didn't try to hug him as he had in the past. "He wouldn't even shake my hand," Wilson recalled.

A month later, in November, Ahmad came to the base but Omar refused to see him. Ahmad persuaded a guard to give Omar a note that explained that he just wanted to talk and to please reconsider. He would be back the next day.

The next day, he received word that Omar had changed his mind and was being taken to Camp Iguana, the seaside camp outside the confines of Delta where the detainees under the age of fifteen were once held. As Ahmad waited for Omar to arrive, a guard told Ahmad that Omar had again changed his mind. Ahmad ran from the building to try to intercept him. "Wait," he shouted, running to the chain-link fence that separated them. *"Assalaam aliekum,"* he greeted Omar, who looked at him without smiling. *"Waleikum assalaam,"* Omar replied.

Ahmad begged him to come back, "just for fifteen minutes." But Omar replied, "You're not my lawyer any more. I fired you." Ahmad spoke quickly as he looked to the sweating guards on either side of Omar. He told Omar he wasn't interested in legitimizing the commission process, that he understood Omar didn't like Americans and he admitted he might never be able to do anything for him; but could they not just go inside to talk?

Omar relented and the guards led him back inside. For five hours, they spoke in what would be Ahmad's last conversation with Omar. During part of their visit, they filled out a Suduko puzzle. "I'm worried your mind is turning to mush," Ahmad told Omar.

When they emerged from Camp Iguana, the light was soft and the sun about an hour away from setting. Omar and Ahmad walked with the guards to the van that would take Omar back to his solitary confinement. A fence separated them from a cliff that dropped off sharply into the ocean.

Omar stopped and looked out over the waves and setting sun and smiled. "This is the first time I have seen the ocean since I got to Guantanamo," he told Ahmad. For a moment they remained still: two guards, a Washington law professor and a twenty-year-old Canadian looking out at the waves and the world beyond Guantanamo.

10

Law and Disorder

"IN THE NAME OF ALLAH. To my dear and most beloved mother, sisters and brothers and neice [sic]," Omar wrote in an April 2007 letter.

> Peace be upon you and Allahs mercy and blessing here i am back on the lines again and writing you with my hopes that this letter will reach you and find you in best health and good feelings and high spirit and every thing is fine and going will, about me nothing really new as they say same old same old except that i'm starting to dicrease my food i'm not fat but i feel that i'm fat i just think i'm just a little paraoide but all is will besides this everything is good my stomich is a little bad its ok and fine and i really miss you and love you all from my heart and wich to be with you soon and my spirits are high praise be to Allah my writing have changed a little as you might have notice i'm trying to improve my english as you have told me to. NOW how are you all and how is life back in canada i hope its fine and that nobody is giving you all hard time and how is Abdullah and did you win the bill i hope so and he is out untel the government want to make its mind on what it wants to do with him i've really lost hope in them and my only hope is in Allah and how is every body school and life i hope easy and fine and about my commission nothing is going on these day i'm waiting and we'll see what they want to do with me but i dont care let them do what they want for Allah is with us and will allwasch be with us if we beleaved in him. Your ever loving son and brother Omar Ahmed Khadr.

In the bottom right corner of the letter, he drew a heart.

ONLY THREE DETAINEES faced charges under the new military commissions in early 2007: Australian David Hicks, Yemeni Salim Ahmed Hamdan and

Omar Khadr. Omar was charged with murder in violation of the laws of war, attempted murder, conspiracy, providing material support and spying.

A new lawyer had joined Omar's team as J.J. Merriam had been deployed to Germany by the time Omar's second round of charges was laid. Navy Lt.-Cmdr. William Kuebler was a baby-faced lawyer with round glasses, short dark hair, conservative views and a habit of crossing his arms tightly over his chest and sighing before he answered questions.

Military law was Kuebler's second life. His first had ended with the death of his mother in 1999, when Kuebler was just twenty-eight, which led him to question his comfortable, but unfulfilling, life as a corporate lawyer in San Diego. Within two months of his mother's death, he had enlisted in the navy and followed in his sister's footsteps to become an Evangelical Christian. Over the next two years, his new-found faith would be challenged, but also bring him comfort when his father died and his eldest brother, a judge in Arizona, was killed in a car accident in 2001.

Kuebler was a JAG, a navy lawyer officer in the Judge Advocate General's Corps, working at a submarine base in Connecticut when he learned in 2003 that the Office of Military Commissions was looking for defense lawyers. Kuebler volunteered. His first case at Guantanamo was to defend a Saudi detainee named Ghassan Abdullah al Sharbi, who had been captured in Faisalabad, Pakistan, and was accused by the Pentagon of high-level al Qaeda connections. What made the case particularly challenging was the fact that al Sharbi didn't want Kuebler's help. He had made it clear that he would not permit anyone to defend him, and most certainly not an American in uniform. By the time al Sharbi's case was heard in court in 2006, Kuebler had met him just once, only to be told by al Sharbi to go away. When the presiding officer asked al Sharbi if perhaps he wanted a different military lawyer, al Sharbi replied, "Same circus, different clown."

Al Sharbi was bright and U.S.-educated, and made a convincing argument at his hearing as to why he should be able to defend himself. But the presiding officer turned down his request, citing the military commission rules which stipulated that detainees must have military counsel. Kuebler was ordered to defend him.

Self-representation is a right that has been accepted in American law for more than two centuries, a fact that made the order troubling. How could Kuebler ethically defend a client who didn't want his help? Only in rare circumstances, such as a defendant who was mentally unfit to represent himself, could a lawyer be forced to represent an accused. Bar associations could otherwise impose sanctions or revoke a lawyer's license for such an ethical breach.

But what would happen if Kuebler refused a military order? Surely locking up lawyers would not help the military commission's beleaguered image and was something the Pentagon wanted to avoid.

Another lawyer facing the same predicament was Maj. Tom Fleener, an energetic army reservist who seemed to have the ability to make his chin quiver with outrage on cue. Fleener represented Ali Hamza al Bahlul, the alleged al Qaeda propagandist who had dramatically boycotted his hearing. Fleener had also been ordered by a presiding officer to defend his client, even though it was clear al Bahlul wanted nothing to do with him, or the trial. "I was horrified," Fleener said of the presiding officer's decision. "In America, you don't have a justice system like this."

The issue ended up resolving itself with the Supreme Court's ruling in June 2006 that quashed the first military commissions as illegal. Under the Military Commissions Act that was signed into law in October 2006, neither al Bahlul nor al Sharbi was charged (although they remain at Guantanamo as enemy combatants, along with the more than 250 other detainees still there).

The new military commission law allows detainees to represent themselves.

LT.-COL. COLBY VOKEY, Omar's lead counsel, didn't believe Omar would ever get a fair trial at the military commissions and started to look outside the law for answers. He wanted to generate the same public and government pressure that had forced the Pentagon to release other detainees. Omar and David Hicks were the only Western prisoners left at Guantanamo.

David Hicks's father, a modest, simple man who had never left Australia or courted attention before his son was detained in Guantanamo, had been waging a public campaign to bring his son home for years. In July 2003, he went to New York City where he donned an orange jumpsuit and stood inside a cage on Broadway, staring silently at the steady flow of pedestrians as they passed. He had gone to Afghanistan to retrace his son's steps with a documentary film crew. It was a dangerous trip but one that earned him sympathy in Australia. By the end of 2006, his campaign had gained momentum. "This is my son, David," Terry Hicks said on a television ad, over the pictures of his son as a freckled nine-year-old. "He's been missing for five years, held in Guantanamo Bay, without trial." The ad ended with Terry Hicks saying, "Please, let's bring David home."

The "Fair Go for David" campaign was bolstered by Hicks's tireless military lawyer, Marine Maj. Michael Mori, who spent months traveling Australia with Terry, giving interviews, organizing protests and speaking about David to anyone who would listen. The pressure put Prime Minister John Howard on the hot seat as he fought for re-election in 2007. Howard was a Bush ally who had publicly supported Guantanamo and sent troops to Iraq but the outcry forced him to intervene in Hicks's case. In February, he raised the case with U.S. Vice President Dick Cheney during his visit to Australia. By March, Hicks had a deal. He appeared before the military commission and pleaded guilty to a charge of supporting terrorism in exchange for a nine-month sentence he could serve in Australia.

Reaction was mixed. Hicks's plea gave the Pentagon a conviction under the military commission system. But without a trial and with a lenient sentence for someone who had been once classified as the "worst of the worst," it was a feeble victory.

Vokey was worried about legitimizing the military commission and had planned to challenge its legality in Omar's case. But he also recognized that the Hicks deal had one essential outcome. It got Hicks out of Guantanamo. "And I'd plead guilty to the Kennedy assassination if that would get Omar home to Canada sooner," Vokey said. But Vokey didn't have a sympathetic family he could rely on. "Hicks's dad never stood up and said, 'I'd rather my son be a suicide bomber than sell drugs in the streets of Melbourne,'" Vokey lamented.

Instead, Vokey attempted to attract some star power to the case and tried calling around Hollywood. His main target was Bono, the lead singer of the Irish band U2, who, during a November 2006 concert in Australia, interrupted the band's signature song, "Sunday Bloody Sunday," to tell the audience of 50,000, "We call for David Hicks to be brought back to Australia." Bono had also insinuated himself into Canadian politics a few years earlier by threatening to become a "pain in the ass" to Prime Minister Paul Martin if he didn't follow through with his promise to increase humanitarian relief to Africa and help end the scourge of AIDS. Perhaps Bono would come to Omar's aid?

Vokey then turned to Gerry Spence, one of America's most recognized lawyers, as familiar a face on CNN in his trademark buckskin jacket as in the courtroom in his suit. At seventy-eight, Spence had a track record of not having lost a criminal trial or a civil case in more than three decades. "I'm the best lawyer I ever knew," he once told Ed Bradley on *60 Minutes*.

Spence had first come to fame in 1979 with the victory for the family of Oklahoma nuclear-power plant worker Karen Silkwood. Silkwood was an American union activist who died in a mysterious car crash while investigating claims of wrongdoing at the nuclear plant—her story later portrayed in the Hollywood hit *Silkwood*. Spence's roster of clients included big names like Imelda Marcos and a host of underdogs, such as the small ice-cream company that won a $52-million verdict against McDonald's for breach of contract. Spence was also a prolific author; his latest release *Bloodthirsty Bitches and Pious Pimps of Power* was described as targeting the "the new conservative hate culture."

Vokey had attended one of Spence's law courses in October 2005, just a month before the Pentagon first charged Omar. Spence ran a school called The Trial Lawyers College, which was advertised as "dedicated to training and educating lawyers and judges who are committed to the jury system and to representing and obtaining justice for individuals; the poor, the injured, the forgotten, the voiceless, the defenseless and the damned, and to protecting the rights of such people from corporate and government oppression." Vokey had been so impressed with Spence that he invited him to Camp Pendleton to hold a session for about sixty defense attorneys. When Omar's charges were laid again in 2007, Spence invited Vokey to his Santa Barbara home to talk about the case and offer his services.

Vokey was delighted to have Spence join the defense team. He wanted him to take over his role of lead counsel and submitted his name to the Pentagon to start the long security-clearance process.

But not everyone was happy with the decision.

ON MAY 9, William Kuebler and Muneer Ahmad checked into the Sheraton in downtown Toronto, across the street from the courthouse where Dennis Edney and Nate Whitling were making arguments in the extradition case of Omar's brother, Abdullah. When the hearing wrapped up for the day, the four lawyers went to dinner.

The Washington lawyers had come because they were worried. Omar had refused visits from his American lawyers since the fall of 2006 when Muneer Ahmed had spent a few hours with him at Camp Iguana. He had even written a statement saying he wouldn't accept American counsel. "I Omar A. Khadr withdrow every/all/any lawyer from representing me in Habeas Corpus, Military Commission or any form of U.S. Courts. And do not allow any body to do any thing on my behalf in any way in any form of U.S. Court or military Commission. And do not allow any U.S. lawyer to do any thing on my behalf and pull all my atharaizations that I have given them," he wrote on October 30, 2006. In March 2007, Omar reiterated his wishes in a call to his grandmother, mother and sister, Zaynab—the first he had been permitted since his capture. Omar told them he planned on boycotting upcoming hearings and would talk only to his Canadian lawyers.

Kuebler was uncomfortable with bringing Spence on board. And by that time, the proposed defense team had grown significantly. Vokey and Kuebler were appointed as military counsel; Ahmad, Wilson and Kristine Huskey, another Washington lawyer the professors had enlisted, were Omar's civilian lawyers. Now Spence. And where did that leave Dennis Edney and Nathan Whitling?

Kuebler hadn't told Vokey he was coming to Toronto or that he disagreed with him. As far as Vokey was concerned, the whole team would arrive in Guantanamo a few days before Omar's next hearing, which was scheduled for the first week of June. Vokey's plan was to meet Omar and introduce him to Spence. Then Omar for the first time would meet with his Canadian lawyers. Kuebler disagreed with Vokey's plan and didn't think Vokey should be on the case since Omar had fired him. Edney and Whitling, the only lawyers whom they knew Omar would agree to see, should meet him first, and then introduce him to Kuebler.

It wasn't the first time that Omar's legal team had disagreed on how to handle the case; there had been many heated arguments in the past between Vokey and Edney, Edney and Ahmad, and even between Ahmad and Rick Wilson. The law was new, the issues were emotional, and all these lawyers were used to taking the lead. Sometimes it was difficult to tell, however, if the clashes involved the law or egos. Sometimes it was both.

Defending Guantanamo detainees was certainly a difficult task and unquestionably took a toll, both professionally and personally. Civilian lawyers took the cases largely at their own expense. Edney and Whitling had missed family gatherings—birthdays, hockey games, school plays— and spent thousands in travel. For them, defending Omar was a matter of principle but it had a cost.

The military lawyers also made personal sacrifices and had the uncomfortable task of confronting the government they had vowed to serve. They were defending men accused of trying to kill their military brothers fighting in Afghanistan. Defending a Guantanamo detainee was not a good career move for someone hoping to rise up through the ranks.

But something about Guantanamo attracted lawyers. Maj. Tom Fleener liked to say, "Gitmo's got legs." Ahmad called it the "playpen of intellectual curiosity." It was like a law school exercise in real time. History was being made. Previously unknown lawyers became celebrities. Ahmad and Wilson were even featured in the pages of *Rolling Stone* in an article titled "The Unending Torture of Omar Khadr." "I grew up thinking to end up in *Rolling Stone,* you had to play a guitar," Ahmad later laughed. Fleener and Kuebler were profiled in the men's magazine *GQ* and while Kuebler may have been described as looking like an "insurance adjuster" and speaking about fundamental legal rights with the panache of an "office manager discussing, say, the supply of ink cartridges and paper clips: dryly and succinctly, as if he is making statements of fact no more or less obvious than the color of the sky," it was still a profile in *GQ*, a magazine normally reserved for Hollywood heart throbs or professional athletes. "There's a sexiness to Guantanamo which is a bit disgusting," Ahmad would reflect. "The law was so fascinating that it was easy to forget that there were men who continued to be held behind bars."

When Kuebler and Ahmad left Toronto, the lawyers had agreed on one thing. Edney and Whitling must get the blessing from the Pentagon as "foreign attorney consultants" and then obtain access to Omar. Vokey was out of the country, having flown on May 10 to Okinawa, Japan, and then to Hawaii, where he was instructing trial advocacy courses for Marine lawyers.

Two weeks after meeting in Toronto while Vokey was still abroad, Kuebler was on a military flight with Edney and Whitling to Cuba.

OMAR HAD BEEN through the drill many times before. The guards would arrive early in the morning, shackle him and cover his eyes and ears for the drive to Camp Iguana where he would wait for his visitors while chained by the ankle to a hook bolted to the floor. That morning, he remained there for hours until Edney and Whitling were led in. The Edmonton lawyers had been fighting for Omar for four years but had never met him. They could hardly believe they were standing in front of him.

Omar smiled. His family had written to him about his Canadian lawyers and had sent a picture they had taken during one visit, so Omar knew the men before him were Dennis and Nate. But his family hadn't prepared him for Edney's accent. Omar had been exposed to many languages inside Guantanamo and had even picked up a Saudi accent, but he had never heard anything quite like Edney's Scottish brogue. Omar began laughing as Edney talked, cutting through the tension.

For two days, Edney and Whitling tried to get to know Omar. Together they ate the picnic lunch of olives, cheese, bread and candies that they had brought, Edney tussling with Omar to make sure he received his fair share of the sweets. Edney talked almost as much as he listened. He told stories about Omar's family and told him about Kareem and Abdullah. "Your sister Zaynab is always trying to bully me," Edney said and flashed a smile. Edney told Omar about his sons and showed him pictures "You've got to have hope, Omar," Edney told him just before he left. "Without hope, we all die."

"I won't give up on you," Omar replied, "but you'll give up on me. Everyone does."

Omar hugged them and asked Edney if he could keep a photo of Edney's son Duncan in his hockey uniform. Then he gave Whitling a paper origami bird and asked him to give it to his wife as a present.

They did not talk much about the law, but Edney and Whitling did ask Omar whom he wanted to represent him. They made him write it down, confirming what he had written in October. "I, Omar A. Khadr, confirm my decision above," he wrote. "I dismiss all lawyers, including: Lt. Col. Colby Vokey, Capt. John Merriam, Muneer Ahmad, Richard Wilson and Kristine Huskey and anybody else from doing anything on my behalf except Dennis Edney and Nathan Whitling." The letter didn't include Kuebler. "Kuebler had asked me to send his regards to Omar," Edney recalled. "I did that and told Omar he would be okay."

Kuebler gave Omar's note to Guantanamo's chief defense counsel, Col. Dwight Sullivan. Vokey was in Pearl Harbor when Sullivan called his cell phone to tell him. "I felt very helpless. I think I had a pretty good idea why Omar wanted to do it and I don't blame him at all, in some ways I kind of agree with him. But I wanted to go down there, and see Omar and talk to him about it and I would have been at ease saying, okay, this is what Omar wanted," Vokey later said. "I didn't know who was telling him what, why he was making this decision. I still had a lot of information I hadn't been able to talk to him about. I was pretty upset."

On May 29, Vokey's plane touched down in Orange County, and he switched on his Blackberry. An e-mail from Sullivan confirmed he had been "released" from Omar's case.

AFTER FIVE YEARS in custody and nineteen months since the Pentagon first charged him with war crimes, Omar was finally going to trial. On June 4, 2007, Omar was again escorted into the makeshift courtroom on a windswept hill at Guantanamo.

Now twenty, Omar looked remarkably different than he had the year before. His beard was fuller and he was wearing a tan-colored prison uniform and flip-flops, a purposeful move by Edney who wanted Omar to be seen as a prisoner. Omar barely raised his head during the proceedings. Beside him sat Edney, Whitling, and then Kuebler, dressed in his navy whites right down to his leather shoes.

Under the Military Commissions Act of 2006, the presiding officer was called a judge, and Army Col. Peter Brownback, a tobacco-chewing Vietnam vet and former Special Forces soldier, had been chosen to preside over Omar's case. Every hearing at Guantanamo was news and a few dozen journalists and court observers had been flown in for the proceeding. No one expected much would happen. The most pressing question seemed to be Omar's representation. The rules restricted the Canadian lawyers to a diminished role of "foreign attorney consultants." How would Omar deal with Kuebler who had remained on the case because commission rules required a military lawyer be detailed? And the prosecution had raised another issue that could further complicate matters. They asked the judge whether Edney and Whitling were in conflict since they also represented Omar's brother Abdullah, who was in Toronto facing extradition to the United States on charges of providing weapons to al Qaeda. What if the legal strategies of the two cases conflicted? What if something said at Omar's hearing would convict Abdullah, or vice versa?

At 8 p.m., the night before the hearing, both the defense and prosecution had met with Judge Brownback in a closed-door meeting in the commission building. They expected the discussion to focus on what would happen the next morning. "We said, 'Look, we need time,'" Kuebler recalled. "We told him if we went forward that day, there was no guarantee that Omar was going to accept any counsel." The lawyers discussed the issue until Brownback took a short break and left the room. When he came back he was smiling and no longer talking about Omar's lawyers.

"I intend to raise jurisdiction," he said, over-enunciating the word so it sounded more like "jur-is-dic-tion." Brownback paused so the lawyers could absorb what he had just said. Was he telling them that he didn't have the authority to hear the case?

"The judge got up and walked out," Kuebler recalled. "[Prosecutor Jeff] Groharing and I are looking at each other and saying, 'What do you think just happened? What do you take that to mean?' "

The next morning, Brownback wasted little time getting to the issue of jurisdiction. He explained that the Military Commissions Act, under which Omar was charged, gave the Pentagon authority to try "unlawful enemy combatants." But Omar, like all detainees at Guantanamo, had been designated an "enemy combatant" by the Combatant Status Review Tribunal (CSRT). Whether he was "unlawful," or, in other words, not recognized as a legitimate wartime combatant, had never been decided. That meant, Brownback argued, he couldn't face trial.

The prosecution had spent the evening preparing arguments to counter Brownback's position that he lacked jurisdiction to hear the case and assistant prosecutor Capt. Keith Petty was quickly on his feet. Petty argued that it was merely semantics. The CSRT had ruled that Omar had connections to al Qaeda; the military commission law's definition of "unlawful enemy combatants" included those who are connected to al Qaeda. President Bush had also defined "unlawful enemy combatants" in his February 2001 directorate as members of al Qaeda. The definitions, Petty argued, were one and the same.

"Therefore because of Omar Khadr's membership and his participation with al Qaeda, he is an unlawful combatant. Therefore, read together, he is an unlawful enemy combatant," Capt. Petty argued.

If those arguments didn't convince Brownback, then Petty said the prosecution was prepared to present a case to convince him of Omar's status.

"The government will produce a video showing Omar Khadr engaged in unlawful combat activities including wearing civilian attire and making and planting roadside bombs. The bottom line, Your Honor, is that Omar Khadr deserves his day in court. Justice in this case will be best served without further delays. In order to avoid these delays the status of Omar Khadr should not be re-litigated." Petty then paused.

"You stopped?" Brownback asked.

"Yes, Your Honor."

"Okay. I'm not picking on you, Captain Petty, but what does the MCA say the CSRT has to say?"

"Unlawful enemy combatant, sir."

"Does the CSRT say that?" Brownback asked.

"No sir, the CSRT says . . . "

"It doesn't say that, right?"

They debated the definitions, but it was clear Brownback would not be swayed. He called a recess just twelve minutes after the hearing began and returned fifteen minutes later with a seventeen-paragraph ruling, which he read to the court. Brownback paused before reading the final sentence. "The charges are dismissed without prejudice."

Reaction inside and outside the commission room was swift. "If the U.S. government is wise, this will be the fatal blow to the commissions," Jennifer Daskal, the U.S. program director for Human Rights Watch, told reporters who were frantically working to get the news out.

Col. Dwight Sullivan called the ruling "enormous" and hoped it would prompt Washington to move Khadr's case to the U.S. federal courts. "What we've seen today is the latest demonstration that the military commission does not work. There is a readily available alternative which has proven that it does work, which is the federal civilian court system."

"HOW MUCH LONGER must Omar Khadr, a young Canadian citizen, be caught up in the judicial farce that U.S. president George Bush created to deal with 'enemy combatants' after the 9/11 attacks?" began a *Toronto Star* editorial the day after Omar's charges were dismissed. It continued:

> This is legal anarchy. Washington appears determined to rewrite the rules until it manages to secure a conviction. Prime Minister Stephen Harper, who has refused to intervene because Khadr has been "before the courts," should advise Bush that the process is irredeemably tainted. By Canadian standards, this "child soldier" has served virtually a full sentence, without being convicted. Releasing him into Canadian custody, with a bond to keep the peace, should not outrage America's sense of justice, cheapen Sgt. Speer's death or bring the law into disrepute. What it would do is put an end to a travesty of justice.

The dismissal of charges seemed to touch a nerve in Ottawa. Deputy Liberal leader Michael Ignatieff said Canada finally had an obligation to take up the case and rescue Omar from his "legal limbo": "Whatever we may think about Mr. Khadr and his past, he is a Canadian citizen with the rights of a Canadian citizen and the government should take up his case actively with U.S. authorities," he said. Members of the New Democratic Party demanded action.

But the Conservative government did not budge. "It is our understanding that the decision is a procedural one at this stage," said a spokesperson for Federal Affairs Minister Peter MacKay in dismissing Brownback's ruling. A week later, MacKay told reporters he had spoken with U.S. Secretary of State Condoleezza Rice and asked that Omar be given increased access to his lawyers, family and educational materials. But he repeated that Canada would not intervene in the case until "the appeals process has been exhausted."

On July 6, the Pentagon formally announced it would appeal Brownback's decision before a hastily convened military appeals court which had only existed on paper when Omar's charges were dismissed. That same day MacKay was in Washington meeting with Rice and Mexico's foreign affairs secretary, Patricia Espinosa. He repeated that Canada would take a hands-off approach to the case and was satisfied the U.S. would give Omar a fair trial. "[Omar] has legal representation and this is a process, because of the nature of these allegations, which has to run its course," MacKay said. "We have received assurances that he will receive due process."

But the Canadian public was starting to squirm. An Angus Reid Strategies poll showed that just over half of Canadians wanted the Conservative government to bring Omar home. The June survey of 1,058 people found that fifty-one per cent believed Ottawa should actively intervene.

The Canadian Secretary General of Amnesty International, Alex Neve, invited reporters to Parliament Hill on June 14 as he presented the federal government a letter signed by an impressive list of Canadians, urging Harper to personally intervene in Omar's case. Among the signatories were twenty-five current and former politicians, including former Liberal Foreign Affairs Minister Bill Graham, former Prime Minister Joe Clark, nine civil rights organizations and 111 lawyers, academics and social activists. "His case now almost stands alone in terms of individuals who have been abandoned by their governments," Neve told journalists. Neve blamed the government's inaction, under both the Liberals and Conservatives, on the unpopularity of the Khadr family and the general reluctance to press the United States on security issues out of fear of being labeled "soft on terrorism." But he also acknowledged that the family's reputation had kept even grassroots and civil rights groups away from the case until now. "There has been some nervousness about the dynamic associated with the Khadr family," Neve said. "But I think it has become clear as time has passed that this truly is a deep, unforgivable injustice."

Even within Bush's inner circle, criticism of Guantanamo was building. On June 21, the Associated Press reported that a meeting of senior cabinet secretaries and intelligence and military officials was to take place in Washington the next day to discuss closing Guantanamo. Following the report, National Security Council spokesperson Gordon Johndroe said the meeting was canceled but gave no reasons as to why. The White House issued a statement saying President Bush was looking for alternatives to Guantanamo, but denied that a decision to close the internment camp was "imminent."

ON AUGUST 11, 2007, Bill Kuebler stood nervously at a podium in Calgary's Convention Centre. It was the first day of the Canadian Bar Association's annual meeting and before him were members of the organization's governing council. This was Kuebler's chance to convince the country's largest legal organization that the military commissions were deeply flawed and encourage them to take up Omar's cause, much as the law societies in Australia and Great Britain had done for their detainees. He took a deep breath and began a twenty-minute PowerPoint presentation.

"It's a system designed to launder torture," Kuebler said as the audience fell silent. "I know that's a strong statement. But I actually think it is true because the intelligence-collection regime that we established at places like Guantanamo did not use the safeguards and procedures the law enforcement agencies routinely use when gathering information from suspects to ensure that that information is reliable. . . . After 9/11 our government initiated what we call 'the War on Terror,' which involved putting much greater emphasis on gathering intelligence. And to do that it was believed that we needed to establish a system which would permit the aggressive interrogation and detention of people that we believed were involved in international terror. Now it was important that this system take place without the ordinary legal constraints that were applicable to the criminal justice system, or the conventional law of armed conflict. And so we developed an elaborate legal justification for why we could detain and hold terror suspects virtually indefinitely, and subject them to just about any interrogation method or procedure that we deemed necessary. What we obtained from this process is 'evidence,' if you want to call it that, that would not be admissible in any regular court, and so we had to devise some sort of a new set of procedures for essentially laundering this information and being able to obtain convictions from some sort of court."

Kuebler then turned his attack to the military commissions themselves, which he said were merely show trials at Guantanamo, which he called a "modern day Devil's Island," and to the Bush administration's new definition of war crimes. "If you are in a war, there are certain things you can't do. You can't attack a civilian. You can't shoot a PoW who has surrendered. You can't attack a church. What the law of war doesn't do is say that it's illegal to engage in combat. So they created this concept of 'unlawful enemy combatant,' which was unknown both in international law of armed conflict and . . . the United States' understanding of the armed conflict before 9/11, and it essentially says that anyone in Afghanistan who resisted the U.S. invasion was guilty of a war crime."

When Kuebler finished, the lawyers jumped to their feet, clapping wildly.

"I think it's time for all Canadians to be speaking out to end this horrendous lack of due process," association president Parker MacCarthy told reporters at a news conference immediately following Kuebler's speech. By the next day, MacCarthy had drafted a letter to Harper, again demanding that the government negotiate Omar's release from Guantanamo. MacCarthy broke into a previously scheduled session to read from the letter and the lawyers again were on their feet for a standing ovation.

The Canadian Bar Association's endorsement helped Kuebler arrange a meeting the following month with Liberal leader Stephane Dion. "It's a matter of rights," Dion told reporters after the Toronto meeting. "When you have the last Western citizen in Guantanamo and the government is not intervening, then the question comes into our minds: Why other countries did and not Canada?" Dion said. He too called on Harper to personally intervene and demand that Khadr be tried in a civilian court in the United States. "If it's not something that the U.S. authorities are willing to accept, then we will ask for the repatriation of this citizen."

But despite this seeming groundswell of support, Harper did not respond and government spokespeople once again uttered the oft repeated media lines: the Canadian government would not interfere in Omar's trial.

OMAR'S LEGAL TEAM was once again at odds over how to handle the case. Rebecca Snyder, a U.S. Department of Defense civilian lawyer who had worked on the Hicks case, had been assigned to help Kuebler. During a week of speaking engagements in Canada, they started to clash with Edney, who was annoyed that Kuebler had been calling himself Omar's "lead counsel." Edney also demanded to know why he had been shut out of the Dion meeting. Kuebler said Dion had wanted to meet alone with Omar's military counsel. "When pressed," Kuebler wrote in an e-mail to Edney, "there was a concern expressed about the public perception of you and Nate as the 'Khadr family lawyers,' and consequent preference for meeting with Omar's military counsel."

Edney decided to take the issue public. "Here we have Canadian politicians choosing to speak to an American military lawyer who is not Omar's chosen lawyer . . . and who was appointed by the same U.S. authority that gave us Guantanamo Bay and all its horrors," Edney lashed out to the *Globe and Mail* newspaper. Privately, he said he felt "duped."

But Kuebler was equally as furious at Edney's public statements and complained that he was undoing all he had accomplished in Canada to build sympathy. Kuebler also pointed out that the first time he met with Omar, the day after his June 4 hearing, Omar had agreed to Kuebler's representation upon Edney's urging.

Eventually, the two lawyers couldn't talk to each other without yelling.

The night before Edney was scheduled to fly to Washington, where he would take a military flight with Kuebler and Snyder to Guantanamo, Kuebler sent him an e-mail:

Dear Dennis:
This will inform you that I have elected not to take you to Guantanamo Bay with me on 24 September. We extended an invitation to Nate to travel in your stead, but he is unavailable to attend.

Your actions to date leave me with little choice but to conclude that it is not in Omar's best interests, at present, for you to meet with him. Your conduct and statements indicate you are unable to accept (at this time) the necessary realities of our relationship to each other and to the client in light of your status. Previous discussions we have had give me reason to believe that your conduct may be motivated by one or more conflicts of interest, which I require further time to investigate and evaluate. There is almost no doubt in my mind that if permitted to speak with Omar in Guantanamo this week, you would use the opportunity to undermine the relationship we have all invested a great deal of time and effort cultivating between Omar and his U.S. counsel. This would be inconsistent with Omar's interests, and, as a result, I feel that I am obliged (as a matter of conscience and professional responsibility) to avoid fostering the circumstances in which so much damage could be done to this representation.

Kuebler and Rebecca Snyder went to Guantanamo alone and spent time with Omar.

Two weeks after their visit, the newly inaugurated military appeals court overturned Brownback's ruling and reinstated charges against Omar. His trial was once again set to resume.

OMAR'S LAWYERS WEREN'T THE ONLY ONES who were fighting among themselves. News that there were problems in Guantanamo's prosecution office first came to light at the end of September, in the pages of the *Wall Street Journal*. "A dispute between the chief Guantanamo Bay prosecutor and a Pentagon official has roiled the government's system of terrorism trials, the latest snag in a six-year bid by the Bush administration to establish an offshore court," began an article by Jess Bravin. "According to people familiar with the matter, the prosecutor, Col. Morris Davis, has filed a formal complaint alleging that Brig. Gen. Thomas Hartmann, legal adviser to the administrator overseeing the trials, has overstepped his mandate by interfering directly in cases. . . . The dispute between the two Air Force officers has left the prosecution office in disarray, according to officials familiar with the matter. Prosecutors are uncertain who is in command and which cases they should pursue. Col. Davis has refused to file additional charges against Guantanamo inmates until the dispute is resolved."

Under the Pentagon's regulations, Guantanamo's chief prosecutor reports to a legal advisor, who is supposed to be impartial, Davis argued.

"If someone above me tries to intimidate me in determining who we will charge, what we will charge, what evidence we will try to introduce, and how we will conduct a prosecution then I will resign," Davis said in a written statement to the newspaper.

This wasn't the first time there had been a scandal in the prosecution's office. In 2004, two U.S. Air Force prosecutors quit, saying they couldn't participate in what they viewed as rigged trials. Capt. John Carr and Maj. Robert Preston accused fellow prosecutors of acting unethically by ignoring allegations of torture, failing to provide the defense with potentially exculpatory evidence and withholding information from their superiors. The Pentagon launched an investigation but concluded that the claims were unfounded.

Davis's allegation about political interference was a tremendous blow, since the outspoken colonel had been the Pentagon's most ardent supporter. At the January 2006 press conference where Davis called Omar a terrorist and lambasted the media for its sympathetic coverage, he spoke in glowing terms about the military commissions. "We want the world to see that we are extending a full, fair and open trial for the terrorists who attacked us," Davis said. "Full, fair and open" were three words that Davis said often. "If I hear 'full and fair trial' one more time, I am going to be sick," Maj. Tom Fleener had told reporters.

But Davis never strayed off message. "It would suit me if these trials were broadcast on Court TV so everybody could watch because the mystery adds the aura that there's something shady going on and there's not, we'd like to have it as open and transparent as possible," he said in an interview with the *Toronto Star* in June 2007.

Davis had a carefully constructed media strategy in which he viewed it as his job to counter the widespread criticism about Guantanamo. "To maintain the public's trust and confidence, particularly considering today's age of instantaneous access to news and information, requires greater effort and more attention than ever before," Davis wrote in the *Air & Space Power Journal* under an article titled "Effective Engagement in the Public Opinion Arena: A Leadership Imperative in the Information Age": "Proactive engagement enables the military to help shape the debate and maximize or mitigate, as the case may be, its influence on public opinion. It is time to take the offensive and influence the story rather than wait until forced to go on the defensive."

Davis's allegations sparked a Pentagon investigation, which concluded that there wasn't any undue interference by Hartmann, the legal advisor. As he had threatened to do, Davis resigned and, all of a sudden, the Pentagon's cheerleader turned critic.

"As things stand right now," Davis said in various media interviews after his departure. "I think it's a disgrace to call it a military commission—it's a political commission."

WHO IS OMAR KHADR NOW? No one really can say. His family has talked to him only in two hour-long phone calls and through censored, superficial letters. His lawyers have met him only a handful of times. There have been at least three rotations of guards in the time he has been detained. Interrogators have come and gone. Perhaps the most consistent visits he has had have been with the Canadian Foreign Affairs bureaucrats who have had "welfare visits" with Omar in 2006 and 2007. But the Canadian government will not allow them to speak publicly.

Omar has interacted with other detainees; some likely even knew his father or maybe ranking al Qaeda members, and others, like Britain's Tipton Three, were cleared of any wrongdoing. His answers to psychological tests show he is likely suffering from Post-Traumatic Stress Disorder and harbors suicidal thoughts, but he has never undergone an independent psychiatric examination. The Pentagon maintains he's a danger if released.

There's likely no consensus among those who have met Omar since his July 27, 2002, capture as to who the twenty-one-year-old has become. And it's likely in that time there have been many Omars.

On November 8, 2007, Omar appeared again before Justice Brownback for his arraignment. In overturning Brownback's dismissal of the charges, the three-member military appeals court ruled that Brownback did have jurisdiction to hear the case but should hold a mini-hearing to determine first if Omar was an "unlawful enemy combatant" as the Military Commissions Act requires.

Edney and Kuebler still had not settled their differences by the time of the hearing, so only Whitling traveled to Guantanamo and met with Omar. "The rules of the military commission say, of course, that Canadian lawyers cannot be the trial counsel in this proceeding," Whitling told reporters. "I don't think any of us are particularly happy about that, but the rules are what they are and we're working within them, certainly it's our view that Omar needs to be represented by counsel. If it can't be us, it should be Lt.-Cmdr. Kuebler."

Once again, the hearing did not last long. The prosecution had surprised Omar's lawyers with new evidence two nights before the hearing—a statement from a government witness to the 2002 firefight who prosecutors said could give the defense exculpatory evidence. Brownback said he wasn't going to allow the hearing to go forward until the defense had time to prepare and examine the new information, much to the prosecution's annoyance.

Omar came to the November 2007 hearing as a man. His beard was thick and his curly hair long and tucked under a cap. He wore a white prison uniform, meaning he had been designated as "highly compliant." It also meant that he had been transferred to Camp Four where the detainees ate and prayed together. Omar later told his family in a December 2007 phone call that he had been working on his English and reading more often. Sometimes he played basketball with the other prisoners.

This time Omar appeared relaxed in the courtroom. He looked around, smirked at the reporters and even laughed when Brownback made a few jokes during the proceeding. At one point, he draped his arm over the back of his chair, trying to lean back, until a guard told him to put his hands back in front of him. The hearing lasted less than two hours.

Two days later the lawyers, journalists, government spokespeople and human rights observers who had been brought to the island to watch Omar's hearing, left on a military flight to Washington.

And Omar went back to his cell.

Afterword

The Pentagon wants Omar Khadr's case wrapped up before the U.S. presidential election in the fall of 2008. Prosecutors chose his case as one of the first partly because they thought it would be the most straightforward. "One of the attractions of that case was that it's stuff that people understand," Guantanamo's former chief prosecutor, Col. Moe Davis, told me. "It's not like some of the other facilitators and stuff where it's kind of like chasing a money trail and plane tickets, connecting the dots to show how this guy facilitated terrorism. Murder is something that everybody understands. It's not one where you have to explain the legal theory behind it—people get it."

But Omar hasn't been charged with murder under its traditional definition and the case has been anything but straightforward. As his lawyer Lt.-Cmdr. Bill Kuebler says, "Omar Khadr is not alleged to have strapped explosives to his back and gone into a shopping mall or hijacked airplanes." Omar is charged with "murder in the violation of the laws of war," and the laws of war were re-written by the U.S. administration after 9/11.

At the time this book was written, there were many court challenges outstanding and international pressure on the Canadian government to demand Omar's repatriation was starting to build. In December 2007, Britain's top five legal bar associations condemned the Canadian government for not intervening in Omar's case. Radhika Coomaraswamy, the UN Special Representative for Children in Armed Conflict, launched a formal protest about Omar's case with John Bellinger, senior legal advisor to U.S. Secretary of State Condoleezza Rice.

At the beginning of 2008, the most pressing question was whether Omar should be considered a child soldier in need of protection, not prosecution. Kuebler argues that trying Omar for war crimes he allegedly committed at fifteen would violate international laws for armed conflict that protect children under the age of eighteen. This is not, Kuebler contends, what Congress intended when approving the Military Commissions Act. The Pentagon maintains that international law allows the prosecution of someone fifteen years or older, and as Davis has often pointed out, Omar was fifteen years and ten months old at the time of his capture.

Davis also notes that fifteen-year-olds are regularly prosecuted in Canada and the United States for crimes. But again, Khadr is not charged in a domestic court. "We prosecute children for crimes. We hold them criminally responsible on the general theory that at a certain age you require a basic understanding of right and wrong and you can be held accountable for your actions," Kuebler explained.

"There's a general idea that, hey, a fourteen- or fifteen-year-old probably knows that it's wrong to steal, it's wrong to kill, it's wrong to do various things that are anti-social. In war, those norms don't apply. In war, it is okay to kill, it is okay to destroy property, it is okay to do things [that are] not otherwise okay in normal life to do."

That's why, Kuebler argues, children who were indoctrinated into war can't be expected to understand the laws of armed conflict. He asks, "Is it any way reasonable to expect a child to understand these highly nuanced, sophisticated concepts of the war of armed conflicts that say you can kill people but you can only kill people if you're wearing certain clothes?"

There's another question to ask. Did Omar throw the grenade that killed Christopher Speer? Until February 4, 2008, the assumption had been that when the grenade was thrown, Omar was the sole survivor in the compound. But a document that was mistakenly released to reporters during Omar's pre-trial hearing in February showed that wasn't the case. The five-page document is based on the testimony of an unnamed U.S. commando, referred to as OC-1, in which he describes the moments after the grenade was thrown. It states:

> He heard moaning coming from the back of the compound. The dust rose up from the ground and began to clear, he then saw a man facing him lying on his right side . . . The man had an AK-47 on the ground beside him and the man was moving. OC-1 fired one round striking the man in the head and the movement ceased. Dust was again stirred by this rifle shot. When the dust rose, he saw a second man sitting up facing away from him leaning against the brush. This man, later identified as

Khadr, was moving . . . OC-1 fired two rounds both of which struck Khadr in the back. OC-1 estimated that from the initiation of the approach to the compound to shooting Khadr took no more than 90 seconds, with all of the events inside the compound happening in less than a minute.

The document confirms that no one saw Omar throw the grenade. But Guantanamo's current chief prosecutor, Army Col. Lawrence Morris, told reporters the day after the document's release that the lack of an eyewitness will not harm the Pentagon's case. "We're confident," Morris said, "that we'll prove the case beyond a reasonable doubt once we get to the courtroom."

Appendix
List of Principal Characters

Muneer Ahmad: A Washington law professor who first visited Omar Khadr in November 2004. He represented Omar before the military commissions at Guantanamo Bay until Omar fired him in 2007.

Amer Ahmed: Canadian friend of Essam Marzouk who stayed with the Khadr family while in Pakistan. Killed by U.S. air strikes on al Qaeda training camp in Afghanistan in August 1998, two weeks after the bombings of the American embassies in Africa.

Ruhal Ahmed: A British citizen captured in Afghanistan and detained in Guantanamo Bay for two years until his release in 2004. Became known as one of the "Tipton Three" because he was arrested with two of his childhood friends from Tipton. Lives with his family in West Midlands.

Saif al Adel: His real name is not known although it's suspected he may be a former Egyptian military officer, Mohammed Ibrahim Makkawi. Became al Qaeda's military commander after 9/11. Lived in the same neighborhood as the Khadr family in Kabul.

Yaqoub Al Bahr: Zaynab's second husband and father of Safia. He is believed to be a Yemeni whose real name is Sameer Saif. Now living in Saudi Arabia.

Abd al Hadi al Iraqi: An advisor to Osama bin Laden whose real name is Nashwan abd al-Razzaq abd al-Baqi. He was held in an undisclosed location by the CIA until his transfer to Guantanamo Bay where he remains today.

Hamza al-Jowfi: An Egyptian leader who after 9/11 took on greater responsibility in al Qaeda, reportedly as a weapons purchaser. His wife, Umm Hamza, died while giving birth as the family hid in Waziristan in 2002.

Ibn al Khattab: A mujahid who came from Saudi Arabia to Afghanistan to join the jihad in 1980s. Went to Chechnya in 1994 and became an internationally recognized figure in the Muslim separatists' fight against the Russian government. Killed in 2002 allegedly by a poisoned letter delivered by Russia's Federal Security Service.

Abu Faraj al-Libi: Commander of Libyan forces in Afghanistan whose real name is believed to be Mustafa al Uzayti. U.S. president George W. Bush described him as one of Osama bin Laden's "top generals" when he was captured in 2005. He was held in an undisclosed location by the CIA until his transfer to Guantanamo Bay where he remains today.

Abdullah Almalki: A Canadian engineer born in Syria who worked with Ahmed Said Khadr in Pakistan with Human Concern International. Investigated by the RCMP and tortured and detained without charges for two years in Syria. Now lives in Ottawa with his family.

Abu al Walid al Masri: Egyptian Mustafa Hamid who is often referred to as al Qaeda's ideologue but has written pieces critical of the terrorist organization. Former husband of Australian Rabiyah Hutchinson and father-in-law of Saif al Adel. Captured in Iran.

Abu Hafs al Masri: Member of Ayman al Zawahiri's al Jihad who became al Qaeda's military commander. His real name is Mohammd Atef. Killed by an American air strike in November 2001.

Ayman al Zawahiri: An Egyptian doctor and leader of al Jihad. Worked at the Kuwaiti Red Crescent Society where he met Ahmed Said Khadr in 1986. Became ideological leader of al Qaeda once he joined forces with Osama bin Laden in 1996. His whereabouts are unknown.

Abdullah Anas: An Algerian mujahid who fought with Ahmed Shah Massoud, whose real name is Boudejema Bounoua. Was close with Abdullah Azzam and Osama bin Laden. Now an imam at London's Finsbury Park mosque.

Maher Arar: A Canadian engineer born in Syria who was part of an RCMP terrorism investigation. He was arrested and rendered by the U.S. to Syria where he was tortured and held without charges based partly on erroneous intelligence from Canada. The Canadian government issued an apology and $11.5 million in compensation. He lives in Ottawa with his family.

Abdullah Azzam: An influential Palestinian cleric who issued a *fatwa* calling Muslims to the jihad against the Soviets in the 1980s. He was murdered in a November 1989 bombing that remains unsolved.

Nazim Baksh: A CBC producer specializing in national security issues who co-produced the March 2004 documentary titled, "Al Qaeda family" featuring Abdurahman Khadr.

Moazzam Begg: A British citizen detained in Pakistan after 9/11 and held with Omar Khadr at Bagram air base before his transfer to Guantanamo Bay. Was released in January 2005 and now lives with his family in Birmingham. He wrote about his experiences in a book titled *Enemy Combatant*.

Osama bin Laden: Founder of al Qaeda whose whereabouts now unknown. Born in Riyadh in January 1958, he had four wives who became known as Umm Abdullah, Umm Hamza, Umm Khaled and Umm Ali (he divorced his fourth wife while living in Sudan).

Peter Brownback: An army colonel currently presiding as the judge over Omar Khadr's war crimes trial.

George W. Bush: The 43rd President of the United States. Declared in February 2002 that detainees at Guantanamo Bay were not entitled to protections of the Geneva Conventions.

Robert Chester: A Marine colonel who served as the presiding officer during Omar Khadr's first military commission hearing in 2006.

Jean Chrétien: Canada's 20th Prime Minister. Retired in 2003 after thirteen years as Liberal Party leader.

Damien Corsetti: A former U.S. Army interrogator who met Omar Khadr at the American base in Bagram. He was charged with prisoner abuse but acquitted and resigned from the military with an honorable discharge.

Morris (Moe) Davis: The former Chief Prosecutor of Guantanamo's Office of Military Commissions who called the sympathetic portrayal of Omar Khadr's case "nauseating." He stepped down from his position in October 2007 citing political interference in the process.

Stockwell Day: Canada's Public Safety Minister since February 2006. Served as the Opposition's Foreign Affairs Critic before the Conservative Party won a minority government in 2006.

Abdul Rashid Dostum: An Uzbek commander who has often switched his loyalties in the fight for Afghanistan. After 9/11 he joined forces with the Northern Alliance and rounded up hundreds of prisoners for the U.S. Forces. Most recently a member of Afghanistan's opposition party, the United National Front.

Dennis Edney: Omar Khadr's Canadian lawyer. Lives with his family in Edmonton.

Ahmed Elmaati: An Egyptian-born Canadian investigated by the RCMP for terrorism offences. He was detained in Syria and Egypt and held without charges before being released. He lives in Toronto. His brother Amer, remains wanted by the FBI, his whereabouts unknown.

Maha Elsamnah: Omar Khadr's mother. Born in Egypt to parents of Palestinian decent. Grew up in Saudi Arabia before coming to Canada when she was seventeen. Married Ahmed Said Khadr.

Helmy Elsharief: A Canadian born in Egypt who worked briefly for Human Concern International and co-founded Health and Education Project International with Ahmed Said Khadr.

Jim Gould: A career Foreign Affairs official who visited Omar Khadr in Guantanamo when he was the deputy director of the department's International Security Branch. Now retired and living in Ottawa.

Bill Graham: Canada's Foreign Affairs Minister from January 2002 until July 2004 when he became the Liberal Party's Defence Minister. Retired in July 2007.

Jeff Groharing: A Marine major assigned to prosecute Omar Khadr during the military commissions.

Stephen Harper: Sworn in as Canada's 22nd Prime Minister on February 6, 2006. Co-founded the Conservative Party of Canada in 2003.

Gulbuddin Hekmatyar: The Pashtun leader of the Hezb-e-Islami who enjoyed the backing of the Pakistani government during the Soviet occupation. Responsible for the deaths of thousands during the Afghan civil war in the early 1990s. Fled to Iran when the Taliban took power but returned after 2001. His whereabouts unknown.

David Hicks: An Australian accused of connections to the Taliban and held at Guantanamo Bay for more than five years. After serving a nine-month sentence at home he was set free in December 2007.

Aly Hindy: A Canadian engineer born in Egypt who serves as an imam at the Salaheddin mosque in Toronto. Longtime friend of Ahmed Said Khadr.

Jack Hooper: Former head of Canada's spy service, the Canadian Security Intelligence Service (CSIS). Retired in April 2007 to western Canada.

Rabiyah Hutchinson: An Australian Muslim convert of Scottish heritage. Married to a follower of the Jemaah Islamiyah before going to Afghanistan and marrying Abu al Walid al Masri. Now living back in Australia.

Abu Imam: A Moroccon spy who infiltrated al Qaeda camps in the 1990s. His identity is unknown but he wrote *Inside the Jihad* under the pseudonym Omar Nasiri.

Abdul Kareem Khadr: The youngest Khadr son born in Pakistan in 1989 (later became a Canadian citizen). Shot and partially paralyzed at the age of 13, during the October 2003 fight with Pakistani forces when his father was killed. Now lives in Toronto with his mother and sisters.

Abdullah Khadr: The eldest Khadr son, born in Ottawa in 1981. Currently in a Toronto jail fighting extradition to the United States where he has been indicted for terrorism offences. Boston prosecutors allege he procured weapons for al Qaeda both before and after his father's 2003 death.

Abdurahman Khadr: Born in Bahrain in 1982 (later became a Canadian citizen), the second eldest Khadr son. Captured in Afghanistan in November in 2001 and agreed to work for the CIA. Returned to Canada in 2003. Currently lives in Toronto.

Ahmed Said Khadr: Born in Egypt in 1948 and came to Canada to complete his master's in engineering. Married Maha Elsmanah and had seven children, one of whom died as an infant. Moved to Peshawar in 1985 where he became closely aligned with Osama bin Laden and Ayman al Zawahiri. Accused of financing al Qaeda's attacks. Killed by Pakistani forces in October 2003.

Ibrahim Khadr: The third-born son in the Khadr family who died from heart problems in 1988 when he was two.

Maryam Khadr: The youngest Khadr child born in 1991. Lives in Scarborough with her mother, sister and brother, Kareem.

Omar Khadr: The second youngest Khadr son born in Toronto in September 1986. Captured on July 27, 2002, after a firefight with U.S. forces in Afghanistan during which Sgt. Christopher Speer received fatal wounds. Currently in Guantanamo Bay awaiting trial for war crimes.

Zaynab Khadr: The eldest Khadr child, born in Ottawa in October 1979. Twice divorced and mother of daughter Safia. Currently living in Scarborough and under investigation by the RCMP for terrorism offences.

Khalid Khawaja: A former air force pilot and member of Pakistan's Inter Intelligence Service. Once close with Osama bin Laden and Jamaat al Fuqra leader Sheikh Mubarak Ali Shah Gilani. Allowed Maha Elsamnah and her children to live with his family after Ahmed Said Khadr was killed in October 2003.

William Kuebler: Navy lieutenant commander assigned to defend Omar Khadr in February 2007. He lives in Washington with his family and is currently Omar's chief military counsel.

Peter MacKay: Appointed Canada's Minister of Defence in August 2007 in Stephen Harper's Conservative government. Was formerly Canada's Foreign Affairs Minister.

Essam Marzouk: An Egyptian and former Vancouver resident who was tried and convicted during a 1999 trial for connections to Ayman al Zawahiri's al Jihad. Met Ahmed Said Khadr during early days of jihad against the Soviets and convinced Vancouver friend Amer Ahmed to come to Afghanistan.

Ahmed Shah Masood: Pashtun warlord revered for his military skills during the jihad against the Soviets. He joined forces with President Burhanuddin Rabbani, later becoming the head of the Northern Alliance when the Taliban came to power. He was assassinated on September 9, 2001.

Layne Morris: Retired U.S. Special Forces soldier blinded in one eye during the July 27, 2002, firefight where Omar Khadr was captured. Now lives in Utah with his wife Leisl and four children.

Azza Nowhair: Ayman Zawahiri's wife who was friends with Maha Elsamnah. She was killed with her daughters in a U.S. air strike in November 2001.

Keith Petty: An army captain assigned to prosecute Omar Khadr during the military commissions.

Ahmed Ressam: An Algerian who lived in Montreal after training at an al Qaeda camp in Afghanistan. He was arrested crossing into the United States in December 1999 with a trunk full of explosives destined for Los Angeles Airport. He was convicted in 2005 and currently serving a twenty-two-year sentence in a Seattle prison.

Abdul Rasul Sayyaf: Afghan warlord who was supported by Saudi Arabia during the jihad against the Soviets. He was at times closely aligned with both Ahmed Shah Masood and Osama bin Laden. He is now a member of Afghan president Hamid Karzai's government.

Christopher Speer: The twenty-eight-year-old Delta Force soldier who was fatally wounded in the July 27, 2002, firefight where Omar Khadr was captured. Left behind his wife Tabitha and two children, Taryn and Tanner.

Abu Ubaydah: Zaynab's first husband whose real name is believed to be Khalid Abdullah. Now jailed in Egypt after a 1999 trial in Cairo where he was sentenced for connections with Ayman al Zawahiri's al Jihad.

Colby Vokey: A Marine lieutenant colonel assigned to defend Omar Khadr at the military commissions in late 2005. In 2007, Omar fired him and Lt.-Cmdr. Bill Kuebler became the lead counsel in the case.

Nathan Whitling: Omar Khadr's Canadian lawyer. Lives with his family in Edmonton.

Rick Wilson: A Washington law professor who first visited Omar Khadr in November 2004. He represented Omar before the military commissions at Guantanamo Bay until Omar fired him in 2007.

James Yee: A U.S. Army chaplain who served at Guantanamo Bay for ten months until he was arrested in September 2003 on suspicion of terrorism offences and kept in isolation in a South Carolina brig. He was later cleared of all charges and left the military.

Notes

Unless otherwise noted, quotes are from interviews with the author.

Chapter One: "Shoot Me"

1 **The grenades came down:** details of the battle were reconstructed through interviews with soldiers Layne Morris, Mike Silver and Scotty Hansen.

4 **They looked to be in:** an examination of photos of the three deceased men, identified as KIA 1, 2, 3.

Then someone from a nearby: Attachment B, in a defense pre-trial motion submitted at the February 4, 2008, military commission for Omar Khadr. Document details the testimony of a U.S. commando identified only as OC-1.

The ABC News feed: Michelle Shephard and Scott Simmie, "Big Apple on guard – Giuliani recalls spirit of the Blitz," *Toronto Star*, October 8, 2001.

5 **New Yorker Lucille Ferbel:** interview with author, Times Square, New York, October 7, 2001.

"There is nothing to negotiate": Kathy Gannon, "U.S. launches second week of air attacks, police battle Taliban sympathizers in Pakistan," Associated Press, October 14, 2001.

In the end, it took: "Operation Anaconda: Taking the Fight to the Enemy of Afghanistan," *Army Magazine*, April 1, 2002.

6 **Put two head shots:** Stephen Kinzer. "Commandos Left A Calling Card: Their Absence," *The New York Times,* September 26, 2001.

7 **Chris Speer, the youngest:** details of Speer's life were provided by Tabitha Speer, although she would not confirm Speer was a member of Delta Force.

8 **His roommate at the Carlisle Barracks:** Barry Hugo, "Fallen Heroes of Operation Enduring Freedom," www.fallenheroesmemorial.com.

9 **But Layne Morris:** details of Morris's life were provided through interviews with Morris, his wife Leisl and children.

12 **I can assure the parents:** Paul Duggan, "Father Recalls Son For Whom Army Was 'My Other Family,'" *Washington Post*, January 6, 2002.

Chapter Two: Al Kanadi

17 **Maha Elsamnah was:** interview with author.

18 **Khadr was the son:** interview with Ahmed Fouad Khadr.
partly due to a speech impediment: ibid.

19 **he was almost thirty:** interview with Qasem Mahmud.

20 **Khadr had joined:** interview with Maha Elsamnah and Zaynab Khadr.
Khadr had arrived in Canada: ibid.

21 **Khadr would ask his wife:** ibid.

22 **I remember this:** interview with Azzam Tamimi.

24 **Others in Peshawar:** *The 9/11 Commission Report*, p. 55.
The most influential: interview with Abdullah Anas; Lawrence Wright, *The Looming Tower*, pp. 95-98.

25 **set up an organization:** *The 9/11 Commission Report*, p. 56. Rohan Gunaratna, *Inside Al Qaeda*, pp. 18-19.
Lajnat al Dawa: Terry McDermott, Josh Meyer and Patrick J. McDonnell, "The Plots and Designs of Al Qaeda's Engineer Khalid Sheikh Mohammed, the man believed to be behind 9/11, hides in plain sight—and narrowly escapes capture in Pakistan," *Los Angeles Times*, December 22, 2002.
The U.S. Treasury Department: statement of Richard A. Clarke before the U.S. Senate Banking Committee, October 22, 2003.
joined permanently in 1998: interview with Kaleem Akhtar.
he stood out from other Arabs: interview with Abdullah Anas.

27 **In Peshawar, now with:** interview with Maha Elsamnah.

28 **Some of them are:** Jack Cahill, " 'Pretty toys' maiming Afghan kids Soviet troops disguise mines Canadian says," *Toronto Star*, September 25, 1986.
The year Omar: interviews with Maha Elsamnah, Zaynab Khadr, Abdullah Anas.
"Now we want to speak": Lawrence Wright, *The Looming Tower*, pp. 54-56.

29 **Osama bin Laden sometimes:** ibid., p. 127, interview with Maha Elsamnah.
It was not until: Peter Bergen, *The Osama bin Laden I Know*, pp. 49-50, interview with Abdullah Anas.

32 **On August 11:** *United States v. Enaam M. Arnaout.* Wright, *The Looming Tower*, p. 131.

"I am only one person: Peter Bergen, *The Osama bin Laden I Know,* p. 123.

The name 'al Qaeda': Osama bin Laden interview with al Jazeera correspondent Tayseer Alouni in October 2001. Translated by CNN and posted, http://edition.cnn.com/2002/WORLD/asiapcf/south/02/05/binladen.transcript/index.html.

33   **Azzam sought advice:** interview with Abdullah Anas.

  But when Khadr: ibid.

  "I'm not a spy": interview with Maha Elsamnah and Zaynab Khadr who recall Khadr telling them about the confrontation. Abdullah Anas also has a similar recollection. There is also a footnote in *United States v. Enaam M. Arnaout* that mentions a "dispute" that broke out between two relief organizations. Although the Saudi Red Crescent Society is mentioned in the documents, Abdullah Anas says the dispute was over the funding of al Tahaddi.

  The city buzzed: interview with Abdullah Anas.

  The trial was held: *United States v. Enaam M. Arnaout,* interview with Abdullah Anas, recollections of Khadr as told to his daughter, Zaynab.

34   **Khadr was visibly distraught:** interview with Abdullah Anas.

  "Ahmed Khadr is": Bill Taylor, "Worker seeks aid for Afghan kids," *Toronto Star,* October 10, 1989.

  He no longer: video titled "Afghanistan, The Untold Story," from September 1991 at the Markham Islamic Centre.

  "Muslim people have": ibid.

35   **HCI officials maintain:** interview with Kaleem Akhtar.

  His son Abdurahman: interview with Abdurahman Khadr.

  Orthopedic surgeon: interview with Maha Elsamnah.

36   **"Let's go see papa":** ibid.

  On his weekends away: ibid.

Chapter Three: The Khadr Effect

37   **Khadr had rented:** interviews with Maha Elsamnah.

  There was also one: ibid.

38   **He often held:** ibid.

  They would watch: interview with Zaynab Khadr.

  The staff and volunteers: interview with Abdullah Almalki.

39   **Two senior managers:** ibid.

40   **Khadr still maintained:** ibid.

  "world's orphaned conflicts": Ahmed Rashid, *Taliban,* p. 207.

  Bin laden focused: Lawrence Wright, *The Looming Tower,* p. 141.

The camp's constitution: ibid, p. 142.

41 Masood's closest ally: Kathy Gannon, *I is for Infidel,* p. 11.
Sayyaf's reputation seemed: interview with Hassan Almrei.
Each night, he slept: ibid.
His only indulgence: ibid.

42 When the Taliban: Kathy Gannon, *I is for Infidel,* p. 51.
but the Pashtun: Ahmed Rashid, *Taliban,* p. 21.
Dostum's brutality: ibid, p. 56.
"I innocently asked": ibid.

43 reportedly Sayyaf who: Kathy Gannon, *I is for Infidel,* p. 32, "A Glass Half Full," *The Economist,* September 17, 2005, as quoting "Blood-Stained Hands: Past Atrocities in Kabul and Afghanistan's Legacy of Impunity," *Human Rights Watch* report, July 2005.
In March 2007: Henry Chu, "Some 'forgiven' deeds can't be forgotten; Afghanistan's amnesty for warlords-turned-politicians reflects the fear they still inspire," *Los Angeles Times,* April 29, 2007.
Khadr managed to deal: interviews with Abdullah Almalki, Maha Elsamnah, as confirmed by Kaleem Akhtar.
He would joke: interview with Abdurahman Khadr.
Khadr said he envisioned: interview with Kareem Khadr, Zaynab Khadr and Maha Elsamnah.
Omar said: ibid.

44 The youngest daughter: ibid.
In 1994, when: interview with Abdurahman Khadr.
Khalden, a prestigious: Farouk was the more specialized al Qaeda camp but Khalden would become better known due to its famous alumni. Montreal resident Ahmed Ressam, the "Millennium Bomber" who failed in his attempt to bomb Los Angeles airport, had trained at Khalden in 1998. Ressam was pulled over in December 1999 by an observant Seattle border guard who thought he looked a little nervous when he tried to cross from Canada into the United States. A subsequent search of his car revealed a trunk full of explosives.
Richard Reid, the so-called "Shoe Bomber" who was convicted in Britain for attempting to bring down a commercial airline with plastic explosives stored in his shoe, had also trained at Khalden.
run by a Libyan: interview with Abdurahman Khadr.
"This is Hamza": Omar Nasiri, *Inside the Jihad: My Life with Al Qaeda. A Spy's Story,"* p. 199. Nasiri, who was known at the camps as Abu Imam, later identifies the boys in the camp as Abdurahman and Omar, but Omar was not in a camp at that time and the ages don't match. Abdurahman Khadr said in an interview that at the camp he was known as "Osama" and his

brother as "Hamza." He said he did not remember Abu Imam but does remember the incidents he writes about.

45 **He was shocked:** ibid, p. 199-202.

"Abdurahman, we're going back": recollections of Abdurahman Khadr.

46 **"cancer of the family":** ibid.

One evening: Omar Nasiri, *Inside the Jihad: My Life with Al Qaeda. A Spy's Story,"* p. 201.

Night after night: ibid.

Isn't that stupid: ibid, p. 202.

one carried a briefcase: Lawrence Wright, *The Looming Tower,* p. 217.

The other drove: Kathy Gannon, "Car Bomb Kills 15 at Embassy in Pakistan," Associated Press, November 20, 1995.

a ten-foot crater: ibid.

picture of Egyptian president: ibid.

47 **"The bomb left":** Lawrence Wright, "The Man Behind Bin Laden," *The New Yorker,* September 16, 2002.

On June 26: "U.S. Department of State: Patterns of Global Terrorism," April 1996.

series of indiscriminate: ibid, p. 215.

Among the suspects: John Stackhouse, "Pakistan reveals charges against Canadian Ahmed Said Khadr under investigation regarding terrorist bombing, government says," *Globe and Mail,* January 16, 1996.

known by his *kunya*: interviews with Abdurahman Khadr, Zaynab Khadr.

she had no interest: interview with Zaynab Khadr and Maha Elsamnah.

a wedding contract: ibid.

Elsamnah had spent: ibid.

48 **barricaded the door:** ibid.

one of her father's guns: interview with Maha Elsamnah and Abdurahman Khadr.

more than $10,000: Alistair Lyon, "Canadian said held for Egyptian embassy blast," Reuters, December 14, 1995.

"Does a criminal": ibid.

Naseerullah Babar told: ibid.

Seven police investigators: Mark Duguay, "Independent Counsel Review and Report: Our File No: 96-024," July 22, 1996.

49 **On December 14, Pakistan:** ibid.

A clearly traumatized: interview with Maha Elsamnah.

more than 300 business: Anthony Wilson-Smith, "Chrétien visits India," *Maclean's,* January 22, 1996.

publicity and clout: Barrie McKenna, "Team Canada off again as the third big Chrétien trade mission hits the road, officials extol benefits of showcasing

Canada. Generating good PR back home doesn't hurt either," *Globe and Mail,* January 2, 1996.

"Jean Chrétien in youth,": Lawrence Martin, "Who will lead us?", *Globe and Mail,* August 30, 1997.

50 **"The art of politics":** Jean Chrétien, *Straight From the Heart.*

"Captain Canada": Anthony Wilson-Smith, "Chrétien visits India," *Maclean's,* January 22, 1996.

"What, you might ask": Editorial, "A shameful silence on China's repression," *Globe and Mail,* June 3, 1995.

51 **are implicitly suggesting:** Anthony Wilson-Smith, "Chrétien visits India," *Maclean's,* January 22, 1996.

"Today, there are": David Israelson, "Team Canada gets message on child labor: Fight abuse, youthful rights advocates urge," *Toronto Star,* January 9, 1996.

"All of us must": "Canadian PM criticizes child labor in India," Agence France-Presse, January 13, 1996.

52 **"I am a hostage":** Michelle Huang, "Bombing suspect pins 'last hope' on Chrétien: 'I am a hostage,' Canadian held in Pakistan attack tells The Star," *Toronto Star,* December 30, 1995.

Elsamnah who implored: John Stackhouse, "Canadian weak from hunger strike. Aid worker protests against detention by Pakistani authorities over embassy bombing," *Globe and Mail,* January 8, 1996.

Opinions are divided: Samir Raafat, *Cairo Times,* November 16, 2000, Glen McGregor, "Egyptians see red over plaque, pink: Ambassadorial residence: Cairo citizens fuming at Canadian snub of Queen Farida's stay," *National Post,* January 9, 2001.

The spectacle of: interview with Marie Andree Beauchemin.

She had met: ibid.

Consular officials had: ibid.

53 **Beauchemin knew what:** ibid.

At times, the meeting: interview with Peter Donolo.

"He lies in a hospital": John Stackhouse, "Canadian suspect in limo. His family plans an appeal to the Prime Minister, but Ahmed Said Khadr remains detained without charges in a Pakistan hospital bed," *Globe and Mail,* January 15, 1996.

"The media contingent": James Bartleman, *Rollercoaster: My Hectic Years as Jean Chrétien's Diplomatic Advisor, 1994-1998,* p. 228.

54 **"All it demonstrates":** John Torode, "Religion—Pakistan on brink of anarchy, warns blasphemy lawyer—extremism on the rise," *Independent On Sunday,* March 5, 1995.

Once, I was the son of a farmer: Terence McKenna, Nazim Baksh, Michelle

Gagnon, Alex Shprintsen, "Al Qaeda Family," *CBC—The National,* March 3, 2005.

"This is a new tendency": John Stackhouse, "Pakistan reveals charges against Canadian Ahmed Said Khadr under investigation regarding terrorist bombing, government says," *Globe and Mail,* January 16, 1995.

Khadr was charged: Mark Duguay, "Independent Counsel Review and Report: Our File No: 96-024," July 22, 1996.

55 **The Special Courts had:** ibid.

Hooper had grown: interviews with Jack Hooper.

"In the popular": Trevor Fishlock, "Canada—Of myth and mounted policemen. The lure of colonial policing—both the glamour and the . . ." *Daily Telegraph,* December 2, 2000.

56 **The RCMP team:** interview with Hooper.

57 **O'Neill was a:** ibid.

Khadr may never: ibid.

58 **a new term:** briefing note to RCMP Commissioner Giuliani Zaccardelli, April 30, 2003, entered as an exhibit in the "Commission of Inquiry into the Actions of Canadian Officials in Relation to Maher Arar."

"no legal evidence": Mark Duguay, "Independent Counsel Review and Report: Our File No: 96-024," July 22, 1996, Appendix 4.

doubted Khadr was: interview with Kaleem Akhtar.

59 **Canadian government:** ibid.

forced by its: "In the matter of a complaint filed by Human Concern International pursuant to Section 41 of the Canadian Security Intelligence Service Act," File No: 1500-301, April 12, 2007.

registered a company: Corporations Canada. Corporation #2401801, incorporated November 16, 1988.

"I have commitments": interview with Aly Hindy.

"No one wants": Michelle Shephard, "Toronto man held in Egypt; 3rd principal of Scarborough Islamic school to be detained. Family says he's been denied consular access, right to lawyer," *Toronto Star,* February 21, 2004.

60 **by late 1996:** interview with Aly Hindy.

One day, Omar: interview with Zaynab Khadr.

61 **farm belonging to:** interview with Maha Elsamnah.

called the compound: interview with Zaynab Khadr. Other publications, including the *9/11 Commission Report,* spells the compound as Nazim Jihad.

which she abhorred: interview with Zaynab Khadr.

Bin Laden had: ibid.

62 **He had married:** Lawrence Wright, *The Looming Tower,* p. 78.

although polygamy: ibid, p. 81.

Umm Hamza was also: interview with Zaynab Khadr and Maha Elsamnah.

obsessing about: ibid.

not everyone in: ibid.

Khadr had not: ibid.

63 **"I don't want":** interview with Maha Elsamnah.

were taken on: Peter Bergen, *Holy War Inc.,* pp. 1-23.

Taliban leader Mullah: Lawrence Wright, *The Looming Tower,* p. 247. Interviews with Maha Elsamnah and Zaynab Khadr.

64 **"Do not come back":** interview with Abdurahman Khadr.

an Egyptian named: ibid.

He phoned from: interview with Zaynab Khadr.

Khadr finally agreed: ibid, *The Attorney General of Canada on the Behalf of The United States of America and Abdullah Ahmed Khadr,* "Second Supplemental Record of the Case for the Prosecution," section (s).

66 **Abdullah resurfaced:** interviews with Maha Elsamnah, Zaynab Khadr and Abdurahman Khadr.

"Albania returnees": Susan Sachs, "An investigation in Egypt Illustrates Al Qaeda's Web," *New York Times,* November 21, 2001.

had angered Zawahiri: Lawrence Wright, *The Looming Tower,* p. 269.

Frank Pressley: *United States of America v. Usama bin Laden, et. al.,* testimony transcript January 8, 2001, New York, NY.

fumbled with: ibid.

he was able: interview with Abdurahman Khadr.

67 **Marzouk's relationship:** Stewart Bell, "Bin Laden's B.C. helper," *National Post,* October 13, 2005.

Canada's spy service: interview with Jack Hooper.

visited often: ibid.

68 **Omar also liked:** interview with Zaynab Khadr.

He was angry: interview with Abdurahman Khadr.

"It built rage": interview with author. He repeated what he had previously told the CBC documentary "Al Qaeda family."

Chapter Four: Flight or Fight

69 **On September 11:** Details of the hijackings and events that morning were reconstructed through the account in "We Have Some Planes," *9/11 Commission Report,* pp. 1-46, and through the transcripts of conversations that day, most helpful was Stephen Kiehl's report, "'I think we're getting hijacked.' Woven Together in Real Time, The Conversations Amid The Calamity of 9/11 Produce a Narrative of Desperation and Anguish,

Foretelling A Changed America. 9/11 Five Years—2001/2006," *Baltimore Sun,* September 10, 2006.

71 **turned on the radio:** interviews with Maha Elsamnah and Zaynab Khadr.
"It is difficult": Kate Clark as quoted in "The Lion of Panshir," BBC News Online, September 11, 2001.

72 **refrained from:** interview with Zaynab Khadr.

73 **Omar was especially:** ibid.
telling the children: ibid.
a Yemeni named: interview with Abdurahman Khadr.

74 **guests snuck up:** interview with Kareem Khadr.
neighbor was Australian: interview with Maha Elsamnah and Zaynab Khadr.
bin Laden's sons: ibid.

75 **Khadr ran into:** ibid.
bin Laden instead chose: Lawrence Wright, *The Looming Tower,* p. 248.

76 **suffered bouts:** interview with Maha Elsamnah.
Zawahiri's knocks: interview with Zaynab Khadr.
more affordable location: interviews with Maha Elsamnah and Zaynab Khadr.
Abu Walid's importance: Mohammed Al Shafey, "The Story of Abu Walid al Masri: The Ideologue of the Afghan Arabs," *Asharq Alawsat,* February 11, 2007.
al Libi was also: interview with Maha Elsamnah and Zaynab Khadr.

77 **had been a relative:** Aamer Ahmed Khan, "Pakistan and the 'key al-Qaeda' man," BBC News Online, May 4, 2005.
The Pentagon accuses: transcript of Combatant Status Review Tribunal Hearing for ISN 10017: http://www.defenselink.mil/news/transcript_ISN10017.pdf. Transcript of Administrative Review Tribunal, February 8, 2007, http://www.defenselink.mil/news/ISN10017.pdf#1.
Also announcement of transfer to Guantanamo: http://www.odni.gov/announcements/content/DetaineeBiographies.pdf.
communicated by walkie-talkie: interview with Maha Elsamnah and Zaynab Khadr.
Saif al Adel: ibid.
Khadr and Elsamnah decided to spend: ibid.

78 **Omar and Abdurahman:** interview with Abdurahman Khadr.
the walkie-talkie: interview with Maha Elsamnah.

80 **"It looks like after":** interview with George Crile, "Omar Khadr: The Youngest Terrorist?" CBS's *60 Minutes,* November 18, 2007.
knock at the door: interviews with Maha Elsamnah and Zaynab Khadr.
knew how to fire: ibid.

81 **And they were all:** interviews with Zaynab Khadr.
he was forced: interview with Maha Elsamnah.

82 **They wanted Omar:** ibid.
"It wasn't supposed": ibid.

82 **Abdurahman first encountered:** interview with Abdurahman Khadr.

83 **The Pentagon would:** Notification of Swearing of Charges, Office of the Chief Prosecutor, Office of Military Commissions, Department of Defense. http://www.defenselink.mil/news/d2007Khadr%20%20Notification%20of%20Sworn%20Charges.pdf.

donned an ammunition vest: *United States of America v. Omar Ahmed Khadr,* "Brief on Behalf of Appellant," in the Court of Military Commission Review, July 4, 2007.

he would keep sending: interview with Zaynab Khadr and Kareem Khadr.

84 **Umm Hamza:** interview with Maha Elsamnah and Zaynab Khadr.

By 2003: *The Attorney General of Canada on the Behalf of The United States of America and Abdullah Ahmed Khadr,* "Second Supplemental Record of the Case for the Prosecution," section (bb).

Al Iraqi, whose: U.S. Department of Defense Background: http://www.defenselink.mil/news/Apr2007/d20070427hvd.pdf.

85 **Sheik Essa, also known:** *The Attorney General of Canada on the Behalf of The United States of America and Abdullah Ahmed Khadr,* "Second Supplemental Record of the Case for the Prosecution," section (t). The record signed by James B. Farmer, Chief of the Anti-Terrorism and National Security Section, United States Attorney's Office, dated April 19, 2007, lists Essa as "Sheikh Aissa" although most local Pakistani press spells his name Essa.

Khadr told Kareem: interviews with Zaynab Khadr relaying what was told to her by brothers Kareem and Abdullah Khadr. Abdullah had spoken with Sheikh Essa after his father's death.

Chapter Five: "Don't Forgat Me"

87 **converted to a prison:** Tim Golden, with Ruhallah Khapalwak, Carlotta Gall and David Rhode, "In U.S. Report, Brutal Details of 2 Afghan Inmates' Death," *New York Times,* May 20, 2005. Also earlier report by Carlotta Gall, "Military Investigating Death of Afghan in Custody," *New York Times,* March 4, 2003.

separated by concertina wire: Chris Mackey and Greg Miller, *The Interrogators: Inside the Secret War Against Al Qaeda,* p. 244.

detainees called it The Barn: interview with Moazzam Begg.

88 **He was charged:** Moazzam Begg, *Enemy Combatant: My Imprisonment At Guantanamo, Bagram and Kandahar,* pp. 87-90.

He worked to: interview with Moazzam Begg.

one British interrogator: Tim Golden, "Jihadist or Victim: Ex-Detainee Makes a Case," *New York Times,* June 15, 2006.

89 **"The guards":** interview with Moazzam Begg.

blankets had once: ibid.

forced to stand: ibid.

90 **"Cell Number One":** ibid.

91 **weren't experienced:** Tim Golden, "In U.S. Report, Brutal Details of 2 Afghan Inmates' Death," *New York Times,* May 20, 2005.

"Often the first task": Chris Mackey and Greg Miller, *The Interrogators,* pp. xxii–xxiii.

92 **American soldiers had all:** Joseph Margulies, *Guantanamo and the Abuse of Presidential Power,* pp. 78–79. George S. Prugh, *Law at War,* "Enemy in Your Hands," card reproduction, Appendix H.

94 **Some guards later said:** Tim Golden, "In U.S. Report, Brutal Details of 2 Afghan Inmates' Death," *New York Times,* May 20, 2005. Documents from the investigation were also released through the ACLU FOIA request: http://www.aclu.org/projects/foiasearch/pdf/DOD048473.pdf.

95 **Damien Corsetti:** ibid.

Sometimes he would: interview with author.

logged more than: ibid.

"The President of the United States": Tim Golden, "Years After 2 Afghans Died, Abuse Case Falters," *New York Times,* February 13, 2006.

During his free time: interviews with Moazzam Begg, Damien Corsetti.

96 **As a present:** Moazzam Begg, "Guantanamo's Catch-22: Defining the Rules of the Road," *Boston Globe,* September 14, 2006.

part of a screening team: interview with Damien Corsetti.

Begg negotiated a: interview with Moazzam Begg.

97 **Omar had been told:** ibid.

Omar's name was written: ibid.

98 **"The naval base is a dagger":** Dan Gardner, "Tenant from hell: The rent's paid and the U.S. has no plans to move its controversial Cuban naval base, Guantanamo, despite fiery threats from the landlord, Fidel Castro," February 27, 2005.

an ailing Castro: Anthony Boadle, "Castro: Cuba not cashing US Guantanamo rent checks," Reuters, August 17, 2007.

99 **"One by one,":** Carol Rosenberg, "Prisoners Arrive in Cuba—More Taliban, Al Qaeda Members Coming," *Miami Herald,* January 12, 2002.

100 **"These represent the":** ibid.

He wrote his father: Leigh Sales, *Detainee 002: The Case of David Hicks,* 21.

guards would nickname: interview with Ruhal Ahmed.

101 **their story started:** story of the Tipton Three from interview with Ruhal Ahmed, their documentary, *The Road to Guantanamo* and David Rose's, "How we survived jail hell," *The Observer,* March 14, 2004.

102 **His 'in-process weight':** "Measurements of Heights and Weights of Individuals Detained by the Department of Defense at Guantanamo Bay, Cuba," released by U.S. Department of Defense March 16, 2007: http://www.dod.mil/pubs/foi/detainees/measurements/ISN_680-ISN_838.pdf.

post-9/11 Pentagon policy: The definition of juvenile has always been unclear at Guantanamo. The military says juveniles are under the age of sixteen, while international and domestic law states under eighteen. Clive Stafford Smith explores this issue in *Bad Men: Guantanamo Bay and The Secret Prisons,* pp. 144-146. Also by Neil A. Lewis, "Some Held at Guantanamo Are Minors, Lawyers Say," *New York Times,* June 13, 2005.

They were allowed to watch: Ted Conover, "In the Land of Guantanamo," *New York Times,* June 29, 2003.

American football and letter: Barbara Jones, "The Innocent Children of Guantanamo Bay," *The Mail on Sunday,* February 22, 2004.

103 **Two things surprised:** interview with author.

A small group of soldiers: interview with Mike Silver.

104 **The tape featured:** as described by Abdurahman Khadr who said he was shown the tape while living in a CIA safehouse in Kabul. Also clips of the video were shown on "Omar Khadr: The Youngest Terrorist?" CBS's *60 Minutes,* November 18, 2007.

FBI even had a yacht: Michelle Shephard, "The Other Side of 'Gitmo,'" *Toronto Star,* January 14, 2006.

One week featured: Excerpt of interview at Moon Hall, Fort Bragg, North Carolina. Released by U.S. Government June 15, 2006 due to FOIA request by the ACLU. Posted by the UC Davis Center for the Study of Human Rights in the Americas:

http://humanrights.ucdavis.edu/projects/the-guantanamo-testimonials-project/testimonies/testimonies-of-interrogators/testimony-of-a-female-second-lieutenant.

military interrogators received: released through ACLU FOIA request: http://action.aclu.org/torturefoia/released/061906/Schmidt _Furlow-Enclosures.pdf.

105 **underlying principles:** Chris Mackey and Greg Miller, *The Interrogators,* pp. 479-483.

106 **a man who called himself Izmarai:** All of Omar's allegations of abuse are contained in *O.K. v. George W. Bush, President of the United States, et. al,* "Application for Preliminary Injunction to Enjoin Interrogation, Torture

and Other Cruel, Inhuman, or Degrading Treatment of Petitioner," and also in *Omar Ahmed Khadr by his Next Friend Fatmah Elsamnah and The Attorney General of Canada and The Minister of Foreign Affairs, "Affidavit of Muneer Ahmad.* "Author also interviewed lawyers Muneer Ahmad and Rick Wilson to confirm their recollections of the allegations. Allegations were also compared against independent reports of abuse such as the FBI e-mails, accounts as told by other detainees and reports from Guantanamo investigations.

107 **one of the best rooms:** interview with Chaplain James Yee.
   Omar seemed to prefer: interview Ruhal Ahmed.
   Nothing bonded: ibid.

108 **"Walk-in consultations":** Advertisement in the Joint Task Force Guantanamo publication, *"The Wire,"* Volume 4, Issue 25, March 5, 2004.
   a report in: Bill Gertz and Rowan Scarborough, "Inside the Ring," *Washington Times,* October 2, 2002.

109 **"Every single time":** Erik Saar and Viveca Novak, *Inside the Wire,* p. 154.
   Miller didn't encourage: ibid, p. 225.
   Saar writes of: ibid, pp. 221-228.

110 **conducted an investigation:** Brig. Gen. John T. Furlow's report: http://www.defenselink.mil/news/Jul2005/d20050714report.pdf.
   there was one story: interview with Ruhal Ahmed.

Chapter Six: The Elephant and the Ant

113 **They came with:** the interrogations with Omar Khadr have been reconstructed through interviews with Jim Gould, other Canadian and U.S. government officials, government reports summarizing the interrogations that were obtained through Federal Access to Information legislation and exhibits in the case of *Khadr v. Canada,* docket T-536-04.

115 **International Security Branch:** Before 9/11, few Canadians even knew the Foreign Affairs Department was in the business of collecting intelligence. Today, there are still many unanswered questions as to its role and scope of its powers. Even the name of the division is something of a mystery, since it is commonly referred to as the ISI, not the ISB which would be the proper acronym. One explanation is that ISI dates back to the days when the department communicated by telegraphs, and each division in Foreign Affairs corresponded to a letter. The "I" division, presumably was responsible for security and intelligence. After September 11, Foreign Affairs was among the federal departments to receive a share of the billions of dollars in new funding for security. This caused concern among some

higher-ups at Canada's spy service who worried that untrained bureaucrats were encroaching on their territory. Unlike its American counterpart, CSIS was not permitted to collect foreign intelligence that didn't directly impact Canada's security. While the CIA engaged in offensive missions, CSIS was primarily a defensive agency, which meant there were strict guidelines governing the actions of agents posted abroad. *What exactly were diplomats working out of Canada's embassies doing to collect intelligence?* It was a concern for Canada's senators as well. "There seems to be a great deal going on in your shop," Senator Wilfred Moore said to ISI's assistant deputy minister Colleen Swords during a committee meeting in May 2007. "The issue is really about information. Foreign intelligence is also about information," Sword replied. "Obviously, if you are representing Canada abroad, you are doing a wide range of things. Part of it is trying to understand the country, which is all about gathering information on that country." "Is there anything that you cannot do?" Moore persisted. "The statutes that you cite as your authorities gives your branch the authority to gather information on individuals, foreign countries, as you wish." "We do not gather information as we wish but rather through open sources," said Swords. "We are not operating covertly. When in a country abroad, you meet a wide number of people in government, the academic community, the NGO community, or the opposition parties. You are gathering information from quite a large number of sources. That is part of the mandate that diplomats have abroad under the Vienna Convention on Diplomatic Relations."

116 **The Dip Note:** all correspondence between the U.S. government and Canadian federal officials, plus e-mails, letters, reports, internal communication and press lines, was obtained through the Federal Access to Information legislation either by the author or Canadian lawyers for Omar Khadr.

118 **"Should we have":** Manley's comments were made during the Commission of Inquiry Into the Actions of Canadian Officials In Relation to Maher Arar. A transcript can be found here: http://www.stenotran.com/commission/maherarar/2005-05-31%20volume%2018.pdf.

119 **They had killed:** David Pugliese, "Inside JTF2's deadly Afghan mission: Canada's commandos played frontline role in the war on terrorism," *Ottawa Citizen,* September 28, 2002.

Canada insisted it: David Pugliese, "Canada's JTF2 captives vanish at Guantanamo: U.S. stymies request for information about Afghans caught in raids," *Ottawa Citizen,* February 14, 2005.

refused to extradite: Sam Dillon, with Donald G. McNeil Jr., "Spain Sets Hurdle for Extradition," *New York Times,* November 24, 2001.

"It was not imprudent": Sheldon Alberts, "PM calls Bloc terrorist

sympathizers: Chrétien 'kneeling in front of U.S.,' Duceppe fires back,"
National Post, February 7, 2002.

"We don't have": "Canada refuses to question U.S. over prisoners in Guantanamo," Agence France-Presse, January 28, 2002.

120 **"She may have":** Mike Trickey, "PM rejects Ducros' resignation: Chrétien accused of double standard over favoured aide's 'moron' remark," *Ottawa Citizen,* November 23, 2002.

121 **"Canada is just":** Tonda MacCharles, "We're both at risk, Powell tells Canada: Border dominates discussion—Tighter border control designed to protect vulnerable. Terror threat a wakeup call for us all, Graham says," *Toronto Star,* November 15, 2002.

123 **Ahmed Elmaati:** Ahmed Elmaati had returned to Canada in the 1990s and became a truck driver, which worried the RCMP because of his frequent trips across the border. Elmaati had also once taken flying lessons at Buttonville Airport, about an hour's drive north of Toronto, which also was viewed as a threat after 9/11. In the end, all three of the men—Arar, Almalki, Elmaati—were held at Syria's notorious prison, the Far Falestine, and just how they got there became a national scandal. Instead of terrorism charges, Project A O Canada ended in two multi-million dollar public inquiries, lawsuits, the resignation of the RCMP Chief and an $11.5-million (CDN) settlement and apology to Maher Arar. Arar's ordeal was the most celebrated case because he was a victim of the American practice of rendition; a program whereby terrorism suspects are seized and flown to countries known to employ torture during interrogations. American officials detained Arar on September 26, 2002, during a stopover at New York's JFK airport. After two weeks in custody, he was flown in a private jet to Jordan where he was driven across the border to his birth country which he had left seventeen years earlier. At Far Falestine, he was tortured for almost two weeks and then held for ten months in a grave-like cell. A federal inquiry into Canadian officials involvement in Arar's detention disclosed that the RCMP had handed all its files to the United States without including the critical caveats normally attached when two countries share intelligence. In one RCMP database, Arar was labeled an "Islamic extremist" with ties to al Qaeda, which likely led to his arrest in New York. Khadr loomed large over the investigation for two reasons. Anyone connected to Khadr was deemed suspicious. But the "Khadr effect" that emerged from Chrétien's intervention in Pakistan in 1996 also dictated how the Canadian government responded when the men were detained in Syria. "The Members of Parliament are seeking the intervention at the Prime Ministerial level for the release of Arar and his return to Canada. The lobbyists are pressuring for quick intervention in an attempt to effect

a return prior to Arar being charged by the Syrians," an April 2003 briefing note the RCMP Commissioner Giuiliano Zaccardelli stated. "The potential embarrassment exists should the Prime Minister become involved in a similar fashion to the incident (involving) the Egyptian bombing in 1995 in Pakistan. In that situation, the Prime Minister intervened on behalf of Ahmed Said Khadr, an Egyptian-Canadian, who was subsequently released from Pakistani custody. Khadr is now recognized internationally as a high-ranking al Qaeda member and wanted by the Egyptians for the bombing. The intervention of the PM has been raised on a number of occasions in an attempt to embarrass the government."

Chapter Seven: "We Are an al Qaeda Family"

130 **was a "sham":** Donovan Vincent, "Lawyer walks out of terror hearing—Protests 'abuse' of client accused of ties to radicals," *Toronto Star,* March 12, 2002.

On the verge: Joseph Hall, "Threat scares lawyer away from clients; Galati drops national security cases. Fears for his life without protection," *Toronto Star,* December 5, 2003.

"We made it": Stewart Bell and Anne Dawson, "Canada 'welcomed' man freed from Guantanamo, Martin says: Officials deny Khadr refused re-entry," *Ottawa Citizen,* November 26, 2003.

"lying through their": Bill Dunphy, "Galati, part spit and part polish, makes his case; Toronto lawyer known for hyperbolic outrage cranked out in defence of those whom very few are willing to defend," *Hamilton Spectator,* November 26, 2003.

133 **Baksh's family was:** interview with author.

"Down, down USA": Mira L. Boland, "Sheikh Gilani's American Disciples: What to make of the Islamic compounds across America affiliated with the Pakistani radical group Jamaat al-Fuqra?" *Weekly Standard,* March 18, 2002, Volume 007, Issue 26.

134 **"(T)hey become":** ibid.

CBC radio program: Nazim Baksh, report aired December 3, 2003: http://www.cbc.ca/news/viewpoint/vp_baksh/20031204.html.

135 **ran a front-page:** Michelle Shephard, "Khadr denies 'spy' deal. Khadr denies co-operation; Didn't lead U.S. to father, contacts Canadian released from Guantanamo," *Toronto Star,* December 31, 2003.

136 **e-mail with the:** e-mail sent December 31, 2003 at 7:38 a.m. by Terry Colli. At 9:30 a.m. the e-mail was forwarded by Patricia Fortier with the text, "Hmmm…." E-mail obtained through Access To Information legislation.

We are in troublesome: Mike Sadava, "Edmonton lawyer takes on United States: Dennis Edney to fight for rights of Ontario youth held incommunicado in prison camp in Cuba," *Edmonton Journal,* January 10, 2004.

141 **The first CIA agent:** interviews with Abdurahman Khadr.

142 **was a tall:** Lawrence Wright, "The Agent: A Reporter at Large," *The New Yorker,* July 10, 2006.

known as "the Wall": ibid.

he would watch: interview with Abdurahman Khadr.

143 **went to a nearby bar:** ibid.

147 **"We have to":** "CIA paid me to spy: Abdurahman Khadr," CBC News Online, March 5, 2004.

online petition: Michelle Shephard, "Khadr family return deeply divisive. Get-them-out online petition quickly gathering signatures. Imam admits being unsure whether to help mother and son," *Toronto Star,* April 13, 2004. The online petition has been taken offline but had been started by Scarborough resident Donna Campbell and received more than 2,500 signatures in about six months.

150 **an interview with:** Christiane Amanpour, *CNN: Special Investigations Unit,* February 10, 2007. Transcript posted here: http://transcripts.cnn.com/ TRANSCRIPTS/0702/10/siu.02.html.

151 **"I am what":** Khalid Khawaja, "Comment: Engage with Islam's voices of reason," *Financial Times,* August 24, 2005.

"we have secret": "Canadian Arab family claims Pakistan holding relatives," Agence France-Presse, December 30, 2003.

"These poor innocent": Isabel Vincent, "Bin Laden ally backs Khadr civil suit: 'Poor innocent ladies': Family suing Pakistan in bid to find father, brother," *National Post,* December 31, 2003.

152 **"If you want to understand,":** Bruno Schirra, *die Welt,* April 2, 2004.

Schirra met: interview with Bruno Schirra.

153 **"Canadian citizenship":** Chris Wattie and James Cowan, "Son, wife of al Qaeda fighter return: Emergency passports: Conservatives' Day says re-entry sends a 'terrible signal,' " *National Post,* April 10, 2004.

Chapter Eight: "It's Destroying Us Slowly"

156 **Baltimore's police commissioner:** Scott Shane, "Cases hint of terrorism, fizzle into the mundane; Investigations: As the nation sorts out how to deal with threats, the burden falls on law enforcement and Muslim visitors," *Baltimore Sun,* November 19, 2002.

158 **"Despite our persistent":** Navy Rear Adm. Harry B. Harris Jr., "Inside

Guantanamo Bay," *Chicago Tribune,* May 17,.2006.

interrogators would often: Erik Saar and Viveca Novak, *Inside The Wire,* p. 67.

Striking an iguana: ibid, p. 42. The law regarding iguanas was also discussed during oral arguments in *Rasul v. United States,* April 20, 2004.

159 **"These are people":** Sue Anne Pressley, "Detainees Arrive in Cuba Amid Very Tight Security," *Washington Post,* January 12, 2002.

"I want you to": Erik Saar and Viveca Novak, *Inside the Wire,* p. 111.

shouting through: Tim Golden, "Battle for Guantanamo," *New York Times,* September 17, 2006.

160 **"We're going to":** CBS *60 Minutes Wednesday,* November 3, 2004.

161 **Omar had been sitting:** interviews with Muneer Ahmad and Rick Wilson.

162 **"Your life is in":** interviews with Muneer Ahmad and Rick Wilson. Omar's allegations are also contained in *O.K. v. George W. Bush, President of the United States, et. al,* "Application for Preliminary Injunction to Enjoin Interrogation, Torture and Other Cruel, Inhuman, or Degrading Treatment of Petitioner," and also in *Omar Ahmed Khadr by his Next Friend Fatmah Elsamnah and The Attorney General of Canada and The Minister of Foreign Affairs, "Affidavit of Muneer Ahmad."*

they used their: interviews with Muneer Ahmad and Rick Wilson.

163 **"As a mother":** Michelle Shephard, "'A spectacular failure'; Canada has done nothing for teen jailed, tortured at Guantanamo Bay: Lawyers Ottawa's 'so-called silent diplomacy,' has failed to change the plight of Omar Khadr," *Toronto Star,* February 10, 2005.

164 **a song titled:** Michelle Shephard, "Mounties uncover 'Al Qaeda' cache; Bin Laden's voice on tape, documents say. Plans, tapes, diaries seized at Pearson. Zaynab Khadr denies they belong to her," *Toronto Star,* June 14, 2005. Details were contained in a seven-page affidavit by RCMP Sgt. Konrad Shourie filed with the Ontario Court of Justice.

165 **"I take it that you're":** transcript of Hooper's testimony, submitted in *Omar Ahmed Khadr by his Next Friend Fatmah Elsamnah and The Attorney General of Canada and The Minister of Foreign Affairs.*

167 **"It's disgraceful":** Colin Freeze, "Judge orders Canada to stop quizzing teen in Guantanamo," *Globe and Mail,* August 10, 2005.

168 **Miller reportedly wanted:** Josh White, "General Asserts Right On Self-Incrimination In Iraq Abuse Cases," *Washington Post,* January 12, 2006.

Omar was among: details of the hunger strike are from Tim Golden, "Battle for Guantanamo," *New York Times,* September 17, 2006. Allegations by Omar Khadr as told to Muneer Ahmad and reported in his affidavit. Diaries of Sami Muhyideen al Hajj and Omar Deghayes. And Clive Stafford Smith, *Bad Men: Guantanamo Bay and the Secret Prison,* pp. 188-228.

170 **"Mr. Sands was":** R.W. Apple Jr., "Mrs. Thatcher Says Death of Sands Won't Alter London's Ulster Policy," *New York Times,* May 6, 1981.

172 **131 prisoners:** Tim Golden, "Tough U.S. Steps in Hunger Strike at Camp in Cuba," *New York Times,* February 9, 2006.
"restraint chairs": ibid.
"Well, yes, we": Press briefing by Scott McClellan, February 9, 2006: http://www.whitehouse.gov/news/releases/2006/02/20060209-7.html.

173 **condemning force-feeding:** David J. Nicholl, Holly G. Atkinson, John Kalk, William Hopkins, Elwyn Elias, Adnan Siddiqui, Ronald E. Cranford and Oliver Sacks, on behalf of 255 other doctors, "Force-feeding and restraint of Guantanamo Bay hunger strikers," *Lancet,* vol. 367, p. 811.
two psychological tests: *O.K. et. al. v. George W. Bush et. al., civilian action No. 04-1136,* Opinion by John D. Bates, July 12, 2005.

174 **"huge cultural gulf":** David Rose, "Operation Take Away My Freedom: Inside Guantanamo Bay on Trial," *Vanity Fair,* January 2004, p. 88.
But this also caused: interviews with Rick Wilson and Muneer Ahmad.

175 **"I want you to":** James Gordon, "Fears for Khadr's mental state as lawyers sacked," *National Post,* September 22, 2005.

176 **"I sat in the middle":** *Layne Morris, Tabitha Speer v. Ahmed Sa'id Khadr,* "Affidavit of Tabitha Speer," District of Utah, Central Division. 04CV00723.

177 **awarded them:** "Injured Utah soldier wins damages against man for Afghanistan attack," Associated Press, February 18, 2006.
amounted to: interview with Maha Elsamnah.
charged him with: charges posted by Department of Defense: http://www. defenselink.mil/news/Nov2005/d20051104khadr.pdf.
"Even if you dress": Jonathan Turley, "Even if you dress it up, a kangaroo is still a kangaroo," *Los Angeles Times,* March 21, 2002.
"Omar Khadr is a child": Tim Harper, "U.S. charges Omar Khadr with murder, aiding enemy; To be tried by military tribunal at Guantanamo. Attempted murder also alleged in Afghanistan attack," *Toronto Star,* November 8, 2005.

178 **the Pentagon stated:** Beth Gorham, "Pentagon goes on record to say Canadian teen Khadr won't face death penalty," Canadian Press, November 9, 2005.

Chapter Nine: "There Are No Rules"

179 **"You'll see evidence":** Michelle Shephard, "T.O. teen 'indeed a terrorist,' U.S. insists; Prosecutor says Khadr deserves life. Hearing begins today in Guantanamo," *Toronto Star,* January 11, 2006.

180 **personally delivered:** interview with Jeff Groharing.

183 **"This life will go on":** Michelle Shephard, "Khadr faces accusers; Canadian teen appears before U.S. military panel. Charged in deadly grenade attack in Afghanistan," *Toronto Star,* January 12, 2006.

184 **One transcript quoted:** Andrew Selsky, "Pentagon releases Guantanamo Bay transcripts, shedding light on detainees," Associated Press, April 3, 2006.

that terrorists favor: Greg Miller, Mark Mazzetti and Josh Meyer, "Documents Reveal the Stories of Prisoners at Guantanamo Bay," March 4, 2006. The use of an inexpensive model of Casio wristwatch appears in almost a dozen CSRT transcripts as part of the summary of evidence.

185 **"What were purported":** Lt.-Col. Stephen Abrahams' statement is posted by the U.S. Supreme Court weblog, www.scotusblog.com: http://www.scotusblog.com/movabletype/archives/Al%20Odah%20reply%206-22-07.pdf.

Omar's CSRT hearing: Hearing report contained included in *O.K. et. al. v. George Bush.*

"Detainees are permitted": Tim Harper, "Gonzales defends conditions at American prison camp; Guantanamo detainees treated well, attorney general says. Dismisses calls for controversial facility to be closed down," *Toronto Star,* March 8, 2006.

186 **I have delivered:** Joseph Margulies, *Guantanamo and the Abuse of Presidential Power, "* p. 214.

187 **nickname Danger:** Vokey explains his nickname in a 2006 interview— "A few years ago when I was a major, a few captains gave that to me, kind of making fun of me. We were actually playing a card game and I was playing seven-card stud and not looking at my own cards and just betting without looking at my cards face own, and I kept doing it over and over again and I kept winning. When I was doing it I was quoting Austin Powers where he's sitting at the poker table saying 'I too like living dangerously.' They just kept saying, 'Oh, Danger.' It kind of stuck."

192 **"We play only a win-win":** Michelle Shephard, "Rooting out rebels on the border. 'You love to live. We love to die.'" *Toronto Star,* May 13, 2006.

193 **"The American people":** Tim Golden, "Battle for Guantanamo," *New York Times,* September 17, 2006.

194 **shortly before midnight:** ibid.

asymmetric warfare: ibid.

"They're determined": Julian E. Barnes and Carol J. Williams, "Guantanamo's First Suicides Pressure U.S. Three prisoners, all held without charges, are found hanging in their cells. Human rights advocates urge an immediate shutdown," *Los Angeles Times,* June 11, 2006.

plans had changed: Michelle Shephard, "The view from Guantanamo Bay," *Toronto Star,* February 2007.

195 **"They have never":** ibid. Quotes from *Huzaifa Parhat, et. al. v. Robert M. Gates,* United States Court of Appeals District Columbia Circuit, Case No. 06-1397.

On June 2: Michelle Shephard, "Terror Cops Swoop; How Internet monitoring sparked a CSIS investigation into what authorities allege is a homegrown Canadian terror cell," *Toronto Star,* June 3, 2006.

197 **whom they knew:** interviews with Zaynab and Kareem Khadr.

199 **"Steve was a Caucasian":** Affidavit by Heather Cerveny, dated October 4, 2006.

200 **gag order:** interviews with Colby Vokey and Heather Cerveny.

accused her of making: Michael Melia, "U.S. military investigation reports no evidence guards beat Guantanamo detainees" Associated Press, February 7, 2007.

"The detainee has": interview with Rick Wilson.

Chapter Ten: Law and Disorder

204 **accused by the Pentagon:** Ghassan Abdullah al Sharbi's charges posted by the Department of Defense: http://www.defenselink.mil/news/Nov2005/d20051104sharbi.pdf.

only to be told: Sean Flynn, "The Defense Will Not Rest," *GQ* magazine, August 2007.

"Same circus": Carol Rosenberg, "Tenth war-crimes court defendant confesses –in English," *Miami Herald,* April 27, 2006.

205 **"I was horrified":** Michelle Shephard, "The Other Side of 'Gitmo,'" *Toronto Star,* January 14, 2006.

In July 2003: Leigh Sales, *Detainee OO2: The Case of David Hicks,* pp. 89-90.

"This is my son": Penelope Debelle, "The Image David Hicks' family hopes will set him free," *The Age,* February 5, 2007.

206 **raised the case:** Leigh Sales, *Detainee OO2: The Case of David Hicks,* p. 229.

207 **"I'm the best lawyer":** Brandon Griggs, "Frontier Justice: Gerry Spence, the Great Defender, Charges Ahead," *Salt Lake Tribune,* September 15, 1996.

"dedicated to": Gerry Spence's school advertised here: http://www.triallawyerscollege.com/.

because they were worried: interviews with Dennis Edney, Bill Kuebler and Muneer Ahmad.

208 **"I, Omar A.":** Letter released by Department of Defense: http://www.defenselink.mil/news/Nov2007/Khadr%20ROT%20d20071108Vol_IIArraignment(Redacted).pdf.

Omar told them: interview with Maha Elsamnah and Zaynab Khadr.

209 **"Gitmo's got legs":** interview with Bill Kuebler.

pages of *Rolling Stone*: Jeff Tietz, "The Unending Torture of Omar Khadr," *Rolling Stone,* August 10, 2006.

Fleener and Kuebler were: Sean Flynn, "The Defense Will Not Rest," *GQ* magazine, August 2007.

he remained there for hours: interview with Dennis Edney.

210 **a Saudi accent:** interviews with Maha Elsamnah and Zaynab Khadr.

"I won't give up": interview with Dennis Edney.

"I, Omar A": Letter released by Department of Defense: http://www.defenselink.mil/news/Nov2007/Khadr%20ROT%20d20071108Vol_IIArraignment(Redacted).pdf.

212 **over-enunciating the word:** interviews with Dennis Edney and Bill Kuebler.

213 **"How much longer":** *Toronto Star* editorial June 5, 2007.

214 **rescue Omar from:** Susan Delacourt, "It's time to step in, opposition tells PM," *Toronto Star,* June 5, 2007.

"It is our understanding": Michelle Shephard, "Victory puts Khadr in limbo; Canadian no closer to knowing his fate after U.S. military judge dismisses terror charges," *Toronto Star,* June 5, 2007.

he repeated: Les Whittington, "Ottawa waits on appeal of Khadr ruling," *Toronto Star,* June 14, 2007.

would take a hands-off: Tim Harper, "Ottawa unbending in Khadr case; Committed to U.S. military trial for Canadian accused of throwing grenade that killed soldier," *Toronto Star,* July 7, 2007.

The June survey: Angus Reid Strategies poll: http://angusreidstrategies.com/uploads/pages/pdfs/2007.06.26%20DFAIT%20Press%20Release.pdf.

"His case now": Michelle Shephard, "Campaign presses for Khadr's release from Cuba," *Toronto Star,* June 15, 2007.

215 **the Associated Press:** Matthew Lee, "Bush Administration close to shutting down Guantanamo, but Friday meeting canceled," Associated Press, June 21, 2007.

denied that a decision: Press briefing by Dana Perino: http://www.whitehouse.gov/news/releases/2007/06/20070622-4.html.

"It's a system designed": Cristin Schmitz, "American military courts 'launder torture': Navy Lawyer," *Lawyers Weekly,* August 31, 2007, Vol. 27, No. 16.

216 **"I think it's":** Tracey Tyler, "Khadr plea wins ovation," *Toronto Star,* August 12, 2007.

"It's a matter of rights": Steve Rennie, Canadian Press, September 19, 2007.

217 **"Here we have":** Colin Freeze, "Dion takes on Khadr issue, plans to meet suspect's lawyers," *Globe and Mail,* September 19, 2007.

Privately he said: interview with Dennis Edney.

Omar had agreed: "Affidavit of Lt.-Cmdr. William Kuebler," *Omar Ahmed*

Khadr and Minister of Justice and Attorney General of Canada et. al., Federal Court of Appeal, Court File Number A-184-06.

"conflicts of interest": Edney presumed Kuebler was referring to his representation of Omar's brother Abdullah when writing about potential "conflicts of interest." The issue has not been raised by Kuebler during Omar's military hearings to date.

218 **"A dispute between":** Jess Bravin, "Dispute Stymies Guantanamo Terror Trials," *Wall Street Journal,* September 26, 2007.

219 **two U.S. Air Force:** Jess Bravin, "Two Prosecutors At Guantanamo Quit in Protest," *Wall Street Journal,* August 1, 2005.

To maintain the public's: Col. Morris D. Davis, "Effective Engagement in the Public Opinion Arena: A Leadership Imperative in the Information Age," *Air & Space Power Journal,* November 5, 2004.

220 **two hour-long:** both calls (March and November 2007) were made to an Ottawa government office.

In overturning Brownback's: United States Court of Military Commission Review: http://www.scotusblog.com/movabletype/archives/CMCR%20 ruling%209-24-07.pdf.

221 **December 2007 phone call:** interview with Maha Elsamnah and Zaynab Khadr.

Select Bibliography

Bartleman, James. *Rollercoaster: My Hectic Years as Jean Chrétien's Diplomatic Advisor 1994-1998*. Toronto: McClelland & Stewart, 2005.

Begg, Moazzam. *Enemy Combatant: My Imprisonment At Guantanamo, Bagram, and Kandahar*. London: The Free Press, 2006.

Bergen, Peter L. *Holy War: Inside the Secret World of Osama bin Laden*. New York: Free Press, 2001.

Bergen, Peter L. *The Osama bin Laden I Know: An Oral History of al Qaeda's Leader*. New York: Free Press, 2006.

Burke, Jason. *Al Qaeda: Casting a Shadow of Terror*. London: I.B. Taurus, 2003.

Clarke, Richard A. *Against All Enemies: Inside America's War on Terror*. New York: Free Press, 2004.

Conot, Robert E. *Justice At Nuremberg*. New York: Carroll & Graf Publishers, 1983.

Gannon, Kathy. *I is for Infidel: From Holy War to Holy Terror: 18 Years Inside Afghanistan*. New York: Public Affairs, 2005.

Golden, Tim. *Battle for Guantanamo*. New York Times, September 17, 2006.

Grey, Stephen. *Ghost Plane: The True Story of the CIA Torture Program*. New York: St. Martin's Press, 2006.

Gunaratna, Rohan. *Inside al-Qaeda: Global Network of Terror*. London: Hurst, 2002.

Hersh, Seymour M. *Chain of Command: The Road from 9/11 to Abu Ghraib*. New York: HarperCollins, 2004.

Ignatieff, Michael. *The Lesser Evil: Political Ethics In an Age of Terror*. Toronto: Penguin Canada, 2004.

Mackey, Chris and Greg Miller. *The Interrogators: Inside the War Against Al Qaeda*. New York: Little Brown and Company, 2004.

Margulies, Joseph. *Guantanamo and the Abuse of Presidential Power*. New York: Simon & Schuster, 2006.

Musharraf, Pervez. *In the Line of Fire: A Memoir*. New York: Free Press, 2006.

Nasiri, Omar. *Inside the Jihad: My Life with Al Qaeda, A Spy's Story*. New York: Perseus Books Groups, 2006.

National Commission on Terrorist Acts Upon the United States. *The 9/11 Commission Report*. New York: Norton, 2004.

Rashid, Ahmed. *Taliban*. Yale University Press, 2000.

Ratner, Michael and Ellen Ray. *Guantanamo: What the World Should Know*. Vermont: Chelsea Green Publishing, 2004.

Roach, Kent. *September 11: Consequences for Canada*. Montreal: McGill-Queen's University Press, 2003.

Rose, David. *Guantanamo: The War on Human Rights*. New York: The New Press, 2004.

Saar, Erik and Viveca Novac. *Inside the Wire: A Military Intelligence Soldier's Eyewitness Account of Life at Guantanamo*. New York: Penguin Group, 2005.

Sales, Leigh. *Detainee 002: The Case of David Hicks*. Victoria: Melbourne University Press, 2007.

Stafford Smith, Clive. *Bad Men: Guantanamo Bay and the Secret Prisons*. London: Weidenfeld & Nicolson, 2007.

Suskind, Ron. *The One Percent Doctrine: Deep Inside America's Pursuit of its Enemies Since 9/11*. New York: Simon & Schuster, 2006.

Worthington, Andy. *The Guantanamo Files: The Stories of the 774 Detainees in America's Illegal Prison*. London: Pluto Press, 2007.

Wright, Lawrence. *The Looming Tower: Al-Qaeda and the Road to 9/11*. New York: Alfred A. Knopf, 2006.

Yee, James. *For God and Country: Faith and Patriotism Under Fire*. New York: Public Affairs, 2005.

Index

Khadr, Ahmed Said (father) *(continued)*
  in custody, 48–49, 52–53
  death of, 85, 110–111, 151
  effect of disability, 39–40
  explanations of 9/11 attack, 72
  fall of Kabul, 78–79
  family dynamics, 114
  fundraising, 27–28, 34–35, 133
  in Gardez, 80
  injuries, 35–36
  interest in Afghanistan war, 21–22
  in Jaji, 30
  in Kabul, 77
  legal action against estate of, 176–177
  move to Najm al Jihad, 61–63
  move to Pakistan, 22–24
  new charity company, 59–60
  rabbits, 37–38
  visit to Khalden, 45
  Zawahiri and, 28–29
  Zaynab's marriage, 64–65, 73–75
Khadr, Ibrahim (brother), 27, 30–31, 231
Khadr, Kareem. *See* Khadr, Abdul Kareem
Khadr, Maryam (sister), 32, 38, 44, 48,
  81–82, 151, 231
Khadr, Mohamed Zaki, 18–19
Khadr, Omar
  Abdurahman and, 141, 143
  Ahmed's visits, 68
  appearance, xii–xiii
  arrival in Guantanamo Bay, 102–103
  background, 231
  at Bagram, 89–90, 96–97
  birth of, 27–28
  call for intervention of Canadian
    government, 213–215
  in Camp Three, 107
  capture, 82–83
  car accident, 60
  as child soldier, 223–224
  commission hearings, xiii, 179–182, 187–
    190, 218
  connections of, 103
  CSRT hearing, 185
  death of Speer, ix–x, 4, 15–16
  early childhood, 30–32
  family dynamics, 74, 114
  father in custody, 49, 55
  father's injury, 35–36
  hunger strike, 168–171, 172

idea of heaven, 43
injunction against CSIS interviews, 165–
  167
interrogations, 105–106, 113–115, 123–
  125
interview with Gould, 125–126
lawyer representation refusal, 175, 207–208
letter to family, 203
meeting with Ahmad, 200–201
meeting with Ahmad and Wilson, 159–162
meeting with Chrétien, 54
meeting with Edney and Whitling, 209–
  210
mini-hearing, 220–221
move to Logar, 78
move to Najm al Jihad, 61
move to Zormat, 81
murder charge, 177–178
news of 9/11 attack, 72
news of father's death, 110–111
place in family, 44
police custody, 48
psychological assessments, 173–174
religion, 174
request for consular visit to, 116, 120
submission to U.S. Supreme Court, 137
video of, 104
Zaynab's marriage, 64–65, 73
Khadr, Zaynab (sister)
  Abdurahman's views of, 149
  on al Jowfi, 83
  background, 231
  birth of, 19
  birth of child, 74–75
  CBC documentary, 145–147
  evacuation of Najm al Jihad, 64
  family dynamics, 44, 114
  father in Jaji, 30
  interview with Edney, 126
  lawsuit in Pakistan, 151
  marriage to Abdullah, 47–48, 64–65
  marriage to al Bahr, 73, 125
  meeting with Schirra, 152
  move to Bahrain, 21
  move to Khawaja's home, 150
  move to Najm al Jihad, 61
  move to Zormat, 81
  news of 9/11 attack, 72
  in Pakistan, 152
  return to Canada, 163–164